THE ARITHMETIC OF MEMORY

BY ANTHONY RUDOLF

POETRY
The Same River Twice, Carcanet Press 1976
After the Dream, Cauldron Press (St Louis USA) 1979
Broccoli (etching by Paul Coldwell), Culford Press 1989
'Retrospective', *The Poet's Voice* (1/2) 1994
Mandorla (drawings by Merlin James), Delos Press 1999

POETRY TRANSLATIONS: YVES BONNEFOY
Selected Poems, Jonathan Cape 1968
Things Dying, Things Newborn, Menard 1985
Traité du pianiste, Delos Press 1995
New & Selected Poems (co-ed. J. Naughton), Chicago University Press/Carcanet 1996
On Raymond Mason (prose), Delos Press 1999

POETRY TRANSLATIONS: OTHER POETS
Alexander Tvardovsky: *Tyorkin & The Stovemakers*, Carcanet 1974
Evgeni Vinokourov: *The War is Over*, Carcanet 1976
Edmond Jabès: *A Share of Ink*, Menard 1979
Claude Vigée: *Flow Tide*, King's College London/Menard 1992
Ifigenija Simonovic: *Striking Root*, Menard 1996

LITERARY (ETC.) CRITICISM
Byron's Darkness: Lost Summer & Nuclear Winter, Menard 1984
From Poetry to Politics: The Menard Press 1969–84, Menard 1984
At an Uncertain Hour: Primo Levi's War against Oblivion, Menard 1990
Wine from Two Glasses: Trust and Mistrust in Language, King's College/Adam 1991
I'm Not Even a Grown-up: The Diary of Jerzy Feliks Urman, King's College/Menard 1991
Engraved in Flesh: Piotr Rawicz and his novel Blood from the Sky, Menard 1996
Everything is Prepared for the Feast: On the Triple Threshold of Religion, Politics & Literature
    (forthcoming)

EDITED
An Octave for Paz (with R. Burns), Sceptre/Menard 1972
MPT French Anthology, Modern Poetry in Translation, King's College London 1973
Poems for Shakespeare IV, Globe Playhouse Trust 1976
Voices within the Ark: 20th-Century Jewish Poets (with H. Schwartz), Avon Books, NY 1980
Spleen: Nicholas Moore's Baudelaire, Menard 1990
Sage Eye: The Aesthetic Passion of Jonathan Griffin, King's College London/Menard 1992
MPT Bonnefoy issue, Modern Poetry in Translation, Kings College London 1992
Theme and Version: Plath and Ronsard, Menard 1995
Collected Poems & Selected Translations of A. C. Jacobs (with J. Rety), Menard/Hearing Eye 1996

DRAMA TRANSLATIONS
Ana Novac: 'The Soup Complex', *Stand* (13/1) 1972
Ana Novac: *The Thoughts of Chairman Mao* (unpublished)
Eugene Heimler: *The Storm* (verse), Menard 1976

FICTION TRANSLATION
Balzac: *Gillette* or *The Unknown Masterpiece*, Menard 1988

THE ARITHMETIC OF MEMORY

ANTHONY RUDOLF

BELLEW · LONDON

for my mother,
Esther [Rosenberg] Rudolf

to my father,
Henry Cyril Rudolf
(1914–1986)

First published in Great Britain in 1999 by
Bellew Publishing, 8 Balham Hill, London SW12 9EA

Copyright © Anthony Rudolf 1999

ISBN 1 85725 135 0

Typeset by Antony Gray
Printed in Great Britain by
MPG Books Ltd, Bodmin, Cornwall

Acknowledgments

I am grateful to five friends who commented on an early draft of the book: Musa Moris Farhi, Elaine Feinstein, James Hogan, Paula Rego and Alan Wall.

I am grateful to Hyam Maccoby for cheerfully serving as my sounding-board and touchstone whenever I needed to test my reinterpretations and/or remembered interpretations of Jewish orthopraxis and orthodoxy. He is a true *maven*.

I am grateful to several of the authors who are listed in the bibliography (some known personally to me, some not) for having written books which, whether I was directly influenced (see the Afterword for comments on Perec and Roubaud) or not, were *there* when I needed them – some before I started work on my memories, some during the work and some after I had finished.

I am grateful to Carole Angier who, in the context of our mutual admiration for W. G. Sebald's work, suggested that I separate the Themes/Motifs section from the Index.

I am grateful to Richard Wakefield of Hampstead Garden Suburb Residents' Association for supplying a 1946 map of the Suburb.

I was honoured to be invited to contribute to the *Festschrift* for my friend Rafael Scharf, to be published by Fundacja Judaica of Krakow in June 1999 on his eighty-fifth birthday. Given his commitment to memory and remembrance, I offered as my text an abridged and edited version of the Afterword.

Finally, I acknowledge various publishers (all included in the bibliography and discography) of brief passages I have quoted, in particular John Bodley at Faber and Faber for W. H. Auden, David Jones, Robert Lowell, Thom Gunn and Walter de la Mare (also de la Mare's Literary Trustees, courtesy of whom his lines are printed), and NLB for the short passages of Walter Benjamin taken from his collection of essays *One-Way Street*, translated by Edmund Jephcott and Kingsley Shorter.

Prefatory Note

Everything in the unbracketed paragraphs has been remembered. The bracketed paragraphs are a commentary on the memories. The book, like most books, is designed to be read straight through, in the given order. But readers of a theoretical bent can, if they wish, start with the Afterword (and the Themes/Motifs section). Some readers who suspect their interest is specialised in respect of the subject matter can, if they wish, select particular sections of the book from the Contents (backed up by the Names/Places Index).

Woodside Park, Summer 1998

Contents

3

Hampstead Garden Suburb Synagogue

4

Schools outside 'The Suburb'

5
Home and Extended Family

Afterword

page 206

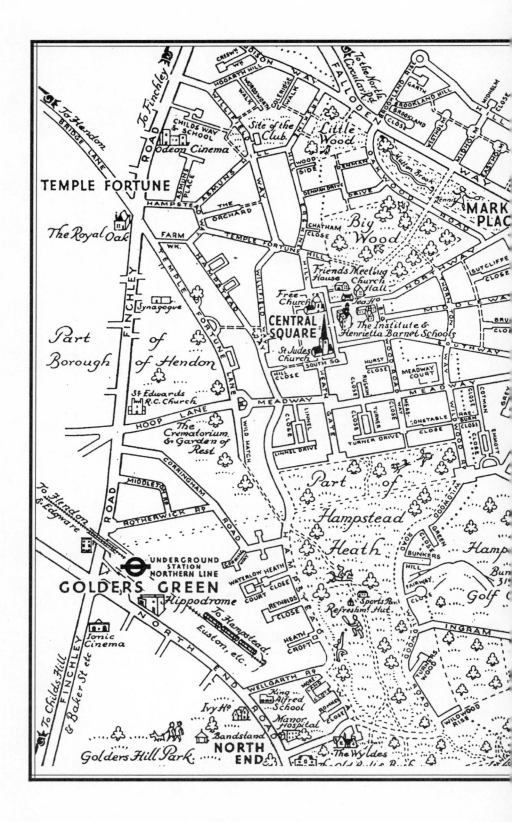

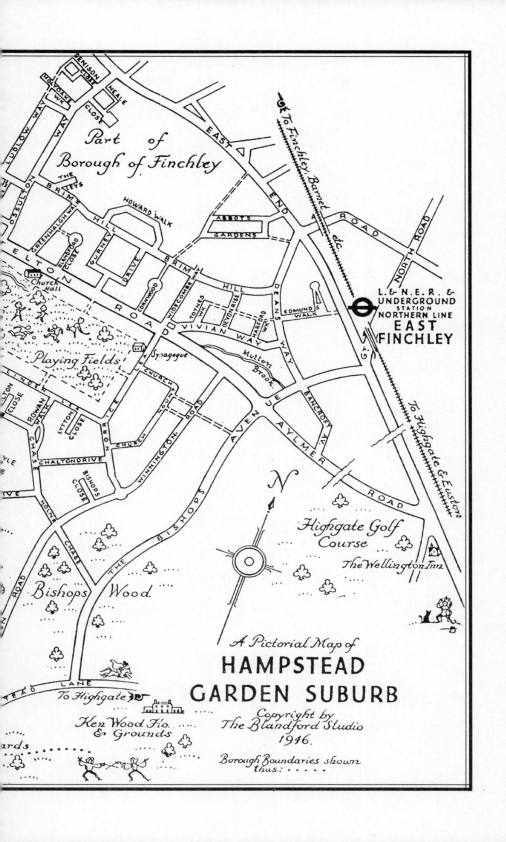

A Pictorial Map of

HAMPSTEAD
GARDEN SUBURB

Copyright by
The Blandford Studio
1946.

Borough Boundaries shown
thus:・・・・・

To divide him inventorially would dizzy the arithmetic of memory

Hamlet, V. ii.117–8
(Second Quarto)

If you can look into the seeds of time,
And say which grain will grow and which will not

Macbeth, I. iii. 58–9

1

Anthony

Language shows clearly that memory is not an instrument for exploring the past but its theatre. It is the medium of past experience, as the ground is the medium in which dead cities lie interred. He who seeks to approach his own buried past must conduct himself like a man digging . . . Remembrance must not proceed in the manner of a narrative . . . I am talking of a space, of moments and discontinuities

WALTER BENJAMIN

(A)

POSSESSIONS

1. I remember my autograph album: some of the signatures were collected personally, some were given to me by third parties who knew famous people, some I wrote away for. My album was not a proper one labelled as such, but an ordinary notebook. I stuck a paper pocket on to the inside back cover for duplicates or for names I didn't really want, sundry cricketers in particular, so that I could swap them later. My uncle Leon Rudolf gave me a programme from a charity dinner, with several signatures he had obtained for me, including the great footballer Stanley Matthews who, however, was not a hero of mine. On one visit to Lords cricket ground I asked the South African off-spinner Hugh Tayfield and his English counterpart, Jim Laker, for their signatures. They refused. *How dare they?* I owned a signed copy of the autobiography of the Scottish soccer international Billy Steele, but I could not bear not having his signature in my album so I cut it out – I knew this was a desecration – and pasted it in. I got the signatures of the Platters at Golders Green Hippodrome. After we had seen Margaret Lockwood in *Peter Pan* at the Scala Theatre I said I wanted the star's signature, so my father walked with me to the stage door,

brushed past the waiting people and said, 'Ask her.' We entered her dressing room.

[Perhaps he said ask her nicely, or ask her politely. But what *chutzpah*! He was like that, my father. I remembered this episode some years later when I read that Margaret Lockwood's daughter Julia was to play Peter, and again more recently when my friend Susannah York told me she herself had played Peter one year. My son tells me that he and my father, his grandfather, replayed family history after a play at the Shaw Theatre – only this time the signature sought was Jill Gascoigne's. My album should be somewhere in this *balagan* of a flat but all I can find is my son's collection. Would I remember the Lockwood episode so vividly if I hadn't had the two boosters as well as the autograph itself? I like the memory of the Tayfield-Laker refusal because by definition there was no written reminder, no visual booster. I recall too from my Lords days that Bill Edrich would never give you his autograph, or rather, to be technical, his signature.]

2. I remember my collection of cigarette cards, including an enormous one, which I thought would make it easier for me to win the cigarette-card game: you had to cover your opponent's cards on the floor by careful targeting of your own. I bought cards – film stars, sports champions – at junk shops: one day I gave them all away to my friend Chris Cooke, across and up my street.

[I wish I had not done this. How could I know the cards would one day be important to me? But, surprise surprise, they are all the more important in their absence. I do not remember that my father, then a heavy smoker, passed them on to me. I think manufacturers had already ceased including them in packets of cigarettes. Nor do I remember using that freak card in an actual game.]

3. I remember my dolls, Woggy B who was large and floppy, and Ickok who was small and thin, and my rocking-horse, whose name I have forgotten, and my sister Ruth riding the rocking-horse.

[I'm supposed to be remembering, not forgetting, but a written childhood incarnates the very interface of remembering and forgetting. I note my implication that the rocking-horse *had* a name: some lapses of memory could be assumptions. But the horse was definitely a he. These thoughts belong in this commentary – a theatre of hindsight and speculation – because, as you will discover, it is not in the spirit of the text to write 'whose name, if he had one, I have forgotten'. 'Ickok' was how I pronounced 'Yitzhok', the Ashkenazi Hebrew name for Isaac (Sephardi pronunciation would require 'Yitzhak', as in Rabin). Woggy B was not a golliwog. If I knew the derivation of Woggy's name I would tell you. It is a classic example of something lost for ever.]

4. I remember my chemistry set and the particular experiment which produced bad smells.

[I wish I could describe this famous experiment or even name its components, but I can't. I didn't get much of a charge from my chemistry set, and chemistry was my worst subject at school by a mile. For some unreason I was not in my element. Not until I read Primo Levi years later did the subject begin to interest me. I did not mention in my small book on him the fact – which I have already passed on to his two biographers, Ian Thomson and Carole Angier – that when I sent him a photocopy of the latest version of the Periodic Table as published in *New Scientist* he confessed that he was glad to have it because, despite his eponymous book, he had not kept up with academic developments in his professional field as a chemist. Mind you, given his sweet character he could have been trying to please me.]

5. I remember my Windsor and Newton paintbox.

[I had more than one paintbox over the years. Two companies made them. I forget the name of the second one. If I remember it in time I will not change the text itself, because the remembered truth or, better, the truthful memory is as above. But it could go in a postscript or in a revised version of this commentary, suitably acknowledged. Thus questions about structure and content are raised as we go along. Texts, like motives and behaviour, are always overdetermined. New thought during cosmetic revision: I have a clear visual memory of a paintbox and a clear visual/aural memory of the name Windsor and Newton but I cannot be certain that the paintbox I am now visualising was not made by the other company since the words Windsor and Newton are not inscribed on the visualised box. Fortunately a book is not a witness box, still less a paintbox, and a writer is not on oath. Why Windsor and Newton and not the other firm? I will never discover at which age I stopped remembering its name. Perec and

Brainard, James Joyce and Sarraute – reader, you are as aware as I am of literary authorities in the matter and manner of memory. But each of us is necessarily his/her own expert, the one and only, in the human science of personal memories unmediated by other people or documentation.]

6. I remember my first geometry set, and being taken in our family car to buy it – at the Village Tuckshop in Highgate Village. The box contained a set square, a pair of compasses, a pointer, a pencil.

[I cannot remember if my father or mother or both were with me. Had we tried and failed to buy the set in Market Place, the shopping parade in Hampstead Garden Suburb, where we lived? Did we make the short journey from the Suburb for the specific purpose of buying the equipment, or were we on our way somewhere else? My guess is that it was a Saturday afternoon. My father would probably have been alone with me. Perhaps we were heading for the second-hand bookshops in Charing Cross Road. (If so we would have driven past Dick Whittington's cat on Highgate Hill and then past the black cats outside the Carreras cigarette factory – the road was not one-way in those days – at Mornington Crescent. The Carreras factory is now called London House. The black cats were huge and I liked them. Why? Doubtless because they were familiar *and* unusual. What became of *them*?). I am fairly sure that we always turned left into Winnington Road from Holne Chase when going to Highgate and/or beyond, though the scenic route is to turn right then left at the top, by Kenwood. Three or four times a year I still have reason to follow that route. I always turn left: I claim it's quicker. Even if that is true – moot point, try it – it's not my real reason is it? One other thing: the Village Tuckshop (the name is still on the fascia) has been closed for *years* now. Who cares? I do. Even now, whenever I drive through Highgate into town, I wonder why. I really do think I will make an effort to find out. A friend, an exact contemporary, has reminded me that the make of the geometry set was Helix, and that the other paintbox company was Reeves. I'm quite pleased I can visualise both boxes clearly and forgot the names. I would like to believe this gives the lie to charges that I am neglectful of the seen, too verbal. A final postscript during revision: over the years I owned more than one geometry set and later bought them for my own children. My memory of the contents has doubtless been mediated by boosters.]

7. I remember I had a balalaika, which I bought on a school trip to the Soviet Union. I remember that a friend of my sister Ruth tuned it for me because I didn't know how to, but he tuned it wrong.

[He must have thought it worked like a guitar. 'Describe!', as Isaac Babel occasionally reminds himself in his marvellous diary written during a Cossack campaign in Ukraine. But Babel is saving the description for a future story. There is no need for me to research and supply my own in this context.]

8. I remember letters from friends, which I never threw away. I remember particularly the letters – and the handwriting – of Susan Leveson and Paul Rochman. Sometimes the letters were on the parental letterhead, sometimes not.

[I still have the letters somewhere. This item belongs in this section but the personal details belong elsewhere, under 'Friends' (3.E.i/ii). Those letters mattered then and matter now. Would that the friends had kept mine, but that could be a sentimental intrusion, and therefore does not belong in this book. I did not start keeping copies of letters I'd written until I had a typewriter – at Cambridge, after the self-imposed time-span of this book's discontinuum – which raises the whole question of archives, one of the several reasons I end this book before leaving for college: see the Afterword.]

9. I remember my bicycle: it had shock absorbers, the only bike in the street with such a feature. They were large and chunky and fixed to the hubs.

[It may well have been a prototype. My father sometimes brought home things his clients gave him. It might be possible to check this one, but if I pursued every ramification the book would become very long – a cross between autobiography and social history – and lose everything. More modest in scope, it is a personal memory bank with all the vicissitudes and avatars that this implies and, sometimes, yields in language. How is a memory renewed? Each time told, it changes the collectivity of representations, reinforces their structures. A memory is always a memory of a memory of the original memory. The story is not *improved* (the legendary caught fish) but deepened in the light of increased understanding. Problems of representation and structure in the field of memory will be raised in passing. Again I proclaim the rule: no consultations with documents or people except in the parentheses and then only sparingly – and own up to them where they occur.]

10. I remember my Meccano set, my Dinky cars and my 3-D lenses.

[I wasn't very interested in the Meccano set, as it involved skills I didn't have. I would guess that Meccano, which was metal, overlapped with the arrival of Lego and then vanished. The 3-D lenses must have had some connection with the latest thing in cinema technology. Nearly half a century later two painter friends of mine, Linda Mariano in New York and Aldous Eveleigh in London, are experimenting with them, as are various conceptual artists or visual writers.]

11. I remember my large toy gun. It was not a cap gun. I remember it used a roll of paper to punch holes in.

12. I remember my stamp collection.

[Taxonomically, this counts as a hobby.]

(B)

CLOTHES

1. I remember wearing Scott's of London shirts. I was different, being the only person I knew who wore that make; the proprietor was a family friend and a client of my father, Bernie Rubin. His factory was in Tottenham. Sometimes the shirts were seconds. Bernie was in or had been in the Communist Party. His nylon shirts were uncomfortable, though it was fun when they crackled with static. The largest rival firm was called Rael-Brook. Bernie or my father told me Rael was short for Israel.

[Wait a minute, *were* the nylon shirts from Scott's? I have a funny feeling Bernie was a pioneer of drip-dry cotton shirts. They had narrow plastic whalebones you inserted into the soft collar.]

2. I remember short-sleeve Airtex shirts and a shop in Market Place called Marshalls' where you bought them, as well as things like underwear and pyjamas. I had a belt which was bought there, fastened by a horizontal metal 's', and ties with different animals on them. Mr Marshall, or his brother, always had a tape measure round the neck, and a brisk cheerful manner.

[A friend tells me the belts were known as 'snake' belts. By mentioning Marshalls' here, C. W. & A. Marshall, gents' and boys' outfitters, I obviate the requirement to mention them in a later section where they equally belong: Market Place and Shops Bordering the Suburb (2A). Marshalls', like most of the shops in Market Place, has gone. One of the shocks of growing older has been the discovery that things change. But I do wonder if the rate of change has accelerated. Was there a more stable period in Britain from the end of World War II until the period when the Tories abandoned the post-war settlement, a settlement which socialists, including my parents, had worked for and, through the Labour Party, carried through? *Why* did Marshalls' close? Retirement? Death? Increased rent? No son and heir? For many people, Tory England has been a harder and more ugly place than the one I grew up in. In terms of community it is a harder and uglier place for everybody, including those who have done well out of deregulation, privatisation and globalisation, but not many of these make the connection. Maybe I will live to see the process reversed by my children's generation. I wish I had as much faith in Tony Blair as my son has. Postscript during final revision: Tony Blair has become Prime Minister since the above was written . . .]

3. I remember tying my tie, including the school tie, with a Windsor knot. The man who taught me the technique was my father's client, Major Stanley Stanley, whose name always made me laugh. Sometimes I tied the knot as wide as possible. I had a shirt with a cutaway collar, perfect for a Windsor knot.

4. I remember my first sports jacket, bought at Montague Burton's on the corner of Tottenham Court Road and New Oxford Street. Burton: 'the Fifty Shilling Tailor'. It was next door a shop which sold gramophones, Imhofs.

[No comment on this item. Not every verse has to be commented on – am I a Talmud scholar or a literary critic or what?]

5. I remember my first pair of long trousers, bought at Horne Brothers on Waterloo Bridge, by the Strand.

[That shop is still there. Horne Brothers appears to have modernised its appeal, unlike Dunns and similar outfitters. This memory is related to another more important memory, because the long trousers were a *symbol*.]

6. I remember a big baggy sweater, called a sloppy joe, and a windcheater.

[I did do train-spotting, with the help of the famous Ian Allan books, but after school, in uniform, thus not wearing a windcheater aka anorak. So, a nerd I wasn't.]

7. I remember I had a pair of brown shoes with immensely thick crape soles. I loved, how I loved, those thick crape soles, and the brown uppers.

8. I remember a period when I had one pair of shoes at a time, because I was growing so fast: the huge feet led my father to call me a right-angled triangle. The first pair of shoes I chose for myself I bought at K Shoes in Oxford Street. From then on, *no way* would I buy shoes with toecaps.

[Until 1992 I continued buying shoes from various branches of K Shoes. Now I love DMs (Dr Martens) and not only because of pressure from my daughter Naomi and her contemporaries. My young friend Rhianon Gale took me to Holt's in Camden Town to buy my first DMs. But K did a very nice shoe. I like that trade usage, as in, 'This is a very nice trouser, sir.' But no one ever asked me which side I dressed, sir. Nor do I recall that tape measures for the inside leg had an inch-long firm bit to minimise intervention in the privates. The DM toecaps caused me grief the other day, at the front security in the Royal Courts of Justice, where they set all the alarms ringing. No way was *no way* used in those days. I date it to the mid-eighties.]

9. I remember a green raincoat with the belt tied tightly round my waist and wearing it on a windswept promenade in Brighton.

[I suppose it was raining that day but I only remember the wind.]

10. I remember Cash nametapes sown into my clothes.

(C)

BODY

1. I remember my parents explaining the small birthmark beneath my left nipple as a coffee stain. I believed them and at the same time suspected they were joking.

2. I remember that my penis gave me neither pleasure nor trouble. It just was.
   [Please understand that in my necessary zeal to avoid a linear narrative and all the consequent distortions the genre is heir to, problems of time-scale are bound to arise. These I can explain, if I feel like it, on a case-by-case basis. Here for example I am saying that the zone in question remained neutral until after the end of the period covered by this book. From my reading and discussion with male and female friends I suspect I was in a minority concerning said organ. Whether this was a good or bad thing remains a moot point. What came later, though occasionally alluded to in these pages, is of no interest or concern – at least in the context of *this* book. 'It just was' can, in this commentary, be glossed: 'It was just as it had been since I was eight days old.']

3. I remember I was embarrassed on one occasion when my pubic hair was seen by my mother and one of my sisters, while I was in the bath.

4. I remember when my facial hair started sprouting. My father instructed me not to start shaving because once you start you have to go on.

5. I remember having spots and using Neutrogena soap and witch-hazel and some prescribed brown cream in vain attempts to clear them up.

6. I remember using different makes of hair cream, including Brylcreem and Silvikrin.

7. I remember once being badly constipated. I was taken to Dr Hirschmann who smeared some kind of cream or gelatine in my *tochus*. When we got home my father came into the bathroom with me and sat on the dirty-laundry box doing *The Times* crossword while I just sat on the toilet. In normal

circumstances I took evening rather than morning dumps.

[But, needless to say, that was not the word we used for bowel movements. What did we say? Perhaps 'going to the toilet'. Or was the word 'business'?]

8. I remember not getting verrucas at school. I hated the word verruca.

[This 'remember not getting' is a genuine memory, different from 'not remember getting'. I suspect the positive nature of the recollection is due to the power which the word, with its unusual cluster of strong consonants and open vowels, had and has on me. Some boys were plagued with the horrid foot warts, spied in the changing-room at the school swimming-pool. Now it sounds like a Scandinavian au pair's name, a big girl, a woman really, admired by the fellows in language school and pub.]

9. I remember flat feet and remedial drill to raise the arches.

[Underneath the arches there was nothing. And Flanagan and Allen's 'Underneath the Arches', always on the wireless when I was young, is now an almost forgotten song.]

10. I remember my first pair of National Health Service specs, prescribed by Mr Flint. Standard issue, they were circular, with gold-plated rims and round earclips. I did not want to wear glasses, I hated them. At prep school I remember touching them the first time a friend saw them, but after a few days I noticed that nobody else cared, so I didn't either.

[Was it John Lennon or Alf Garnett who started the later fashion for them?]

11. I remember the family dentist, David Sigaloff, known to me as Uncle Doddy. He moved his surgery from Harley Street to Uxbridge Road, a long way down the road from the two Shepherds Bush tube stations. Uncle Doddy told jokes and made you feel safe. Once or twice he gave me gas. I remember the gas cylinder and mask – and a second dentist called in from downstairs, as required by the regulations. Before being anaesthetised you had to go for a wee.

[He must have moved from fashionable Harley Street to unfashionable Uxbridge for reasons of lease or money or both. I wonder if novocaine was already an alternative to gas, or does its use post-date my childhood tooth removal? I carried on going to the family dentist for years longer than convenient. Doddy is also included in a paragraph (5.A.iii.2) dealing with the friends of my parents. They were known as uncle or aunt. Believe it or not, young readers, in those far-off days no grown-up was addressed by his or her first name. Doddy was a lover of women, often his receptionists. Today, by chance, my mother left a message on the answerphone that he is in hospital with advanced cancer. A generation is passing. Soon, in terms of my family, the senior generation will have left the scene. Half and quarter generations belong to friends rather than family. When I phoned the hospital Doddy had gone home, having doubtless flirted with the nurses. And now, revising this paragraph, I record that he has died.]

12. I remember going to hospital to have my tonsils out. A nurse dressed me in a smock and took away my cake.

[Perhaps it was a birthday cake. I don't remember that I was given a slice for myself. I suppose I was, but the memory may have been cancelled by the enforced removal of *my cake*.]

13. I remember various childhood ailments and illnesses, mumps, measles, chicken pox.

14. I remember Dr Hirschmann's surgery in Greenhalgh Drive. My parents sometimes sought second opinions from doctors who were conveniently close relatives, Uncle Jack Simon and Uncle Leon Russell, my mother's brother-in-law and brother.

[Dr Hirschmann seemed to be known by everybody. There must have been other doctors in the Suburb but I was not aware of them. Strictly speaking he belongs in the Suburb section but I think that having constructed this section and sub-section, I must include him here.]

(D)

MIND

1. I remember often thinking that grown-ups were different from children, completely different. But on one occasion, in the upstairs bathroom, I remember being *amazed* at the likelihood, indeed the certainty, that I would go to the toilet when I was grown up.

[For 'completely' read 'ontologically', but I do not use the word in the text itself since I did not know it then, and therefore could not have thought in such a conceptually sophisticated way. I wonder what age I was when I had that bathroom thought. I permit myself a rare reference to age: it feels like 10 or 11. I (above) should read 'I', for as children we cannot know, thank goodness, that when grown up we never stop housing the children we were. Here I am reminded of a remarkable phrase about old age, used by the American poet George Oppen in conversation with our mutual friend Paul Auster, who passed it on to me: 'What a strange thing to happen to a little boy.' The phrase might have made a nice epigraph for this book but although it does feel strange to be in my early fifties, I do not classify this as old. One also recalls Psalm 37, verse 25: 'I have been young and am now old.' Yitzhak Rabin or Shimon Peres once misquoted it as, 'I have been young but am now old.' He was vilified by religious members of the Knesset, the Israeli Parliament, for his interpretation of the rest of that verse. One poet, however, said he agreed with the perpetrator's political gloss but that he should be strung up for losing the poetry of the phrase quoted above. It is surely true that the banal copula 'but' destroys the psalmist's delicate poetry.]

2. I remember thinking that if a great glass dome were to cover Finchley my street would remain the same for ever, and how solid the pavements were.

3. I remember that there had to be dark, total dark in my bedroom before I could go to sleep, not one crack of light showing, except my luminous watch.

[This remains true to this day, or should that read night? Go on, say it: I am still in the dark. Even in the daytime. My self-possession gutters as I consult my statements: the current account of memory is not looking too good, even in the black.]

4. I remember wanting to be left-handed in everything. I was pleased that I did in fact bat left-handed at cricket, and played left-handed on the putting green, but that was all.

5. I remember 'the little box' where I placed my most secret thoughts. Only I had access to this part of my mind.

[I have tried to take good care of the little box, which is akin to Montaigne's 'little back shop' as well as Edward FitzGerald's ' . . . magic shadow-show / played in a box whose Candle is the Sun'. This was where I belonged of right, as the Beatles and Winnicott, both echoing Wallace Stevens, were to say (in their own languages) of a similar place or construction. Why do we 'seal the hushed casket' of our souls (in the phrase of Keats)? Perhaps because in the segue of family 'there is no outside, no inclosing wall, no circumference to us', as Emerson wrote and as quoted in John Taggart's book on Edward Hopper. This phrase in turn reminds me of Walter Benjamin's concept of porosity in his essay 'Naples'. You can imagine my delight when I discovered Vasko Popa's beautiful poem 'Little Box' years later, translated by Anne Pennington. I was the first publisher of this poem in English, and produced three editions of it on a single sheet or postcard before it appeared in a book. When I discovered Joseph Cornell, my cup ran over.]

6. I remember nursery rhymes, and how 'real' they were, sometimes frightening. I particularly remember 'Who Killed Cock Robin?', 'Hey Diddle Diddle', 'Rock-a-bye Baby' and 'How Many Miles to Babylon?'.

[Years later I was delighted to find all four in Paula Rego's marvellous engravings of the rhymes: theatrical and mordantly post-Freudian, as Marina Warner calls them in her introduction to the Folio Society edition. Nursery rhymes registered less potently than the Jewish stories of Passover, etc., which had the dual force of myth *and* history, or so it seems when invested with hindsight.]

(E)

READING

1. I remember reading the *Iliad* and the *Odyssey*, translated by E. V. Rieu, on the bus going to my prep school and after lunch there. I remember very well Diomedes and Ajax, Poseidon and limping Hephaestus; Odysseus and Penelope, of course; Circe and the Cyclops. I preferred the *Iliad* to the *Odyssey*, and the Greek names of the gods to the Latin names. Those classics had brown covers. Later I read Balzac and Stendhal in Penguins with green covers. But Penguins mainly had orange covers.

[The last page of my battered copy of the *Iliad* has fragments of a secret language I and a close friend at prep school, the late Colin Macleod, invented.]

2. I remember reading and rereading a prep-school prize, *Redcap Runs Away* by Rhoda Power.

[This was the only prize I ever won from an educational institution, apart from Hebrew classes.]

3. I remember reading several novels by Dickens. Various scenes remain vivid in my mind, including Bill Sykes fleeing to Hampstead after murdering Nancy, to Whitestone Pond *which I knew*.

[According to my uncle Leon Russell, Fagin lived in Steward Street off Spitalfields Market, the same street and perhaps even the same house my maternal grandparents lived in, but I can find no evidence for this in the book! I don't need to 'remember' the books themselves because I still have the complete Dickens Mr and Mrs Philip Lewis (of Lewis & Tucker, estate agents, Hanover Square) gave me for my barmitzvah. One or two volumes were missing so my father said I should telephone Mr Lewis, his client and oldest friend. Philip told me the set had been bought at Boots in Regent Street. I remember going there, upstairs, to complete the set at the Lewises' expense. Had I asked for this present? Was I consulted? Was it their own idea? My father may well have suggested it if in fact they asked him what they should get me. I could phone Philip and find out but, after forty years, would he remember? Almost worth checking out as an experiment, and for the fun of it. Postscript during revision: he too has died recently. Boots, it suddenly occurs to me, is not the most obvious place to buy a set of Dickens, but that branch was only five minutes from Hanover Square and perhaps the nearest 'bookshop'.]

4. I remember reading countless schoolbooks and adventure stories by authors like Percy Westerman and G. A. Henty, and John Buchan in Penguins with orange covers. I had a book called *Shandy at Ringmere*. I regularly borrowed girls' boarding-school stories from Jill Rosenheim across the road. I also remember Billy Bunter, his teacher Squelch (Quelch?) of the Remove, and his Indian friend, Hurree Jamset Ram Singh. I read Kipling's *Stalkie and Co.* which I did not like, and his *Just So Stories* which I did. I remember Mowgli in *The Jungle Book*.

[All the boys' school stories, except one, were set in boarding schools. They often ended with the heroes (ever upstanding or formerly rebellious) going off to run the empire. I'm trying to get hold of *Shandy* – a bookshop in Hay-on-Wye has a search out for it. The book set in a day school was *Three-Guinea Watch* by Talbot Baines Reed, based on my alma mater, City of London School. My grandfather's barmitzvah present to me was a Swiss watch which, oddly enough, cost three guineas. It was a Zodiac. No one else had a Zodiac. Postscript: I finally tracked down a copy of *Shandy of Ringmere School* (the correct title) through a specialist dealer, Robert Kirkpatrick. Rereading it has proved to be a mistake.]

5. I remember reading *Robinson Crusoe* and *Treasure Island*, *The Coral Sea*, *Lord of the Flies* and *Black Beauty*. Several Dumas and loadsa Biggles.

[Biggles and co. were the Famous Five in grown-up gear.]

6. I remember classics like *Children of the New Forest* by Captain Marryat, *Old St Paul's* and other books by Harrison Ainsworth. I remember *Rob Roy* and *Ivanhoe* by Walter Scott.

[Mine must have been almost the last generation of children to read Captain Marryat and Harrison Ainsworth, and definitely the last to read Westerman and Henty.]

7. I remember browsing among my parents' books. Some of them I read. I chose and loved Evelyn Waugh's *Decline and Fall* and *Scoop*, but abandoned Graham Greene. I was much affected by *Doctor Zhivago* and *The Great Gatsby*.

There was a Penguin with a red cover, Turgenev's *Fathers and Sons*, and a deeply boring novel about a boxer, Bernard Shaw's *Cashel Byron's Profession*.

8. Among my parents' books I also remember reading L. P. Hartley's trilogy *Eustace and Hilda* – *The Shrimp and the Anemone*, *The Sixth Heaven* and *Eustace and Hilda* – as well as his *The Go-Between*. I read the multi-volumed *Jean-Christophe* by Romain Rolland when I was ill with flu in the little bedroom above the garage. I found and read *Brave New World* and *Animal Farm*.

9. I remember reading Kenneth Grahame's *Wind in the Willows* and several novels by Arthur Ransome. I enjoyed these tales of a rural world which was not mine. Nor had I ever seen a scarecrow, except in the illustrations to Barbara Euphan Todd's Worzel Gummidge books.

10. I remember a book I read over and over again. It had a bright blue cover: *Hindu Fairy Tales*. And I had an edition of the story of King Arthur. The legend of Bedivere, Lancelot and Guinevere enthralled me.

[*Hindu Fairy Tales* was one of a number of books I now bitterly regret selling when later I moved from my room in Powis Square to Granville Park, Lewisham. Laura Del Rivo, a Portobello Road dealer friend of my neighbour Michael Horovitz, slipped an agreed ten-bob note under my door in payment.]

11. I remember a Penguin with a pink cover, *The Family from One-End Street*. I loved this book and read it many times. Another Penguin I liked also had a pink cover, *Ballet Shoes* by Noel Streatfield. This book mentioned Cromwell Road which I knew from visits to the museums in South Kensington.

12. I remember a cartoon book with a sinister character called Baron de Bong. He was short, had a beard and hat, and possibly a hump. He was a smuggler. The colour blue predominated in this book.

[I would love to see it again. Offers welcome. Thank you.]

13. I remember a children's illustrated Bible, but the only episode which comes to mind from that edition concerns Gideon and his soldiers, the episode involving the drinking of water. [See Judges 7, verses iv–viii.]

14. I remember *Our Island Story* by the children's historian A. W. Marshall. I remember Lambert Simnel, Perkin Warbeck, John Ball, Wat Tyler, and the little princes in the Tower.

[Those initials are wrong: a confusion with the gents' outfitters. Mind you, most of the history involved gents.]

15. I remember the first (apart from set texts) book I read in the original French, *François le Champi* by George Sand, on holiday in Royan with my French exchange friend, André.

16. I remember sports annuals like *The Boys' Book of Soccer* and the Playfair books of soccer and cricket and *Wisden*, and learning statistics off by heart. The highest first-class score was 424 not out by A. C. Maclaren of Lancashire.

[Overtaken since then by Hanif Mohammed and of course, during the writing of this book, by Brian Lara who is forbidden to overtake Denis Compton's 1948 record of runs in one season, though he is allowed to overtake Bill Edrich's total which is second only to Compton's. My 1951 edition of *Wisden* survives, falling apart at the seams like an ancient cricket ball.]

17. I remember subscribing to *World Sports* and also receiving *Motor Sport* free each month because the publisher, Wesley Tee, was my father's client. I was not at all interested in motor racing or cars but looked through the magazine each month. One of the drivers was a Siamese prince known as Bira, who drove at Goodwood. The editor had a funny name: Willy Body. Famous car manufacturers had names like Maserati and Bugatti.

[Today the Siamese prince, whose full name was something like Birabong, would be a Thai. Wesley Tee died recently, aged 93, a senior member of what my father in his later years called the jeopardy generation. Mr Tee was in fact my father's *first* client, an important figure in his development as a chartered accountant and in the growth of his professional practice. As the name suggests, Wesley was a Methodist, and a prominent one. His office, by accident or design, was behind the founder's chapel in City Road.]

18. I remember a book about one of the highest mountains in the world, *Annapurna* by Maurice Herzog.

19. I remember reading by torchlight under the blankets after my light was supposed to be out. I could hear my father's slow footsteps as he came up to check my light was out.

20. I remember Oscar Wilde's *The Happy Prince* on a set of 78s which I played on our gramophone. There was an illustrated text: 'Turn the page' and 'Turn the page and the record'.

21. I remember a book fair at the Royal Festival Hall. My father or I chose John Masefield's *Collected Poems* and the *Albatross Book of Verse* published by Collins. Sir Norman Birkett made a speech. My father said he was a famous lawyer.

[I still have these two books and refer to the latter occasionally. It is possible that the visit was occasioned by book tokens, which were perhaps barmitzvah presents.]

22. I remember Arthur Mee and his *Children's Newspaper* and, later, *Junior Express*. Occasionally I bought comics such as *Rover*, *Hotspur*, the *Wizard*, *Tiger*. They were just about tolerated. *Eagle* was actually encouraged. *Beano* and *Dandy* were forbidden. *Film Fun* and *Radio Fun* contained regular strip cartoons about Petula Clark, Issie Bonn and other stars.

[Adult newspapers will be found on another shelf, along with more on books. See section 5.A.iii.]

23. I remember writing to a magazine edited by Peter Noble, possibly called *Film*, about Harpo Marx: Was he really dumb? They replied that I would be pleased to learn he was not.

(F)

MUSIC

(i) Classical

1. I remember my first two classical records, *Eine Kleine Nachtmusik*, and Delibes' *Coppélia Suite*. These were 45s and were also known as extended plays (eps) – I bought them at HMV in Oxford Street, where you could listen to everything in a booth before making a decision to purchase. I bought the score of the Mozart and tried to follow it.

2. I remember going to concerts at the Royal Festival Hall. I liked sitting in the cheap seats behind the orchestra where you had a good view of the soloist. My favourite pianist was Shura Cherkassky.

[My taste has changed. I prefer quieter pianists, and work written for piano alone rather than concertos, for example Andras Schiff's Schubert. When will he record the Beethoven sonatas?]

3. I remember Classics Club, the earliest club of its kind, with the unprepossessing record sleeves. One of their records was the Tchaikowsky first concerto, with Noel Mewton-Wood as soloist. I had never heard of Mewton-Wood but my piano teacher said he was very good.

[Department of the Lexicon: 'unprepossessing' is indeed the *mot juste* but strictly speaking it should not be included in the text as I would not have used it then.]

4. I remember my piano teacher, a shy New Zealander called Douglas Zanders, who lived in Hurst Close in the Suburb. His handwriting was totally illegible because, like my paternal grandfather, he had been born left-handed but forced to change – he at school, my grandfather in the army.

[Perhaps on the keys this strengthened the fingers of your weaker hand, and was thus a good thing? But maybe it gave you stress – and was thus a bad thing?]

5. I remember the Holland Park Young People's Music Club to which I was introduced by Nadia-Myra Grindea, the daughter of Miron and Carola Grindea, in whose flat at 28 Emperor's Gate SW7 I heard informal recitals.

6. I remember going to a performance of *Let's Make an Opera* ('Listen to the wind . . . ') and listening to a recording of *The Young People's Guide to the Orchestra*, both by Benjamin Britten.

7. I remember various 78s at home, and their labels. HMV had a famous trademark: the dog with its ear to the amplifier. *Peter and the Wolf* was a great favourite of mine. We also owned Solomon playing Chopin mazurkas and polonaises; Walter Gieseking playing Mozart or Schubert; George Kulenkampff playing Beethoven's *Violin Concerto*; and several other symphonies and concertos. Long works involved changing the record every five or six minutes. I thrilled to Beethoven's *Choral Symphony*. I knew that the 'Ode to Joy' symbolised the triumph of the human spirit and, very particularly, demonstrated Beethoven's own survival in the face of personal adversity. My father would sometimes sing along, rather tunelessly, with the Ode. A warped 78 could be heated up and converted into a flower pot.

[Many years later I read Mary Felstiner's fine biography of Charlotte Salomon. She tells how the 'Ode to Joy' accompanies an important episode in the life story and 'story life' of this extraordinary artist. If, at this very moment, I try to visualise the memory of my father singing along, I see him merging with a group of soloists at a prom . . . only for Charlotte's story to overlay them. And then, remembering the time-span of Charlotte's miracle of work on her *Three-Colour Operetta* in the South of France (early 1941 to summer 1942), I try to visualise my mother pregnant with me in London in 1942. And I try to hum Beethoven's famous tune . . . an appropriate musical reminder of Weimar's distinguished daughter, Lotte, creator of one of the great works to emerge from that world.]

8. I remember the Proms at the Royal Albert Hall. One year I won tickets in the ballots for the first and the last night. I liked being a promenader and, on the last night, sang 'Jerusalem' and tried to clap Malcolm Sargent and the orchestra off-beat in 'Saucy Arethusa'. I always went on my own. Friday night was Beethoven night but this I listened to on the wireless, sometimes called radio, because we never went out on Friday evenings.

9. I remember Chopin's music always meant a great deal to me. I asked my

piano teacher to teach me the easier pieces. Frivolously I asked him to play the difficult Minute Waltz in one minute.

[To this day unless I make a positive decision to play a particular work by a particular composer, I put on Chopin: Dinu Lipatti playing the B-minor sonata or Maria Joao Pires the nocturnes, for example. And I still try to play Opus 34, No. 2 on my own upright piano.]

(ii) Popular

1. I remember nonsense songs like 'I'm a Pink Toothbrush . . . ' sung by Max Bygraves. And 'Put Your Shoes on Lucy, You're a Big Girl Now' sung by – who? And the Goons: 'I'm Walking Backwards to Christmas', 'Niddle, Nuddle, Nu' and the Ying Tong Song. One song (sung by ?) began: 'Ay–round the corner, woohoo, bee–hind the berry tree/Ay–round the corner, bee–hind the bush, looking for Henry Lee'.

[These and many others in this section were heard on the wireless, in particular on *Children's Favourites*, which went out on the old Light Pro-gramme. A recent interview with Petula Clark, in her sixties now, so help me, revealed that she sang 'Lucy', but no tampering with my memory above. And who, I wonder, was Henry Lee? Does the song contain sexual innuendo?]

2. I remember cowboy songs like 'A Four-Legged Friend . . . ', sung by Roy Rogers, and 'Champion the Wonder Horse' by Frankie Laine. Frankie Laine also sang 'Jezebel'.

3. I remember many pop songs though I rarely bought them – my father disapproved of pop music. Some of these songs are associated with particular occasions: there was Laurie London's version of 'He's Got the Whole World in His Hands', which he sang on an edition of *Six-Five Special* ('The Six-Five Special's coming down the line/the Six-Five Special is mighty fine'). Someone, my uncle Leon Rudolf I think, had obtained tickets. I took Gillian Posner who lived in Willesden Green (up from Walm Lane, down from the tube) on condition we did not dance. She promised but could not resist, and dragged me on to the floor. I was wearing a beige round-necked pullover. The following Monday I was recognised on the tube. Laurie London was very short, even

allowing for the fact he was only fourteen. Pete Murray was the compère or host, and there was a commère, Josephine Douglas. On one occasion I listened to Frankie Vaughan's hit 'Green Door' at HMV's store.

[So where are you now Gill Posner? Given that I have two children aged around twenty you are probably a grandmother. *Oy veh*, or something. And what became of Laurie London? Thinking again about the programme's signature tune quoted above I suspect I have made a mistake with the second line. It was Lonnie Donegan's 'Rock Island Line' which was 'mighty fine'. The Saturday-evening programme, as you will have guessed, began at five past six. Since the only actual song title I can remember from my HMV forays is 'Green Door' that makes the occasion *memorable*.]

4. I remember Bill Haley singing 'Rock Around the Clock' and 'See You Later Alligator'. The latter song gave rise to a plethora of catch phrases like, 'See you later, mashed potato.'

5. I remember skiffle which I loved, especially Lonnie Donegan's 'Rock Island Line', 'Cumberland Gap', 'Putting on the Style' ('Sweet sixteen goes to school just to see the boys, laughs and screams and giggles at every little noise'), and Johnny Duncan and the Blue Grass Boys singing 'Last Train to San Fernando' ('If you miss this one, you'll never get another one, diddy diddy dum dum to San Fernando').

[I am fairly sure that Tommy Steele emerged from skiffle, which deriving from traditional jazz overlapped with early UK rock and roll on the one hand and folk on the other. He modulated to rock and was perhaps the first UK-born pop star of the new generation. He sang the UK cover version of Guy Mitchell's 'Singing the Blues' ('The moon and stars no longer shine/the girl is gone I thought was mine/there's nothing left for me to do/but cry–y–y–y over you'). Some years later in America I found myself outside a station on the Rock Island Line, and sang a chorus in honour of Lonnie Donegan.]

6. I remember Perry Como and 'Catch a Falling Star' (he pronounced it 'cetch') and I remember explaining to my father in Golders Green Road, in front of a menswear shop where we could not find a grey zipper cardigan as worn by my school friend Warren Pantzer and which I had finally persuaded

my father to buy me, that Perry Como did *not* have a gimmick. Ah, said my father triumphantly, *that* was his gimmick.

[There was no answer to that, as Eric Morecambe would say later. Except, on reflection, the singer without a gimmick might not have been Perry Como but Pat Boone, whose 'April Love' and 'Love Letters in the Sand' I well remember. These days I fall to pieces, recalling things that other people have desired, when I hear Patsy Cline sing 'Love Letters . . . ']

7. I remember the Platters. 'The Great Pretender' and 'Only You' were my favourites among their renditions, apart from 'Smoke Gets in Your Eyes', which I knew was a standard.

[The Platters have worn well. There is a pub in Kentish Town which still has their recordings in its juke box. I wonder if they actually wrote 'The Great Pretender'. One of the finest versions of 'Smoke . . . ' is Jerry Garcia's. It can be heard over the credits of Paul Auster's film *Smoke*.]

8. I remember Guy Mitchell's 'Roving Kind': 'She was a nice girl, a proper girl, but – one of the roving kind', and 'Pat Him on the Po-Po'; and Johnnie Ray ('Little White Cloud that Cried' and 'Too Young' and 'Walking in the Rain'), Frank Sinatra and Doris Day. And Dickie Valentine: 'Someone broke into my heart and stole a beat or two,/The finger of suspicion points at you'. And Valentine again: 'Mr Sandman, bring me a dream,/Make her complexion like peaches and cream'. And: 'The naughty lady of Shady Lane, she's got all the guys in a whirl;/The naughty lady of Shady Lane, me oh my, oh what a girl'. I remember whistling 'Finger of Suspicion' in the alleyway leading from Sutcliffe Close to my road. Johnnie Ray had a hearing-aid and was called a crooner.

[The random nature of recollection is illustrated by the precise reference to Sutcliffe Close, where doubtless I had been visiting a friend, Adrian Barnes or Ivor Shrago. I must have whistled 'Finger of Suspicion' and other tunes many times but this was the one I remember, although – I hasten to add – not 'as if it was yesterday'. It was, and feels like it was, a very long time ago. I admire the words of 'Finger of Suspicion' but do not feel the need to check out the name of the writer.]

9. I remember Tab Hunter and a song called 'Young Love'.

[This was a dreadful song, sung tunelessly by an actor with no voice. I knew that even then, but wasn't bothered.]

10. I remember the Hit Parade in *New Musical Express*, and how I pored over it every week (Friday?), like the football league tables on Sundays.

[Attempt a few years ago to impress thirteen-year-old daughter or at least to show interest: 'What's top of the hit parade, Naomi?' Groaning and eyes rolling: 'The charts, dad, the charts.']

11. I remember the folk songs we used to sing in the car on long journeys: 'Hang my heart on a weeping willow tree . . . ', 'Widecombe Fair', 'Sucking Cider Through a Straw' and 'Clementine'.

12. I remember Harry Belafonte singing 'Scarlet Ribbons' and 'Banana Boat Song'.

13. I remember going with two school friends, Dave Roberts and Alan Bell, to hear Ella Fitzgerald sing at the Gaumont State Theatre in Kilburn. My parents must have been away because I returned to Finchley Central on buses, and slept at the house of Uncle Leon Rudolf, St Paul's Way, number 22, off Long Lane N3.

[Ella Fitzgerald: my great and pre-sexual Platonic love from afar, cognate in my lived life with Hilary Sefton (3.E.ii.5) and Patricia Hammerson (4.C.ii.III.1). Fitzgerald was surely the supreme singer at the interface of popular music and jazz, abolishing the boundary between them in a way that two other great singers, Billie Holiday on the jazz side and Frank Sinatra on the popular side, did not. Ella you are old and ailing now but I want you to know that I was present when you sang in concert and I love you. The Gaumont State is now a bingo hall. Postscript: Ella died recently. May the earth rest as lightly on her bones as her legato lies on our ears.]

14. I remember Chris Barber and Monty Sunshine, and other traditional jazz musicians.

15. I remember Juliette Greco, to whom I sent a love letter c/o the Savoy Theatre, where I went to hear her. She never replied. But I thought she was divine.

[I was not alone. There was Sartre, and Miles Davis . . . and, my friend Z. Kotowicz tells me, Georges Brassens. I still think she is divine. I knew she refused for years to sing songs Sartre wrote for her, until she finally relented with 'Rue des Blancs-Manteaux', a song about the guillotine which stood in the eponymous Marais street in Paris, near the latter-day Picasso Museum. If she could reject *him* it made my own rejection easier to bear. I'm having second thoughts about that love letter. It *feels* like something I would have done pre-college, that is pre-sexual awareness, but something tells me it was post-Ella. The temptation to break the non-documentation rule and check out my collection of theatre programmes is almost overpowering but finally I resist. The time-span of this book ends with my return from Paris shortly before my nineteenth birthday and the beginning of my university life. So, perhaps I went to the Savoy in the summer of 1961. Consider this and in our time-span: that this parenthesis be dropped, but no. There is so *little* to show for all my remembering. And as for chronology . . . what's with the linear autobiographies I've read? . . . Oh, 'marvellous tremor of time', as Chateaubriand, quoted by Gaëtan Picon, wrote in *La vie de Rancé*. (Picon also reminds us that Chateaubriand, speaking of a different matter in *Mémoires d'outre-tombe*, varies the phrase to 'marvellous shortcoming of time'.)]

16. I remember 'Mustafa', and Edith Piaf singing 'Milord'.

17. I remember joke songs and rhymes like 'My Old Man's a Dustman' (' 'e wears a dustman's cap,/'e bought a two-bob ticket to see a football match' and ending: 'we can kick 'em, we can pass, we can kick 'em up the arse/nal'); 'In Days of Old' ('when knights were bold and lavatories weren't invented'); 'On Top of Ol' Smoky' ('where nobody goes, there li–ives Jane Russell, without any clothes./Along came a cowboy, his name was Jock, he pulled down his trousers . . . '), and 'As I was lying on the grass / I felt a nob go up my arse./It wasn't me, it wasn't you,/it must have been . . . '

[. . . Name left unmentioned. After all, why should a person still in public life be embarrassed after serving a jail sentence for an alleged activity none of us knew existed, let alone was illegal? The tendency in these songs is scatalogical, macho.]

18. I remember Eddie Calvert and his golden trumpet – 'O Mine Papa' and 'Cherry Pink and Apple Blossom White' – and Sophie Tucker's 'My Yiddisher Mama . . . '

19. I remember Paul Robeson singing 'Poor Old Joe'. The beauty of his voice and the strength of feeling in his rendition of this folk song about injustice brought tears to my eyes.

[It still does. Serious question: the three greatest black icons of the century: Martin Luther King, Nelson Mandela, Paul Robeson. Discuss. Well, what about Malcolm X, Bessie Smith, Billie Holiday, Louis Armstrong, Jesse Owens, Pelé, Cassius Clay and Rosa Parks?]

(G)

WIRELESS/RADIO

1. I remember 'The Stargazers are *on* the air, and to start our programme this time . . . '

[I can't remember whom 'our' refers to, and whether or not this group existed *off* the air.]

2. I remember *A Song, A Hymn and A Prayer* at five to ten, immediately after *Housewives' Choice* on the Light Programme.

3. I remember *Have a Go*, 'bringing the people to the people', and Barney on the piano and Wilfred Pickles asking his wife Mabel what was on the table this week. 'Give 'er the money, Mabel.'

[W. Pickles, with his gentle northern teasing and joke prizes, was a far cry and a long chalk from later TV programmes where people are routinely discomfited in return for gifts or money. Britain was a *kinder* country than it is now. Even some Tories believed in mutuality or mutualism, and not only because they believed something had to be done to prevent Communism, or more realistically, permanent Labour rule. Old Labour, that is . . .]

4. I remember listening to *Workers' Playtime* and *Music While You Work* and *Mrs Dale's Diary*. I never listened to *The Archers* ('an everyday story of country folk').

5. I remember on Monday nights *Journey into Space*, which followed *Top of the Form*, a school quiz programme.

6. I remember *Dick Barton: Special Agent* ('Open the door, Richard,/and let me in') and *Educating Archie*: 'Hello, Brough.' I used to practise speaking without moving my lips.

[I never realised at the time how *weird*, how *post-modern* it was to have a ventriloquist and his dummy on the *radio*, even though there was a studio audience. Peter Brough must have been very funny to get away with it, no? Or was he already famous in music-hall and pantomime, an institution in his own right? Later, on television, there would be another ventriloquist and dummy, possibly called Charlie McCarthy and Saveen, with the former – presumably – the dummy. Later still there would be the *insufferable* Sooty, well trashed by Nick Hancock recently when the little tosser turned up on his quiz programme in the hands of the son of the original handler, Harry Corbett.]

7. I remember *The Goon Show* on the Home Service on Mondays. Fans sometimes listened to the repeat on Thursdays. The characters included Milligan as Eccles, Secombe as Major Denis Bloodnock and Sellers as Blue-bottle, and all the rest. Once I went to a recording of the show at a theatre – now a dance-hall – in Camden Town. On that occasion I remember unscripted anarchically funny warm-up routines masterminded by Milligan before the session began. At school we repeated catchphrases like 'we'll all be murdered in our beds' and 'he's fallen in the water' and 'there's more where that came from'. On one occasion a rude phrase spoken by Spike had somehow got by in the recording and thus in the first broadcast, but was dropped from the repeat: 'the dual carriage way leading south from Bushey Park to my knees'. Ray Ellington's quartet and Max Geldray's mouth-organ supplied the musical interludes. Even the announcer made jokes – the only programme where this happened.

[I wonder whether Milligan, a true comic genius, and a local hero for his conservationist work in North Finchley where I now live, remembers the rude phrase. The Goons transferred to television, possibly outside this book's time-span, but this decision was the mother of all disasters and, retrospectively, a refracted object lesson in the magic of audio-imaginings. John Cleese at his most inspired combines the talents of Sellers and Milligan in the best *Monty Python* sketches, but I would lay a hefty bet that *Fawlty Towers* will be remembered long after *Monty Python*.]

8. I remember 'At Much-Binding-in-the-Marsh, da dada dada dada dada dum dum' with Kenneth Horne and Richard ('Stinker') Murdoch and Sam Costa.

9. I remember other radio-comedy programmes including Hancock (the best of them all and, like the Goons, much better on radio than on TV) and *Take It From Here* with Ron and Eth, and Beryl Reid as Marlene, and *Life with the Lyons*

('and I'm Bebe Daniels Lyon'). And there was Ted Ray in *Ray's a Laugh*, one of whose characters was the slow-moving Mrs Mazeltov, who always spoke in a broad stage-Jewish accent; her catchphrase was: 'All right, all right, I'm coming. Rome wasn't built een ah die.'

[Mrs Mazeltov was played by Harold Behrens. I passed his grave recently at Bushey Jewish Cemetery. He resides close to Miron Grindea. I suspect that the Jewish community, which is at once more over-sensitive and more self-assertive than when I was a child, would object to Mrs Mazeltov today. In his letters, Kenneth Williams is seriously rude about Hancock, considering him to be completely and utterly dependent on the genius of his scriptwriters. Williams (jealous?) misses the point. Olivier as Hamlet is dependent on *his* scriptwriter's genius too. Put a sock in it, Kenneth, darn it.]

10. I remember a programme starring Charlie Chester whom I found funny and who had the bonus of living locally, so it was said, and whose son Pete Chester floated around the margins of my social circle, or I his, to be more modest – though we never met. I remember Charlie's jingles, and their quondam topical relevance: 'Down in the jungle,/chanting every day,/you should hear the natives,/boom, all say: England beat the Argentina,/what a relief!/shows 'em what we *can* do,/boom, without beef.' Or, 'Down in the jungle,/got a little tent,/better than a prefab, /boom, no rent.'

[I'm surprised this was not recycled during the Falklands War. For obvious reasons it could not be recycled during the World Cup. Mad cows make it even more topical.]

11. I remember setting my alarm for 3 o'clock to listen to the world heavy-weight boxing championship from New York between Don Cockell and Rocky Marciano. I put a Crunchie bar and a glass of orange squash beside my clock. Being British, I was sad when Cockell lost, although he was bound to . . .

[. . . being British. For a moment I hesitated and nearly typed Bruce Woodcock and Lee Savold but I am obliged to type what I remember, even if it's wrong. As it happens, a sports-expert friend confirms the memory, given the approximate date. I like the presence of the Crunchie bar. I remember the little radio: it was brown . . . Bakelite?]

12. I remember listening to *Children's Hour* at 5 o'clock on the Home Service: there were Jennings (and his pal Darbyshire), the detectives Norman and Henry Bones (one of the detectives was played by a *woman*, Patricia Hayes), *Toytown* with Larry the Lamb written by F. G. Hulme Beaman, and *Nature Parliament*. *Nature Parliament* was boring. The presenters were known as David and Uncle Mac: 'Goodnight, children – everywhere.' On Saturday morning I listened to *Children's Favourites*, presented by Uncle Mac, before I went to synagogue for the children's service. Some non-Jewish friends went to Saturday-morning cinema shows.

[Uncle? Yes, uncle. *Le bon vieux temps, quoi*. The *Jewish Chronicle*'s children's page used to be edited by 'Aunt Naomi'.]

13. I remember *Sports Report* and its catchy signature tune every Saturday on the Light Programme at 5 o'clock. I lay on my bed with a cup of tea and one or two chocolate digestive biscuits and noted down the scores which mattered to me. The programme was presented by Eamon Andrews . . .

[before he became famous for *This Is Your Life* on TV . . .]

14. I remember boxing commentaries by Raymond Glendenning, who had thick glasses, with inter-round summary by W. Barrington Dalby.

15. I remember the Home Service weather forecast: 'Lundy, Faroes, Rockall, Malin, Dogger, Irish Sea', perhaps not in that order. I remember the best place to hear about bad weather was your bed.

[Seamus Heaney too remembers the mantra in his book *Field Work* – listing the last four in the same order in the first line of a sonnet.]

16. I remember that on the Home Service books would be serialised and novels adapted as plays. One specialist in adaptations was H. Oldfield Box.

[Many years later I asked a famous Third Programme producer, my friend Geoffrey Bridson, if H's name was in fact a pseudonym. No, it was real. Too good to be true.]

17. I remember Radio Luxembourg on 208 medium wave, the only pop station. It carried advertising and the reception was sometimes bad. One

regular advertiser had a system for success on the football pools: Horace somebody.

18. I remember the cricket commentators, E. W. Swanson and Brian Johnston, and John Arlott with his West-Country accent: 'Alec Bedser's coming up to bowl from the Pavilion End. And he's out. Jack Robertson [or whoever] is out.'

19. I remember my father telling me that he made his own wireless, when he was a boy, with cats' whiskers.

THE ARITHMETIC OF MEMORY

(H)

POPULAR BELIEFS

1. I remember we used to believe that if you swallowed chewing gum you would die. Wrigley's made three kinds of chewing gum: one was called PX.

[Or was it bubblegum which could kill you? I was no good at popping bubblegum.]

2. I remember we, or at any rate I, knew you were supposed to stand still and hold your lapel when a funeral cortège passed by.

3. I remember we believed that Errol Flynn's penis was so large it had to be strapped back between his legs during film shots, in case he tripped over it. Conversely, the entire body of Alan Ladd was so small he had to stand on a box to kiss his leading lady.

4. I remember a rumour that a beehive hairstyle was dangerous because a beetle might lodge there and burrow into your scalp.

5. I remember that if you cut yourself between your thumb and first finger you would get lockjaw.

6. I remember always checking out pennies because one dated 1931 was supposed to be worth a lot of money since only a few were struck.

(I)

SPORTS, INCLUDING HEROES (MAJOR AND MINOR)

1. I remember Denis Compton and Billy Wright. I watched Denis at Lords several times, but I *never* saw Billy play except occasionally on TV. My friends and I took our food with us to Lords, egg-and-cucumber sandwiches for lunch and jam sandwiches for tea. We would buy an ice-cream and a soft drink. Some of us kept the score in our special score-books. Football I regularly listened to on the wireless. I studied and memorised the statistics of both sports in various annuals and yearbooks. I remember learning from Billy's autobiography, which I read several times, the name of his first landlady – Mrs Colley – when he moved to lodgings near the club ground, Molineux, after the manager Stan Cullis agreed that he could join Wolves as a junior. I wrote off for a signed photograph of him which I stuck in my autograph album.

[Compton was my summer hero, Wright my winter hero. My mind was a land fit for heroes, heroes were made to measure for my mind. I did not really approve of Compton's earlier soccer activities – that was encroaching on Wright's field. *Where oh where is my autograph album?*]

2. I remember Johnny Leach. For several years I participated in the annual *Eagle* table-tennis competition which he organised or fronted at St Bride's Church off Fleet Street, near my school. I badly wanted to win the competition, but never got past the second or third round. You could talk to Johnny Leach in person. There he was, twice world champion, already overtaken professionally – I knew – by the Chinese and Japanese, with their penholder grip and thickly rubbered bats. I watched Richard Bergmann at Wembley and admired him for his brilliant long-distance defensive strokes, which was what I did best too. I was amazed when my father's brother, Uncle Isidore, told me about the great Czech champion Bo Vana whom he played against at Brady Boys, a Jewish youth club in the East End: Vana used an HP Sauce bottle as a bat and still won. I admired other great players: the Hungarian Zsoltan Bercik, the Rowe twins, Diane and Rosalind, and Ann Haydon before she became even more famous as a tennis player called Ann Jones. I watched Ann Haydon closely at Manor Place baths, near the Elephant and Castle. Then there was Harry Venner, and photographs of Victor Barna who wore long trousers.

[The fact that I played table-tennis and did not merely watch it entitles it to a place elsewhere in this book. Concerning Isidore, years later my mother's brother Phil Russell told me his sister's future brother-in-law would turn up on a Friday night at their home and Grandfather Russell (then still Rosenberg) would think they were going out for a Sabbath walk, but they had their table tennis bats hidden under their jackets, and would play a few hundred yards down the road at Bishopsgate Institute, where I too played years later. I went to Harry Venner's coaching school in Putney, played for Hampstead Garden Suburb, and was my college champion. Johnny Leach was not a *primary* hero of mine, this honour belongs to Denis and Billy, but table tennis has always been my favourite sport to *play* and figures regularly in my dreams, a kind of ballet, a kind of mobile, a kind of geometry in motion. Sport at its best is art, and the principle of the pleasure it gives is aesthetic. Even under pressure great players are graceful. Full of grace. Crowd reaction – beyond the merely partisan – reveals this.]

3. I remember going to Wimbledon after school and watching Lew Hoad practise on an outside court. I saw many older players at the ground and on TV, including that magical stroke player Pancho Gonzalez, and Budge Patty. Veteran players like Jean Borotra, one of the 'four musketeers', were still performing. Above all I loved Ken Rosewall and was sad he never won the championship, although we were happy for old Jaroslav Drobny, who beat him in the Final one year. I supported the British players of the generation after Mottram and Paish, especially Bobby Wilson (like Denis Compton a local boy, though Denis was Hendon, Bobby was Finchley), who was a member of the same club as my Uncle Phil and who bought his rackets at Preston's in Temple Fortune, where I bought my first and last one. Apart from Wilson there were Billy Knight and Roger Becker, but only Wilson reached even the semi-finals. Mind you, two Britons, Angela Mortimer and Ann Jones, won the women's singles. As did Shirley Fry: I was pleased for her because I was *sure* she minded not being as good a player as her fellow Americans, Doris Hart, Louise Brough and Maureen Connolly, 'little Mo', whose early death moved everybody to tears. One year, on the tube to Wimbledon and in the queue, I was reading a book called *Protest*, a paperback anthology of rebel, beat, existentialist and 'angry young' writers, including Sillitoe and Wain. My own tennis racket, like my cricket bat, was too heavy.

[My heavy bat and racket hindered my development. Perhaps I was meant to grow into them. Today I read the *Guardian* obituary of Lew Hoad by Frank Keating, the most sentimental of all sports writers. It was an excellent piece except that he quoted approvingly a foolish remark by David Gray in which Ken Rosewall is put down – without any acknowledgment whatsoever of the lyric beauty of his ground strokes. Lew Hoad was the most complete player I have ever watched, master of all the genres, but Rosewall was the greater poet and a secondary hero of mine, along with Johnny Leach and, indeed, Lew Hoad. It's a sad day when a hero dies. What finesses the poignancy is the shock horror realisation that Hoad was only seven years older than me, not only when he died, but even in those far off days of hero worship on an outside court.]

4. I remember many Wolverhampton Wanderers players. Wolves were my team because I liked their name, not because they were the top team – they weren't yet, so there. After Billy Wright my favourites were the wingers Jimmy Mullen and Johnny Hancock, Dennis Wilshaw and Bert 'the cat' Williams, Ron Flowers and Bill Slater, all of whom played for England. Bill Slater was an amateur.

[Years later I went to Wolverhampton to see Susannah York play Ranevskaya in *The Cherry Orchard*. I explained the situation to her and she was happy to go walkabout before lunch. We found Ron Flowers' sports shop in the centre of town and I told him about my support for Wolves. He didn't seem all that interested in my past, or in my companion for that matter.]

5. I remember the names of many Middlesex players too, apart from Denis: Jack Robertson, Jack Young, Sid Brown, Bill Edrich, old Jim Sims, J. J. Warr, J. G. Dewes, Don Bennett, Fred Titmus, Leslie Compton, Reg Routledge. Amateurs had initials before their name. I remember wondering if Leslie was jealous of his younger brother Denis. And was Eric Bedser jealous of Alec, across the river at the Oval? I always felt sorry for underdogs. At the same time I felt that it must be quite nice to be an underdog because people felt sorry for you.

[Mind you, Leslie played soccer for England as a full international, Denis didn't. Deliberately, I think of all the underdogs through history and thank heaven they lived, continually. I have an album – the gift of a friend with good reason to hate cricket – by the rock group Half Man Half Biscuit, containing the song 'Fuckin' Hell! It's Fred Titmus'.]

6. I remember watching Roger Bannister on TV, running the first four-minute mile.

[I wrote down the above in my 'I remember' notebook a few weeks before the fortieth anniversary of the historic event was featured in the new *Radio Times*, which I picked up today, the very day I am entering this section into the word processor as part of the latest draft. The coincidence or synchronicity is banal but it does remind me to draw attention to an important point. Some texts, i.e. unbracketed paragraphs, came to me at random, unbidden, others were plucked from the past while I meditated within a particular category. Others were merely the latest in a sequence or series of the same generic memory, but whether they have been 'improved' or survived uncorrupted and more brightly than ever I am not concerned with. The word processor is the symbolic intersection or interface of my *space*: books, pictures, etc., in my apartment in North Finchley in London, etc., just as we used to write those joke addresses on envelopes . . . universe, space, more space, etc., and of my *time*: memories and predictions, death and birth, my father and my daughter. Emotions? They belong elsewhere. As does a deep meditation on space and time, which can bring non-fiction writers to the borders of two areas of material idealisation they are not best placed to handle, and must leave to others: music and painting.]

7. I remember Reg Harris the racing cyclist, Split Waterman the speedway ace, Royal Tan the horse. These and others were my tertiary heroes, after Billy and Denis (primary) and Johnny, Ken and Lew (secondary). I wanted, if possible to find a player or a team to admire in each sport, even sports I had never seen live: golf, rugger (Harlequins, of course), motor racing, etc.

[Wanted = needed, I suppose, in the kind of reading I am not engaged in.]

(J)

HOBBIES, GAMES AND OTHER ENTERTAINMENTS

1. I remember I collected stamps, particularly from the British Empire. When a letter arrived from abroad, anywhere abroad, my father said I should not remove the stamps but keep the envelope. But I preferred to steam them off and place them in my Gibbons stamp album. I had tweezers and a packet of stamp hinges which enabled you to secure the stamp in the album without sticking it down. I used to go on the bus to Gibbons in the Strand to buy catalogues which I studied. I remember you could write off for job lots of stamps or buy them in junk shops, including my regular haunt, the junk shop in Temple Fortune.

[102 or 58 bus from Market Place to Golders Green, changing to the 2 or 13. I don't remember, I can't visualise, 'swapping' duplicate stamps with friends, but I'm sure I did. How can I be sure? Through another way of reading my past. As for envelopes, I now think my father was right. And about other things too . . .]

2. I remember playing draughts and dominoes, jacks and marbles, yo-yos and hula-hoops (though these were more often played by girls), skipping and hopscotch (also mainly for the girls), cap-guns and kites, Monopoly and Scrabble. Ludo and Snakes and Ladders were boring. I remember a Passover game using cobnuts and my grandmother's washboard. We played conkers in the playground. Someone sold me or swapped me a conker saying it was some number or other.

[I was naïve. The conker's number was a pedigree: it meant the conker had a history of defeating that number of conkers in conker duels. Conkers were threaded on a string. You swung the conker at your opponent's, and then it was his turn. The trouble was, my new conker did not have a hole in it! Compare and contrast my experience to that of Stephen Dedalus who says early in *Portrait* that it is 'mean of Wells to shoulder him into the square ditch' (i.e. the school cesspit), 'because he would not swop his little snuffbox for Wells's seasoned hacking chestnut, the conqueror of forty'.]

3. I remember my father teaching me chess. I owned a chess set which was given to me for my barmitzvah by my father's cousin Reg and his family, together with Harry Golombek's Penguin book on chess. We visited Reg and Minnie Forrester and their sons David and John when they lived in Paris. Someone – Reg or my father – read to me from the Nonesuch *Lewis Carroll* with its red cover.

[This was a beautiful chess set which I still have. It is one of my few surviving barmitzvah presents. Surely a perfect gift. The older of David's two younger brothers is John, a Lacanian interpreter of Freud. Forrester had been changed from Flashtig but Rudolf was always the same name. That sort of family stuff belongs in another book. Memo to self: write the 'grandfather' book before you become a grandfather yourself.]

4. I remember a bus conductor uniform, and a Red Indian outfit. I always preferred Red Indians to cowboys because Red Indians were supposed to lose.

5. I remember Finchley Lido, the open-air swimming pool. The pool was always crowded, in and out of the water.

[Lidos were outdoor parallels to Odeons, similar 1930s architecture. Today the Lido, closed down for years, has reopened as the replacement to dear old Squires Lane pool and as part of a huge complex of cinemas, restaurants, etc., the Warner Village. In the old days I must have taken the 102 bus to the Bald-Faced Stag in East Finchley, and then walked. It was always pronounced Lee-doh, correctly given the etymology; but when you phone the new one up the attendant says Lie-doh.]

6. I remember the Rex Cinema in East Finchley, and three cinemas in Golders Green: the Ionic, the Regal and the Odeon. There were other Odeons in Temple Fortune, Tally Ho and Swiss Cottage. I went once to the Swiss Cottage Odeon with Michael Duschinsky and we asked someone to take us into an 'A' film, but the man said, 'Clear off, I'm the manager.' I saw *Davy Crockett* at Tally Ho where I now live. Studios One and Two in Oxford Street showed cartoons and newsreels. I remember films which seemed aimed at children, like the *Titfield Thunderbolt*, and *Goodbye, Mr Chips*, and *Genevieve*. *The Dambusters* had a wonderful theme tune.

['A' films, unlike 'U' films, required children to be accompanied by an adult. According to a friend of mine we should have walked in backwards, pretending we were leaving, like Lord Snooty did in *Dandy* on one occasion! 'X' films were completely forbidden to children under eighteen. On reflection *Goodbye, Mr Chips* was not a film for children, it was a film set in a school. The Rex is now the Phoenix, apparently the oldest surviving purpose-built cinema in the UK. I think the Golders Green Odeon is still the Odeon – probably a multicinema. Temple Fortune Odeon was pulled down. I remember seeing a film at the Regal with Michael Duschinsky called *The Angel Who Pawned Her Harp* – it starred Diane Cilento – and I saw *The King and I* with Richard Hyams after school one day at Golders Green Odeon. Tally Ho Odeon is no more. In an early draft I wrote that *The Dambusters* was an early post-war war film but of course that description was less a kosher memory than a parading of film history so I have transferred the comment to this parenthetical paragraph.]

7. I remember joining the National Film Theatre while still at school and going to see classics like *Intolerance* and *Birth of a Nation*, *Citizen Kane* and *Battleship Potemkin*, *Un Chien andalou* and *Zéro de conduite*. I went often to the Everyman in Hampstead, and the Paris Pulman in Drayton Gardens SW7 or SW3.

[For me, the Everyman was to cinema, or the flicks as we called it, what the Royal Court was to theatre. I remember its proprietor, or manager, Mr Fairfax Jones, a short man with glasses, assessing the queue before allowing it to move forward. More accurately I remember a person who, I learned later, was called Fairfax Jones.]

8. I remember the bowling alley which opened in Golders Green on the site of the Regal cinema. It was the first bowling alley in the country. My friend Pete Goodeve, a Canadian and therefore expert, took me on the second evening. I remember 'spares' and 'strikes' and special boots.

9. I remember throwing tennis balls over our house. More than once I broke a window.

[I am fairly sure I had to pay for a replacement on at least one occasion but I'll take my mother's word for it if I didn't.]

10. I remember the public library in East Finchley, halfway between the Rex and the Lido. I borrowed fiction and sports autobiographies.

11 I remember Big Chief I-Spy, and I-Spy books which you ordered from the *News Chronicle* or bought locally in Ellingtons. I filled them in during long car journeys.

[I-Spy books cannot have survived recent advances in information technology but they were jolly good entertainment and very educational. Completely wrong about their demise, a friend with young children tells me! They're still going strong.]

13 I remember going to the theatre from time to time, either alone or with a friend. On one occasion I remember being in a huge rush to get home after school, have my supper, and return to town in time to meet Martin Lester for a play at the Criterion. I learned from my father the habit of writing the date and name of my companion on the programme and keeping the programme. At Wyndhams Theatre, and perhaps others, you sat on stools provided by the management while waiting in the queue for your gallery ticket.

[I *think* the system involved picking up a reservation in the morning and queuing in the evening. Maybe you went along around six o'clock and queued for an hour or two. I think a ticket cost one shilling. I wonder which play we went to at the Criterion – I could check that from my collection of theatre programmes. Sometimes I wonder what happened to x and y and z, including Martin Lester. Martin could be included in the school friends section but there he would be part of the 'content'. Here his role is structural.]

13. I remember Cinemascope, the wide screen, which was the latest thing in cinema technology. I loved Laurel and Hardy, Abbott and Costello, Charlie Chaplin and the Marx Brothers. In the cinema you bought an ice-cream or Butterkist. Every programme had a main film, a second film, a few cartoons, a newsreel.

[Things are different and worse now: one measly film. The mask slips: breaking the rules and displaying emotion I permit myself a heartfelt sigh for the good old days. I do not remember Harold Lloyd or Buster Keaton, whom these days I prefer to the remembered names above. Was it for reasons of fashion that they were not shown during that period, or did they appeal more to adult taste? And yet my children, when young, much preferred Harold Lloyd to Chaplin.]

14. I remember the Schoolboys' Exhibition at Westminster in the huge hall there. Every interest under the sun was on show including, I remember, model railways, which did not interest me.

[I would be *very* interested to see a catalogue, if such exists, of this splendid event. Perhaps the British Library reading room has a copy. I wonder when it stopped. Just for fun I'll guess that it staggered on until about 1974. The other day in a speech at my uncle Leon Rudolf's memorial service at Kinloss Gardens synagogue my second cousin, Stanley Davis, referred to the Boys' Own Exhibition but he must have meant the Schoolboys' Exhibition. I do however remember the *Boys' Own Magazine*, which probably died around the same time as the *Children's Newspaper*. Their demise either caused or was caused by the founding of *Eagle*.]

15. I remember ice-skating at Queen's Rink in Bayswater and that I kept falling over. I didn't particularly enjoy skating but that did not stop me going.

16. I remember Whipsnade Zoo and London Zoo which many people visited in order to see Brumas the panda.

[Or was he a polar bear?]

17. I remember Whitestone Pond: the Punch and Judy show, the donkey rides, other children sailing their boats.

2

'The Suburb'

They flee from me that sometime did me seek,
   With naked foot stalking in my chamber:
I have seen them gentle, tame and meek,
   That now are wild and do not once remember
   That sometime they have put themselves in danger
To take bread at my hand; and now they range,
Busily seeking with a continual change

SIR THOMAS WYATT

(A)

MARKET PLACE AND SHOPS BORDERING THE SUBURB

1. I remember the 'clinic' which was situated in a kind of barracks. I used to go there with my mother, and my little sister Ruth, for injections and to buy Haliborange and cod-liver oil, as well as the regular orange juice which children drank.

   [I suppose it was an early NHS childcare centre.]

2. I remember, immediately next door to the clinic, Lyttelton Garage, where we bought petrol. Once I saw Harold Wilson there. He lived in Southway, the next street to us. My parents knew him and his wife Mary from local Labour Party circles. I recognised him from the newspapers. He held a big briefcase and was puffing at a pipe.

3. I remember, opposite Lyttelton Garage, Ann's, the sweetshop-cum-café,

which was the first shop on the south side of Market Place. I bought news-papers and sweets there, sherbert which you sucked through liquorice (though I hated liquorice), gob-stoppers and flying saucers (sherbert in rice-paper). I always studied the jars of sweets high on the shelves. Would the toffees need replenishing before the wine-gums? Which jar would win? Once, I remember, our milkman took me to Ann's for a cup of tea and a roll and butter after I'd spent the morning helping him. During the holidays some of us would race to his horse-drawn cart. The winner became his assistant on that round. Dobbin was the name of his horse.

[The jars of sweets were like a three-dimensional graph or league table.]

4. I remember one shop which sold nothing but sweets and chocolates: Lollies, a few doors along from the gents' and boys' outfitters, Marshalls'. Every Monday, during the days of sweet rationing, I took my week's 'points' with me and bought eight packets of Refreshers, my favourite sweet. They never lasted out the week. I spotted that the name of the company, Trebor, which made Refreshers, was Robert backwards. I liked mint chocs and gum drops. 'Goody gumdrops' meant 'good' or 'hurrah'.

[My week's points were my weak point. Ha Ha. But Lollies is still there. It has gone up-market. Memory is a funny thing, as we know: I am one hundred per cent certain that I would sometimes have obtained my sweet ration in Ann's, but I only remember handing over the coupons in Lollies, and I cannot pretend otherwise. Maybe I thought: sweets? Go to Lollies. The point about Ann's would have been that all its products were by-products. 'Trebor' reminds me I was good at spotting language tricks in advertisements, doubtless because of my early training as my father's chief assistant on *The Times* crossword.]

5. I remember next door to Lollies was the hairdressers' shop, Coopers', where I would say hello to my mother while she was sitting under a huge dryer. At the front were the men's barbers, a tall fair quiet-spoken one on the left and a stocky darker one on the right. One day the shorter one, who looked like my Uncle Isidore, was not there. The other barber told me he had left to run the local scouts troop. Once I tried to cut my own unruly hair, at the back end of the parting. The barber had to put it right next time. I always had trouble with my parting.

[Years later I found out the reason for this trouble but if I gloss every item in this book affected by later developments I will be doing myself out of possible sequels! OK, just this once: later on, after I stopped going to another barber, Sam's at the top of Ossulton Way (where my father and I went after Coopers' closed), and found myself my own hairdresser, Johnny Buccheri of Macclesfield Street, Soho (in my mid-twenties following a six-month job attachment in Chicago), the latter took one look and said my natural parting was on the right. I told him I grew up believing this was supposed to be the girls' side but asked him to change it over – he did, and everything was fine. The next time I saw my mother she owned up to having swapped the parting round when I was little. Now, in my fifties, my parting refuses to manifest itself at all. Such sweet sorrow. I learn from Johnny – who now lives in the Suburb and after closing the Soho shop has come to rest professionally at a small shop next door to the side entrance of Golders Green Station – that my vanishing parting is due to texture changes in hair, quite normal. Like changes in teeth and eyes. And mind. Everything changes and nothing does. Our past remains an on-going continuum, a continuum in fact, although a better word would be discontinuum (defined as a meta-narrative where the time of space and the space of time interact or interface like dancers, perhaps the dancers in Anthony Howell's ballet novel), hence the arrangement of this telling. A straightforward non-fictional linear narrative would fail to represent, to recapture, my feel of and for the gone time. Then/there is here/now for ever: memory multiplied by imagination = order multiplied by growth ($M \times I = O \times G$). This is Rudolf's First Law (perhaps I should say Rudolf's Law since it is likely to be the last). I am still the teenager who walked up Ossulton Way with his father to Sam, and to Sam's sidekick Sid, of a Saturday afternoon. Their shop, with its East Finchley catchment area, was more downmarket than Coopers. We used to chuckle at Sid's racy jokes. My father would ask them to turn down the football commentary on the radio. More *chutzpah*.]

6. I remember Hugh Lloyd's, the chemist's shop where I went with or for my mother to collect prescriptions or to buy toothpaste or plasters. I would sometimes nip in to buy Ovaltine and Horlicks tablets for myself, though I never drank the powdered version as a nightcap. I also bought Dexedrine tablets for energy. I remember going there for medicine after my only attack of migraine.

7. I remember Ellington's, a little further down the parade. This was the shop where our newspaper orders were placed and written into a large book with detachable tickets, where biros and stationery were bought and where books could be ordered. Here too I bought *Eagle*, the permitted, indeed approved, comic. During the week we took *The Times* and the *News Chronicle*, and on Sundays *Reynolds News* and the *Sunday Times* and/or the *Observer*, depending. Once I won a five-shilling postal order, third prize in a *Reynolds News* drawing competition. I remember across the road was a general shop called Gamages which was owned by Ellington's and had very little in it. They also owned the sub-post office up and across the road, where I bought stamps and national savings certificates and a few premium bonds as soon as they were introduced by the Chancellor of the Exchequer, Harold Macmillan. I remember Vicky's cartoon figure of Supermac in the *Evening Standard*.

[Still have the bonds. Still haven't won a penny.]

8. I remember a fruitshop called Harrod's.

9. I remember further down the parade, on the next corner, an electrical supplies shop called Wrigley's.

[For years and years you could distinguish the outline of the letters of the old name on the high fascia after the shop had become an optician's.]

10. I remember across the road, Northway, from Wrigley's was Cummings, a general shop like Ann's, with the great advantage of a candy-floss machine. Mr Cummings, or Cumming if it was in fact Cumming's, had a big moustache. He was not very friendly.

11. I remember the last shop on that side of the parade was the Jewish delicatessen, Rosenblatt's. Mr Rosenblatt always said, 'Hello Anthony,' as did his wife. I remember going there in the holidays when my mother needed something. He was short and became more and more stooped. At some point he started wearing a *yarmulka*, a skullcap.

[I'm not sure when Anthony became Tony, probably during my secondary-school years. These days I am still Anthony to some older members of my extended family, and on the covers of books.]

12. I remember Boots on the other side of the parade. Upstairs was the Boots library which was the alternative to the public library in East Finchley and to the travelling library near St Jude's Church – until a branch library was opened in Market Place.

[By that time Boots had probably stopped the library side of their business nationwide. Memo to self, representative common reader: when the necessary curiosity is generated to kill the time available, check out the link between pharmacy and reading in the Victorian era, apart from the obvious joke about improving your health. Many years later I recognised the librarian at my local branch in North Finchley as the woman who ran the Market Place branch library thirty years earlier. I imagine a map of her life overlapping with my map and, by extension, all the maps of space/time this book touches on. Spread them out: to say they would be isomorphs, ontological isomorphs, co-extensive, Borges-style, with the world described, would be an understatement. Fortunately the imagination goes into overdrive when necessary, which is just as well when you are dealing with a world that is always over-determined. ('Each thing is in a space of possible states of affairs,' wrote Wittgenstein. Yet he also wrote: 'states of affairs are independent of one another'. Memo to self: How does this connect with Walter Benjamin's concept of porosity?) How many ways are there of looking at a blackbird or a red wheelbarrow or, for the matter of that, a poet? If your tendency is to enjoy and/or to worry about meta-narrative rather than narrative, historiography rather than history, theory rather than practice, you need to keep it short if you write fiction. It is no accident, as they say, that the greatest writer of such examinings, the said Borges, only wrote short stories.]

13. I remember just up from Boots was Woolworths which sold everything. Once, by mistake, I took a threepenny (pronounced 'thrupny') or sixpenny card from the shop without paying, but as I crossed Market Place at the traffic lights by the garage I realised what I had done. I was too scared to take it back.

14. I remember the Jewish baker's Grodzinski's where you could buy lovely rye bread and *challas* as well as the usual loaves. I remember the day they introduced a bread-slicing machine. Various Grodzinskis lived in the Suburb, including one family in my own road. Grodzinski's also sold Snowcrest kosher

(*parev*) ice-cream, which could be eaten with meat (i.e. it had some kind of milk substitute or cream substitute), and ice-lollies in the shape of a pyramid. I was allowed to eat icecreams but not ice-lollies because my mother said that according to Uncle Jack, a doctor, these were bad for your teeth. Grodzinski's biscuits were delicious but too expensive for regular purchase. My mother baked her own *kuchels* and *mandelbrot*. There was another baker's, next door to Wrigley's, namely Sherrard's, whose egg *challas* were larger and more delicious than Grodzinski's. We all liked egg *challas*, except my father, who preferred the plain ones. Bread prices sometimes included a farthing, the last remaining use for the quarter-penny.

[That branch of Grodzinski's has gone the way of all flesh, as it were, but Sherrard's is still next door Wrigley's 'wot was', and their bread is still good. Presumably bread prices were regulated by the government – if I am right in thinking that no other commodity's price continued to include farthings.]

15. I remember two fishmongers, Stoller's ('prime fish at popular prices') and Richardson's, where we went more often. My mother bought kippers which I loved, especially when fried, and smoked haddock which I didn't. The woman who served in Richardson's wore gumboots.

[More than thirty years later, on a rare shopping trip to Market Place, I recognised the gumbooted woman from Richardson's and she recognised me: 'Anthony Rudolf.' This was almost as impressive as the woman to whose farm I was briefly evacuated during the war: some forty years later, after an outing to Hellfire Caves with my friend Keith Bosley and our young children, I visited the farm which happened to be nearby. I asked the farmer's wife if she could guess who I was. 'You must be Anthony Rudolf.' When you think about it, who else would ask a question like that? But even so, the speed of reaction, the sheer intuitive intelligence, commands admiration. But this story is hard to believe. Is my short-term memory playing tricks? Almost certainly yes. But I don't *remember* improving the story. As for Stoller, at some point everyone knew his daughter had become an actress.]

16. I remember J. A. Pinder and Son, the ironmonger's and hardware shop, with the eternal musty smell of wax and oil, and with gardening and household gadgets and supplies around the place. Old man Pinder had a long thin

mustache. This was where we bought dubbin to clean my football boots and linseed oil for my cricket bat, and the stuff – perhaps called Glittersol – for shining the metal on my school cadet-corps uniform.

[My sister Annie tells me Mr Pinder junior is still there but I am not tempted to pop in. Let Pinder stay put in the deep store of memory, the archetypal shop or store from childhood. Bruno Schulz would have loved it – one could relocate it like a Rachel Whiteread object to his Street of Crocodiles (which I walked down) in Drohobycz. 'Eternal musty smell' is not really a memory, more a literary characterisation of a memory. The other day, at a reception in the French embassy when Susannah York deservedly received a medal for services to French theatre, she told me she would polish her medal with Duraglit – a good housewife supplying me with the word I forgot above. Which goes to show, I know, how little polishing I do at home except, maybe, of words. Postscript: driving through the Suburb recently I saw that Pinder's had closed down.]

17. I remember near Pinder's a dress shop called Cresta, owned by Mr and Mrs Marcuse, whose daughter Carol went to our Hebrew classes.

[Years later I discovered that Mr Marcuse was the brother of the radical theorist, Herbert Marcuse.]

18. I remember behind the shops on our side of Market Place was a private road where shopkeepers would receive their supplies and you could take a short cut from Kingsley Way to Northway, saving about thirty seconds. Above one of these shops, the Victoria Wine Company, lived Miss King, a semi-invalid my parents would drive to Labour Party meetings. I thought it was peculiar a) to live in a flat, b) especially a flat above a shop.

[Thirty seconds is a conservative estimate, but highly theoretical in any case for you could, in fact, save ten minutes or even half an hour; after all, by going the 'long' way round, that is via the shopping parade, you might have found yourself making unscheduled calls on the usual suspects!]

19. I remember Wiseman's gents' outfitters in Golders Green, almost opposite where my hairdresser, Johnny Buccheri, is now. My father knew Mr Wiseman from the old days. There *always* seemed to be a sale on.

20. I remember the Embassy caff at the top of Ossulton Way, frequented by workmen in overalls.

21. I remember Myers', the kosher butcher in Market Place my mother did not go to. She went instead to Frohwein's in Temple Fortune, on the western border of the Suburb. Joe who worked in there had a number on his forearm. Mr Frohwein and Joe would both give me a small slice of *wurst* on occasion. There was a lady, ensconced in a high-windowed cubicle, who took the money.

22. I remember the junk shop in Temple Fortune which I haunted, dropping in for example when picking up repaired shoes for my mother from Fenlon's up the road. I bought cigarette cards there, also job lots of cheap stamps, a magnifying glass, a penknife, a compass, Dinky cars, and various odds and ends.

[These days that old junk shop haunts *me*. Rereading the paragraph above I realise that I cannot in fact remember visiting the shoe-repair shop and the junk shop on the same trip. I well remember visiting both on several occasions and it is certain that I would have taken advantage of a trip to Fenlon's to visit the junk shop. Strictly speaking, though, I have cheated.]

23. I remember Jean's Teashop in Temple Fortune where my mother took me once. We had a pot of tea for two ('please') and buttered toast (already cut into slices).

[Perhaps we had just bought items of school uniform at Pullens almost next door. If Market Place didn't have whatever, you went to Temple Fortune, if Temple Fortune didn't, you went to Golders Green, if Golders Green didn't, you went to Oxford Street. East Finchley was out of it, and Brent Cross did not yet exist. Jean's Teashop involves a classic conundrum: do I remember that visit because we only went once and therefore the uniqueness commended itself to the relevant brain cells or have I conflated several visits? In this instance I plump for the former (because the memory is extraordinarily vivid) but elsewhere in this book there are undoubtedly examples of conflation. I am not, thank goodness, Borges' Funes the Memorious.]

(B)

THE STREETS

1. I remember the network of alleyways. For example, as you look up the street outside my childhood house, the nearest alleyway leads left to Brunner Close and, opposite, right to Sutcliffe Close. These alleyways continue to Southway and to Northway. They were signposted but only people who lived in the Suburb knew about them.

[Something niggled me today, so I checked 'alleyway' in my Chambers dictionary: it would appear that I am talking about 'alleys' not 'alleyways'. But I remember them as 'alleyways'.]

2. I remember the allotments which could only be reached from the ends of the gardens which backed on to them. Fortunately I knew people whose gardens did adjoin, like the Caplins up the road, who moved in after my friend Everard de Westenholz moved out. In the allotment bounded by Middleway, Thornton Way and Northway there was a wonderful tree you could climb and sit in. There was a fireworks party on Guy Fawkes Day in another allotment.

3. I remember Litchfield Way had trees which blossomed a lovely pink every year. Mr Graham who changed his name from Grabo had the most beautiful private garden in the Suburb on the corner of Middleway and Litchfield Way. He cut down his hedges because he, quite rightly, wanted everybody to see his flowers.

4. I remember the pillar box on the corner of Northway and Thornton Way. Sometimes I would rush to catch the last post for my mother. Across Northway from the pillarbox was the entrance to Big Wood where you went for a walk with your dog if you had one, without it if you didn't. I remember the open-air theatre in Little Wood and a performance of *A Midsummer Night's Dream* in the rain.

[To this day any mention of any open-air theatre conjures up that play and that weather. An old friend, Jan Marsh, *née* Penny, now a writer, grew up in Denman Drive round there.]

5. I remember Lyttelton Playing Fields where I played football with my friends and flew my kite – which never worked. Occasionally I kept an eye on my little sisters Mary and Anne when they came along to play on the swings and roundabouts. There was a bowling green where old people played their ball game slowly. Next to the bowling green were our tennis courts. Mutton Brook meandered through the playing fields. Near the entrance at Kingsley Way it was narrow and shallow enough to jump over. I played for the Suburb table-tennis team, captained by Mr Corkhill. Local league home matches were in the sports pavilion by the bowling green. One away game was played in a factory near Neasden, on the North Circular Road.

6. I remember cul-de-sacs like Constable Close, Reynolds Close and Turner Close but I didn't know anybody who lived in one, except my piano teacher – in Hurst Close.

[I was gobsmacked to learn years later that Tony Hancock had lived in the Suburb, in Grey Close. Railway Cuttings it wasn't. As a French translator I must cover my flank and register that the correct plural is *culs-de-sac*.]

7. I remember there was no public transport within the borders of the Suburb except on the main roads (Lyttelton Road and Falloden Way, with Market Place joining them up) which bisected it, and no pubs – not even in Market Place – until you got to the borders themselves. There were no fences, which were forbidden by the Suburb's constitution, only hedges. The Suburb had its own estate agent in Temple Fortune called Coparts, which my parents explained meant co-partners. I knew that Hampstead Garden Suburb was supposed to be a special and unusual place visited by tourists, and was famous with town planners and architects. It was even rumoured that you were only allowed to hang your washing out on Mondays. There was the old Suburb where I lived, and the new Suburb on the other side of the main road where some of my friends lived. The war memorial at Henly's Corner, *La Délivrance*, was known locally as the Naked Lady, which she was.

[There is a pub (Goldie's formerly the Eagle) at Henly's Corner, one at the corner of East End Road (the Bald-Faced Stag), one at Golders Green (the Refectory) and one at Whitestone Pond (Jack Straw's Castle). If these are the four corners of my very own and private universe then . . . so what? Unlike those at the old Caledonian Market these four corner pubs were not planned. But am I the first to notice their collective existence? There are a few other pubs, also on the borders, including the Royal Oak at Temple Fortune and the Spaniards near Kenwood. One of my children, when very young, renamed the Naked Lady the Bum-Bum Lady, which she is.]

8. I remember the Heath Extension at the back of Meadway and Hoop Lane. It stretched to Wildwood Road and Hampstead Way and, beyond, to North End Road and the Heath itself. We knew that Elizabeth Taylor had lived in Wildwood Road and been a student at Aida Foster's drama school in Golders Green.

9. I remember Hampstead Heath very well, although it was outside the Suburb and strictly speaking does not belong here. We went there for walks, and visited the fair at which I never even won a goldfish, let alone a coconut. Dodgems were favourite. One winter it was possible to toboggan on the Heath.

10. I remember the putting green at the bottom of Northway. There was a little hut where you chose your putter and paid the attendant sixpence. Once, playing alone, I called my score the world record. I remember often beating my own record, sometimes cheating, sometimes not. On the other side of Northway there were tennis courts, but I preferred the ones in Lyttelton Playing Fields.

11. I remember the Suburb annual junior tennis competition. I used to do quite well but I never won it. We played these matches on the courts at the bottom of some of the closes. My friend Richard Hyams was a member of Chandos Lawn Tennis Club in Wellgarth Road. I used to enter its annual open competition.
    [Bobby Wilson himself plays at Chandos now, according to my Uncle Phil.]

12. I remember Mr Cohen who lived in my street, across and down. In summer he worked in his garden, at a table covered with books and papers. A man working at home! This was strange.
    [Years later I discovered he was the famous translator and editor, J. M. Cohen, a Buddhist, unlike the Leeds footballer George Cohen, who was a

Roman Catholic. As a translator myself, I wrote to J. M. Cohen. He replied that he remembered I had ginger hair, which meant he was confusing me with my next door neighbour, Ephraim.]

13. I remember the bomb-site on the corner of Middleway and Thornton Way and my father telling me about his occasional experiences as a fire-watcher during the war. I did not know of another bomb-site in the Suburb.

[The house was rebuilt some years later. Just down from it is a very ugly modernisation of the frontage at no 28. This was against all the by-laws of the Suburb. The owners doubtless could not afford to live in Winnington Road, where the frontage would have been appropriate. My father's experiences of fire-watching and other tales ante-dating either my memory or my own life might perhaps have merited a sub-category of their own (see 5.A.v.7 for more on memories of others' memories). What kind of true stories do parents tell their children? Some are volunteered, some are answers to questions. My questions often concerned old photographs, which I loved going through. My pleasure in this activity makes it difficult for me to measure my eidetic skills.]

14. I remember every house had a wooden gate at the beginning of the narrow drive leading to the front door, and two gates at the begining of the drive leading to the garage. Once, fooling around with my friend Ephraim, I fell off our gate. Two or three stitches had to be put in under my chin.

[I do not think a single house has the original gates left. Most of the original garage doors have gone too. I still have the scar under my asymmetrical chin. Was I taken to the Whittington or the Royal Free? Equidistant in miles – and in memory too: memory miles. Your host resists an immense temptation to break the rules and phone his mother for the answer. But what a disgraceful vanity on my part to suppose that the incident remains important enough for her to remember which hospital I was taken to! On the other hand some memories are accidental. And I know she remembers the accident itself.]

15. I remember Bishops Avenue. The part from East Finchley High Street to Lyttelton Road was known jokingly as the 'poor end'. Rumours abounded that film stars and royalty lived in Bishops Avenue. Everybody knew that a radio personality, the Latin-American bandleader Edmundo Ros, lived in a close off

the Avenue. One street off the 'poor end', Bancroft Avenue, was where several of my friends and a cousin of my father – Alex Shiner – lived. Doctor Lorn, my first doctor, had his surgery on the south-west corner of Bishops Avenue/Lyttelton Road. My father told me Dr Lorn did not approve of the idea of the National Health Service and retired to Cornwall in 1948 when the NHS was founded.

[Postscript during final revision: at a conference in San Francisco recently I met a French/Israeli writer Emmanuel Moses, who is married to a German Jewish writer, Gila Lustiger. In conversation it emerged that he is related by marriage to Mr Bernard Lax of Bancroft Avenue. Bernard Lax is related by marriage to the wife of Alex Shiner. Gila Lustiger is a cousin of the Cardinal Archbishop of Paris, Jean-Marie Lustiger. There is a rumour that (in the unlikely event of a non-Italian being chosen) he might become the next Pope, the first Jewish Pope since Peter. In which case I shall be related, by marriage, to the Pope of Rome.]

16. I remember the knife-grinder.

17. I remember the onion man from France.

18. I remember the coal man with the black face and large sack he emptied into the coal cupboard at the side of the house.

19. I remember the junk-cart man: 'Any old iron?'

20. I remember the postman. Some of my letters were addressed to 'Master Anthony Rudolf'.

21. I remember the travelling library behind St Jude's Church at the top of my street. One day I borrowed *The Moon and Sixpence* by Somerset Maugham, an Ellery Queen and a Bulldog Drummond.

[While I can only remember the books I borrowed on one particular occasion, I do remember going on other occasions: compare and contrast Jean's Teashop earlier.]

22. I remember the Teahouse at the top of Northway and the Free Church Hall next door.

(C)

SCHOOLS

(i) Nursery School

1. I remember my nursery school – it was called Auntie Martha's. I went there by bus and in a pushchair, accompanied by my mother or by Lisa who lived with us, and who was, well, Lisa. Auntie Martha's was just past Hoop Lane on the way to Golders Green, a big house on the main road. There was a winding path along a rockery up to the front door, which was painted red.

[I think it was the house next door to Golders Hill School. There is no clue from the outside that it was once a school. Nor from the inside either, I wouldn't be surprised.]

2. I remember two group activities at this school: going to the toilet and lying down to rest. The former involved a queue and performing with the door open.

[Doubtless the queuing accounts for the recollection. I would be interested to hear from any alumni/alumnae or faculty members of this *alma mater*, though perhaps that should be *alma amita*.]

(ii) Junior School

1. I remember my first day at junior school, Henrietta Barnet, at the top of our road. I walked up Middleway holding my mother's hand. The headmistress was Miss Doris Ironside, but she retired soon after I arrived. Her successor was Miss Barbara Harris, who walked with a limp and lived in Temple Fortune. One day, for some reason, three of us went to see her about various matters. Peter Morton's complaint concerned the food. He was dismissed: 'Tell your mother the carrots are fresh, not tinned. You *can* eat them.'

[My friend Betty Scharf, an Old Henrietta, told me only three days ago that Miss Harris died on 23 April 1994.]

2. I remember the gym teacher Miss Wells. Later she went blind. The girls removed their school skirts for gym. Their navy-blue knickers had a pocket for a handkerchief but they kept boiled sweets in them. There was a fat girl called

Mary, and a thin one called Ruth Horn, and Celia Shindler whom I also knew from Hebrew classes. The boys kept their short trousers on for gym. We played 'he', also known as 'it', in the playground.

[Theo Gale and my other friends from the younger generation, who know Henrietta Barnet as a girls-only school, used to find my attendance there a big joke, unless I'd changed sex, which would have been an even bigger joke.]

3. I remember a teacher called Miss Vermer who lived close to our street, in Litchfield Way. And there was Miss Boggan, Sheila Boggan, who was known as toboggan. Once she sent me out of the room for something I had not done. Someone came out and looked down the corridor not up, and therefore did not see me. Toboggan thought I'd vanished.

[Years later I discovered Miss Vermer's name was Miss Vollmayer. It's funny that I can't remember being ticked off for vanishing, on top of my original crime. Memory itself plays tricks, *kuntsim* as they say in Hebrew. Vanishing tricks indeed, into the *trous* of *mémoire*.]

4. I remember Anthony Axon, who lived in Big Wood Court, a block of flats across the road from the school. He had no brothers or sisters. I thought he was very strange – living in a flat and being an only child. Harold Wilson's son, Robin Wilson, who lived in Southway, just up the road from Anthony Axon, was in my class.

[Anthony and I, after different secondary schools, ended up at the same college with the same French tutor.]

5. I remember John Deech who lived in Maurice Walk. After walking down my road, Middleway, from school, the two of us stood outside my house on several occasions and sang a popular song quite loud before John proceeded on to his house: 'You are the apple of my eye, you are the sunshine of my heart.' We burst into laughter because (presumably) why apple? We also compiled lists of tables way beyond the amount required by the arithmetic teacher. John's notebook was red and had lists of weights and measures on the back, including avoirdupois.

[John is now a lawyer and married to the head of an Oxford college. Her name is Ruth. He tells me he lived in Hill Top, not Maurice Walk. I am sure he is the apple of Ruth's eye and she the sunshine of his heart.]

6. I remember telling John Deech a joke: 'When is a door not a door?' and knowing the answer but not understanding it.

[The door of the cupboard where my memories sleep was prised ajar quite late in the composition of this book while I was checking a reference in David Jones' other masterpiece, *The Anathemata*. Having found what I was looking for, I reread Jones's preface where he says that when he was a child 'there was still in vogue the Victorian catch-question "when is a door not a door?" . . . When is a sign not a sign? When is what was valid no longer valid?' Apart from triggering my memory, the quote from Jones (born in 1895) prompts another memory, this time with pre-Victorian connotations, namely being told that if I wasn't good 'Boney will come and get you'. My 'official' first memory (see 5.H.6) dates from early 1946. The two memories in this paragraph date from around 1949, when the nineteenth century was not all that far off. The Irish poet John Montague took me to meet Jones on 26 November 1972. Jones signed and dated my copy of *The Tribune's Visitation* in red, green and black; two treasured possessions: a book and a memory.]

3

Hampstead Garden Suburb Synagogue

> . . . the desire to forget prolongs the exile, and the secret of
> redemption is remembrance
>
> Hasidic saying attributed to the BAAL SHEM TOV

(A)

SERVICES AND PEOPLE

1. I remember when Norrice Lea Synagogue was only one storey high and
there was no ladies' gallery. The ladies sat in the back half of the synagogue and
could be seen more easily than now.

2. I remember when the *bimah* (the raised area for the cantor and other
officiants) was immediately before the Holy Ark and not in the centre of the
synagogue.

3. I remember the joke Yiddish name for the street: Shnorrer's Lea. I knew that
the word meant 'beggar'.

4. I remember the rabbi of the synagogue, Dr Meyer Lew, and the general
rejoicing when he was appointed *dayan*, a religious judge and member of the
London *Beth Din* or ecclesiastical court of the Chief Rabbi. Our families knew
each other from way back, in the East End. I remember a prayerbook at home
signed as a barmitzvah present to my own father by the Reverend Esterson,
future father-in-law of Rabbi Lew.
    [Traditionally any three rabbis constituted a *Beth Din* but the Victorian (and
earlier) Jewish establishment wanted a more formal set up. The Chief Rabbinate

was modelled on Canterbury. The outside world sees the incumbent as the representative of all Jews – quite impossible as Jonathan Sacks has discovered, and indeed he is officially the Chief Rabbi only of one grouping, the United Synagogues of Great Britain and the Commonwealth. At the *shiva*, the week of mourning in my parents' house after my father's funeral, our family was honoured by a visit from Dayan Lew. As a principal mourner, I was in a position to discuss controversial issues with him, since he was there to 'console the mourners in Zion'. Somehow he knew I was no longer an orthodox or orthoprax Jew and to my surprise he mentioned in a respectful way the name of the influential Reform Rabbi Maybaum – mentor of younger rabbis such as Lionel Blue and an influence on Hugo Gryn. Maybaum, I have been told, was rejected on arrival from Germany before the war by the orthodox United Synagogue movement for being *too* interested in theology. I raised the critically important issues of the *agunah* and *mamzerut* (the status of the deserted wife and the status of children of an adulterous relationship) with Dayan Lew: he shook his head, and said that these were tragically difficult issues to resolve. He must have known I was hoping that he, in Beckett's phrase in a rather different context, 'might have passed some remark'.]

5. I remember the *chazan*, the cantor, Reverend Freilich, with his powerful operatic tenor voice, his extraordinary coloratura maintenance of liturgical traditionalism. On Yom Kippur he wore a white gown and a white hat.

[It was a very beautiful voice in the great tradition of operatic cantors from Poland and Germany (the link between art and religion deriving from this tradition is one of the themes in *The Jazz Singer*). I hope there is a tape somewhere of Reverend Freilich's voice. Old and ailing, he was an officiant at the recent funeral of my uncle, Stanley Russell. My friend Felek Scharf heard a famous American cantor sing in Warsaw recently. Felek told him (after they discovered they were second cousins, both being great-grandsons of Rabbi Moshe Yaakov Yekel Scharf of Oswiecim, known in Yiddish as Osptzin) he could have had a career at the Met. 'I know but I didn't want to. I am a Yid.']

6. I remember the caretaker, Mr Chisnel, who was not Jewish.

7. I remember the *shammas*, the beadle, a short fat man in a top hat, Harry Cohen. Sometimes he would joke with the children, sometimes he shouted at us for a breach of decorum.

8. I remember the children's service held every *Shabbos* morning in the synagogue hall and how I tried to avoid the eye of the Hebrew classes headmaster Mr Taylor, who ran it, so that he would not invite me up to sing a solo before the Reading of the Law, the part which concludes (in Hebrew, of course) with the famous words: 'For out of Zion shall go forth teaching and the word of the Eternal One from Jerusalem.' I was always successful in avoiding a public airing of my tuneless voice. After the short service we went into the main synagogue.

9. I remember many prayers and hymns, for example the *shema* and *yigdal*, *hashivenu* and *adon olam*, *aleinu* and the *kaddish* . . .
   [. . . and can still recite them by heart. Today, as a member of a non-orthodox (Liberal) synagogue, I would say, for example, *Shabbat*, following the Israeli and/or Sephardi pronounciation, rather than *Shabbos*. Today, too, I believe that the *aleinu* prayer contains a message about repairing the world – *takken olam bemalchut shaddai* – for the whole of humanity in our precarious ecology. I have written about this elsewhere.]

10. I remember the honorary officers in top hats, Mr Harry Landy, Mr Max Fulder, Mr Frankfurter. Sausage my father called him which even then I did not think was all that funny.

11 I remember the different routes I could take from synagogue to my house in Middleway: the most boring one was via Linden Lea and Kingsley Way. The next best was to follow the main road, Falloden Way. But the best was through Lyttelton Playing Fields where I could dawdle past the tennis courts, over the bridge, and along the stream.

12. I remember sometimes going back to Martin Silk's house after synagogue to play table tennis before lunch. He lived in Church Mount, one minute from *shull*, as we called the synagogue.

13 I remember one Saturday afternoon my parents were driving somewhere and went close to Norrice Lea. Too close. I hid myself on the floor in the back of the car.

[This was because my Jewish friends in the suburb tended to be more religious than me and I didn't want their parents to know that I broke the law. When I was young my father was quite hostile to religion, even the relatively mild Anglo-Jewish compromise which the United Synagogue represented. But he and my mother never joined the Reform Synagogue, nor even Louis Jacobs' Independent Orthodox Synagogue – the forerunner of today's Masorti or Conservative congregations. Coming from an ultra-orthodox (*Machzike Hadath*) family, my mother was always more traditional; unlike my father (whose own father had been orthodox but less so, being a member of Hambros United Synagogue), she has never eaten positively forbidden food. My father loved oysters, etc. But her house was and is strictly kosher.]

14. I remember that two important foreigners would stay with relatives in the Suburb and attend *shull* when in London. One was Danny Kaye (but I never saw him); the other was the Israeli Minister for Religious Affairs, Dr Burg (I did see him).

(B)

HEBREW CLASSES (*CHEDER*)

1. I remember the headmaster, Mr Solomon Taylor, who was a very strict schoolmaster of the old school. He always wore a stiff collar, even on the hottest day, when he would substitute a highly coloured blazer for his suit.

[The blazer was certainly specific to an institution, perhaps his teacher-training college in Leeds. I suspect he was a last-gasp and now vanished combination of the old English elementary-school teacher and the eastern European *melamed*. We were afraid of him. *Melameds* could be fearsome, as the painter Soutine discovered long ago. Mr Taylor was not hated, but he was not loved, *pace* my Suburb contemporary Bernard Taub who wrote the obituary in the *Jewish Chronicle*. Let us say he was respected. But Bernard in addition to being more religious was a better student than me. So, I could be wrong. 'Memory goes on foot, history takes the train,' wrote Charles Péguy in his great and neglected book *Clio*. Given that a fact is an event under description (according to Hayden White), then if the event – the 'event' being our image of Mr Taylor – has two descriptions there is still only one fact: a tale of two competing descriptions. What then is truth? On this reading the geometrical figure of truth is a polyhedron.]

2. I remember Mr Taylor telling us that if we could not speak good of someone we should keep quiet. He used also to quote Talmud to the effect that a willow was stronger than an oak because in a storm the willow would bend but the oak would break. I liked both of his quotes. I also remember one occasion when he stared me in the eye and said that Israel needed farmers not chartered accountants.

[With parents who were anti-Zionist till 1948 (on political rather than religious grounds) and non-Zionist till the Six-Day War in 1967, I had only the vaguest idea about Israel at the time Mr Taylor eyeballed me. But I knew he was making a point about my father. A farmer Henry Rudolf wasn't, as Mr Taylor well knew. This is not the place to go into great detail concerning the question of Jewish anti-Zionism and its different modalities. My ultra-orthodox maternal grandfather Meyer Rosenberg (Russell) was against political Zionism on *theological* grounds, namely one must not anticipate the work of the Messiah.

Like the Grand Inquisitor in *The Brothers Karamazov* he would have argued that the undeserved suffering of one person – let us say the death of a child – raised theological problems no different from, say, the deaths of six million. He would have been familiar with one of the great poems of world literature, the *Book of Job*. But to avoid any misunderstanding I must emphasise that Zion was at the heart of the daily prayers of this deeply pious Jew: 'may the redeemer come unto Zion speedily and in our days'. Had he lived to see it, his contempt for the modern Lubavitch messianic tendency would have known no bounds. He died, ironically enough, on the day the state of Israel was declared. Mr Taylor's remark about keeping *shtum* I remember trying to live up to, and I think I did until when? Until the age this book ends with. This supplies yet another gloss on the rationale for ending it before the author goes to college.]

3. I remember that in addition to Hebrew classes on Sunday morning from ten till one we also attended on Tuesday and Thursday evening from five-fifteen till six forty-five. When the new synagogue hall was being built and the synagogue expanded we used the classrooms of a local school, Childs Way. We were divided into houses on the model of English schools. The houses were Rashi, Hillel, Maimonides and Montefiore. On Tuesday and Thursday evenings after school I went straight to the Dorothy Café in Temple Fortune where I had a cup of tea and a roll and butter and did some school homework before Hebrew classes started.

[Considering that the first three houses were named after three of the greatest Jewish figures who ever lived (all rabbis), the name of the fourth house, Montefiore, that is Sir Moses Montefiore, comes as a surprise. Why not, for example, choose the Vilna Gaon if a more modern name was wanted, or the Baal Shem Tov? – though the latter would have been less likely in those days, when Hasidism was less fashionable than it is now. Montefiore was the most prominent and influential Anglo-Jew of the nineteenth century, leaving aside Disraeli. Perhaps Montefiore's name nods sub-textually or unconsciously in the direction of gratitude to Britain for hosting a Jewish community. Or maybe Mr Taylor chose the houses in thirty seconds during a weekday bus ride or Sabbath walk from where he lived, Hendon, to the Suburb.]

4. I remember other teachers: my very first one, Mrs Miriam Bornstein, and Mr Taylor junior, a thin, quite friendly man who chain-smoked. I was sure that

Mr Taylor senior had been a very strict father when his son was young. There was Rabbi Leperer who was witty and entertaining, the young Rabbi Silberg who was the assistant to Dayan Lew and who once said he would play football with us if we worked harder, Mr Bernard Benjamin who was good at sport and conducted the children's service on Yom Kippur held in the pavilion in Lyttelton Playing Fields (because the synagogue hall was used as an overflow service for grown-ups), Mrs Ehrentrau, who wore a turban, and a young woman called Shifrah Stritzower, who was an anthropologist, whatever that was. A new and bearded teacher, Rabbi Feist, disliked me as much as I disliked him. Rabbi Wilshanski used to stroke his (i.e. his own) beard. When, on one occasion, I parroted the Hebrew words *kaddish* and *mamzer* in their affection-ate Yiddish usage, Rabbi Wilshanski became very agitated. We learned about the liturgy and about Jewish history, and made a start at learning modern Hebrew. At twelve, to prepare for barmitzvah, the boys attended a special class on Mondays: we had to learn our 'portions' (see 3.D.1) and how to 'lay *tefilin*' (see 5.C.ii.4); later we took a voluntary class in Talmud taught by Sidney Leperer. I thought I was spending a lot of time at the Hebrew classes, four evenings a week plus Sunday morning plus the service on Saturday.

[Only Friday was exempt, and Friday evening was the quintessential Jewish moment in our relatively secular/non-orthoprax household. I have racked my brains about the Hebrew classes curriculum and I have to observe that, *pace* Mr Taylor's remark about accountants and farmers, we were not taught about Israel; nor about the Holocaust. You must remember that I finished Hebrew classes quite a few years before the 1967 Six-Day War, which revolutionised the lives of all Jews everywhere, *whatever their convictions, or lack of.* My junior sisters born in 1951 and 1953 probably discovered Israel and the Holocaust (as it wasn't yet known) around the same time as I and my sister Ruth born in 1942 and 1945. And, indeed, a phonecall to my sister Annie confirms what I say. She too has no recollection of being taught about Israel or the Holocaust. I now realise that *kaddish* and *mamzer* were words Rabbi Wilshanski only knew *stricto sensu. Mamzer* is a strict legal category, the product of an adulterous liaison, *not* the product of unmarried people, but it is also used to mean 'little so and so'. *Kaddish*, the memorial prayer for the dead, also means, in popular usage, a little boy, that is the person who will one day grow up to say the *kaddish* at your own funeral. Recently my mother took me to the sixtieth-anniversary dinner of the synagogue. It was good to meet again the sadly emaciated Rabbi Leperer – who has since died – and Mrs Bornstein. Not long ago I obtained from the BBC archive a tape of a programme about Anglo-Jewish poets. Broadcast in 1961 – before the watershed of 1967 – it does not contain a single reference to Israel or to the Holocaust. Today the story would be very different.]

5. I remember that most years I won a prize at Hebrew classes (*cheder*). The first prize I won was a Passover *Haggadah*.

[I still have it, and it is still used at family *seders*, wine-stained and *matsah*-crumbed, and much loved. The illustrations are poor but have become iconic in the temple of my mind. Art Spiegelman should do a *Haggadah*. Before me is the final prize I won, a Soncino Pentateuch with the marvellous commentary by the late Chief Rabbi Hertz, so much better than the ArtScroll edition which has replaced Soncino. I note that the prize bookplate gives the synagogue's phone number as SPEedwell 8126. Ah, the 'intoxication of anamnesis', as Walter Benjamin wrote.]

6. I remember that I and my sister Ruth went with a group from the synagogue to a camp in Seaford. The camp took place three times. We were the only children who went every year. The children slept in dormitories (weaker brethren enduring apple-pie beds), played sports, went to the beach and to the park. One year, Mr Reuben or Rubin, the father of one of the boys in our dormitory, made an appearance for some reason and got angry when he heard me utter a rude word whose meaning meant nothing to me. I had a buddy, Norman Shaffer, who was very freckled. One year, on the last night, he and I put on a play involving a character called 'Casey Cow go Golders Green'. ('Thank you, Archibald . . . Ta, Bert,' went the only exchange I can remember). Two songs were very popular: 'Unchained Melody' and 'The Man from Laramie' ('He had so many notches on his gun . . . [something] was this man's melody? or specialty? . . . There was no cayoot who could outshoot the man from Laramie'). Norman owned a cardigan with a zip and collar. The cardigan was more chunky than Warren Pantzer's. I competed strongly with Bernard Taub and Lawrence Litt for the title of best cricketer.

[The name of the character in the play is doubtless an allusion to some topical person, in our lives or on the wireless. The brief exchange suggests that we were employing class difference, that old English standby, to get a laugh. The two songs just pre-date rock and roll, and were sung by a big star, Jimmy Young. A casual glance at Black's *History of the Jews' Free School* (attended by several members of my family) suggests that the camp we went to had once been their old school camp.]

7. I remember I attended a camp the previous year in Lowestoft under the auspices of Whittingham College, a Jewish boarding school in Sussex, whose headmaster was called Mr Halevi. I remember almost nothing of that holiday except that we sang the hymn *adon olam* to a rousing tune, and the sea was rough, and the toilets were flooded.

(C)

FESTIVALS

1. I remember *Rosh Hashonah*, New Year. I did not like the second day which was more or less identical to the first. We were taught that Jews in the diaspora celebrated two days because you could not have been one hundred per cent sure, in the days before electricity, which time it was in which country.

2. I remember *Yom Kippur*. The final *kaddish* on this day was sung to a particularly rousing tune. At the end of the service, Cantor Freilich would drink a glass of wine and all present congratulated him on his musical efforts, calling out the traditional phrase: *shekoyach*. One year, Mr Eder, our next-door neighbour and the father of Ephraim, tried to tempt some of the under-thirteen boys with oranges and sweets. He failed because it was a point of honour to attempt to fast throughout the twenty-five hours even though it was not obligatory until you were barmitzvah, i.e. an adult in terms of religious responsibilities. My mother's theory or tradition was that it was easier to fast on a small meal, smaller anyway than my father's family could manage on.

[*Shekoyach* is short for, or was how I heard, *Yasher ko'ach* or, more correctly (says my *maven*) *Yisharko'achecha*, may your strength be renewed: the phrase is found in the Talmud. My *maven* also tells me that the rousing tune for the *kaddish* was composed by a Polish cantor called Moses the Hoarse One.]

3. I remember the festival of *Succoth* and the traditional booth, the *succah*, built at the synagogue by Mutton Brook, which ran along the side of the *shull*. I remember the men went down to the brook for the ceremony of *tashlik*, casting one's sins upon the waters.

4. I remember the New Year for Trees.

5. I remember on *Purim* we used to stamp our feet when Haman's name was mentioned during the reading of the Scroll of Esther and wave flags and special rattles (*gregors*). I liked Esther because her action saved our people, but also because that was my mother's name. We had our own scroll which had

belonged to my maternal grandfather. Every *Purim* there was a fancy-dress party at the synagogue. Cartoon films were shown.

[*Purim* is a very popular street festival in modern Israel. Traditionally, cross-dressing and drunkenness have not been discouraged. I can understand why some Jewish women prefer Vashti to Esther, but it is not given to many people, men or women, to be the saviour of their people. One fascinating example is the mother of all role models for Jewish women, the pious, tough and much painted Judith of Jerusalem, who took her kosher lunch with her when she went to bump off the Assyrian general Holofernes. Like Esther, she deployed feminine wiles in order to save the Jewish people, but unlike Esther she did not eat *treif*, non-kosher food, and also unlike her she did not sleep with the enemy. And there is the case of Jael, who killed the enemy Sisera by hammering a tent-peg into his skull, having, according to rabbinic tradition, slept with him first. These are examples of doing good through sinning, a dangerous doctrine which taken to excess leads directly to antinomianism and to Shabbetai Zvi, the subject of a major essay by Gershom Scholem, one of the grandest and most important Jewish thinkers of all time. In a church at Ribeira Grande on San Miguel in the Azores is an extraordinary work of art, the *Arcanum*, by a nineteenth century ex-nun, Marguerite of the Apocalypse. This took her more than twenty years. Contained in a huge glass case are hundreds of scenes from the Bible with thousands of tiny figures made from flour and gum. The Old Testament scenes include the three strong women mentioned earlier. Marguerite surely admired their courage and tenacity. I must check if Rahab is included. Later I visited the delapidated former synagogue, guarded by the last Jew on the Azores, and a Jewish cemetery with ancient graves.]

6. I remember one *Pesach* (Passover) week, during the middle days when you are allowed to work and travel, visiting the print shop in Sun Street, Bishopsgate, of my uncles Leon and Isidore Rudolf. I forgot it was *Pesach* and bought an egg sandwich at the caff on the corner. I ate it. And then I realised what I had done. I waited for God to punish me, to strike me down, for eating bread on Passover. Nothing happened and I remember that this felt like an important moment and required thinking about.

[It *was* an important moment but my later thoughts about theology belong in another book. One interesting consideration, to me at any rate, is that I broke all kinds of laws and never thought I would be struck down. But Passover was special, very special. Uncle Leon died earlier this month. We had our differences, but he was a generous man. The print shop: its ins and outs, its ups and downs, the brothers at war with each other, the question of inheritance, my father's torn loyalties between his siblings, the powerless grandfather, the role of in-laws, all these would have fascinated Balzac.]

7. I remember *Shavuot*, Pentecost, the anniversary of the Giving of the Law. You counted the *Omer*, the days after Passover, till this festival. My mother told me that she and my father were married on *Lag b'Omer*, the thirty-third day of the *Omer*. On all other days of the *Omer* you are not allowed to marry, but on this day you are.

8. I remember how every year, without fail, the festivals came round.
[They punctuated my life sentence. You knew who you were, or what you were.]

9. I remember many other things associated with festivals which took place at home rather than at the synagogue (see section 5.C.i).

(D)

BARMITZVAH

1. I remember my barmitzvah, and the week's Torah portion of *Leh Leha*, when I sang *maftir* (the last section of the Torah reading, which begins 'And Abraham rose early in the morning') and *haftorah* (the commentary from the prophets, in my case Isaiah) in the two traditional chants.

2. I remember standing before Rabbi Lew as he addressed me and then presented me with a prayerbook signed by the three honorary officers and himself. I recited the barmitzvah boy's prayer.

3. I remember going upstairs to the ladies' gallery, as was the custom with all barmitzvah boys, to kiss the mother and the grandmothers, in my case one grandmother, since Grandmother Rudolf had died the year before.

4. I remember an interview with Rabbi Lew in his house in Vivian Way before the barmitzvah.

5. I remember my best school friends being in the synagogue that day. I went to Warren Pantzer's synagogue in Dollis Hill for his barmitzvah. The barmitzvah of my best friend, Michael Duschinsky, took place at the Spanish and Portuguese Synagogue in Lauderdale Road, Little Venice. He was being brought up as a Sephardi by his great-aunt in London, a Pinto by birth. His father, an Ashkenazi rabbi from Hungary living in South Africa, came over to participate.

6. I remember after my barmitzvah there was a celebratory *kiddush* in the *shull* hall for friends and family. Michael Duschinsky ate all the olives.
   [We all thought he was peculiar because he loved olives but I suppose now that he liked them because he grew up as a Sephardi and Sephardim are more Mediterranean than Ashkenazim. The (Anglo-Jewish) irony is that in England, apart from recent immigration from Persia, etc., Sephardim have been here for hundreds of years and are often more English than the English or at any rate than the Ashkenazim. Professor Raphael Lowy, a Sephardi 'convert' from Ashkenazi Judaism, once gave me a copy of his translation into Latin of the Hebrew hymn *adon olam*, and you can't get more English than that.]

7. I remember I had my first pair of long trousers for my barmitzvah. I was the last of the boys in my class to wear long trousers even though I was one of the tallest, perhaps the tallest. I wore my school blazer with the regulation dark-grey flannels. Other boys wore their first suits.

[It must have been a new blazer – see the cover photo, posed for without glasses.]

8. I remember my barmitzvah party at home (see 5.C.ii).

(E)

FRIENDS

(i) Boys

1. I remember always being a little uneasy with my synagogue friends, except the ones who were not religious and the rare ones who lived in my street. Bernard Taub and Lawrence Litt were much more religious than I was. But Bernard was even more religious, more *frum* than Lawrence, perhaps by osmosis from his parents. Bernard once told me a joke about Joshua, Yehoshua Bin-nun: 'Joshua the son of none had no father.'

[I do not remember Bernard or Lawrence coming to my house, but this could not be because they lived a little over a mile away, in the 'new part' of the suburb, since other friends Richard Hyams and Paul Rochman also lived there. But Paul was my *best* non-school friend, and Richard doubled as a school friend and synagogue friend, one of only two. It can't have been the food, because my mother kept a kosher house (although see 4.C.ii.I.5, the paragraph on Ralph Ullmann under school friends, concerning this). The whole question of degrees of friendship is an interesting one. Richard Hyams and Norman Bar really belong with my school friends. Friends from my street appear elsewhere. But I do remember visiting the houses of Bernard and Lawrence in Aylmer Road and Bancroft Avenue respectively. They *must* have visited my house and I have forgotten. Pierre Nora's remark is pertinent: 'Memory is in a permanent state of evolution, open to the dialectic of recollection and amnesia, unaware of its successive deformations, vulnerable to all the ways in which it is used and manipulated, susceptible to long periods of latency and of revitalisation.']

2. I remember Paul Rochman who lived in Manor Court, a flat, which was unusual. He went to Leigh House, the prep school at the entrance to Lyttelton Playing Fields in Kingsley Way, and then as a boarder to Aldenham School. We were in each other's homes all the time during the holidays. Paul's family were even less religious than mine. Even so, their butcher was Schlagmann's, a kosher butcher. Paul's younger brother John was in love with my sister Ruth, or was said to be. Paul and I went on holiday together the summer after O levels, youth hostelling in Luxembourg and Belgium, and visiting the World Fair in

Brussels. We saw two films, *I'll Cry Tomorrow* with Susan Hayward and *A Man Alone* with Ray Milland. The youth hostel in Antwerp was the most luxurious we had ever seen. In Luxembourg we wandered into the grounds of the radio station and met Don Moss, the disc jockey.

[Leigh House is now Lubavitch House, a Jewish junior school. Ironically my parents' friend Ralph Leigh, a complete unbeliever married to a convert to Lutheranism, was born Ralph Lubavitch. I wonder now if Paul's mother bought her meat at Schlagmann's because, being on Aylmer Parade, adjacent to their flats, it was the nearest butcher of *any* description? The son of Schlagmann owns Phaidon Press. Soutine would have smiled at this.]

3. I remember Bernard Taub's cousin Anthony, and Malcolm Austen and Alan Saunders and Peter Collins and the Shrago brothers and Peter Fox and Norman Shaffer; and Neville King and Michael Weizmann even though they were one or two years younger. Neville King's father was an estate agent and a known Conservative. Michael Weizmann's father had a limp. There was John Coberman whose father died, and the Segal brothers who were good at sport. Stephen Segal was left-handed. Other names are Tony and Richard Loftus and the Tarlo brothers; and Tony Corby and Ashley Price and Anthony Taub's brother Brian, but they were older than me. Michael Richards and the Luck sisters pronounced certain vowels of our Ashkenazi Hebrew differently.

[The Hebrew pronounciation probably reflected the eastern European geolinguistic fault line which divided my grandmothers. I saw Michael Richards many years later working out some figures and orders with a waitress in Lindy's coffee house in Golders Green. From which I deduced he was the owner. Which was accidentally confirmed by his and my childhood friend Warren Pantzer in a letter to me from Australia last year. An additional factor concerning Hebrew pronunciation is that it reflected cockney influence among people whose grandparents were born in the East End or arrived when they were very young. Finally, I give myself permission to smuggle in a memory from student days, thus post-dating the book: the name Tarlo reminds me that Jonathan Tarlo and I went one Yom Kippur to an Indian restaurant – an umbilically rebellious but not revolutionary gesture, since we returned to synagogue. Michael Weizmann became a brilliant scholar. His death recently was sadly premature.]

4. I remember Martin Silk. He is in a category of his own because our parents knew each other from the East End and have remained close all their lives. He had unusual birthday parties in their flat at the top of Ossulton Way before they moved to Church Mount: the entire party consisted of a cheerful punch-up followed by tea. He and I also used to box – I owned two pairs of blue boxing gloves. My father said I was more skilful but Martin was stronger. One year Martin and I went youth hostelling around the Box Hill area.

5. I remember on Saturday afternoons we would gather under the benign aegis of Bernard Lax at various houses, but not mine, to celebrate a traditional *Oneg Shabbat*, the Joy of Sabbath. It was primarily social, but each week someone gave a talk. My talk was on the Jewish calendar, which is why I have never forgotten that in the lunar system we have seven leap years every nineteen years (a leap year involving an additional month not an additional day). We also sang pioneer songs of the *Yishuv* (pre-state Israel), such as 'Hafinjan' and 'Kinneret'. One hot Saturday afternoon I was even more sweaty than usual because I had smeared on too much Brylcreem, a commodity which did not do a great deal for my spots.

(ii) Girls

1. I remember my friends' younger sisters, Lois Litt known as kipper for some reason, Hilary Taub, Elizabeth Hyams, Ruth Silk.

2. I remember Sue Leveson who lived just outside the Suburb in Beech Drive, on the border of Muswell Hill, but who went to HGS Hebrew classes. She was petite and had a bloodshot eye. One year she became very ill and began the first of many stays in hospital. We corresponded. I kept all her letters.
   [We remained friends but later lost touch. I renewed contact a couple of years ago to find out if she had kept my letters. She had just disposed of them, after more than thirty years. I have resisted the temptation to look at the many letters she sent me, which would break my rule.]

3. I remember Barbara Wimborne and her aunt Frances who was younger than she was. Or vice versa? Either way, it was funny (peculiar and ha ha). Ruth

Gilbert lived on the main Lyttelton Road. Once I turned up at her house while she was ironing a bra in the kitchen. She laughed unembarrassedly. There was a girl called Madeleine who, according to rumour, had a non-Jewish boyfriend, and two sisters Judith and Marilyn Webber, both older than me, and their brother Jonathan, who was younger. Their father George was a cheerful soul, an admired and senior figure in a morning suit, who always found time to talk to the youth of the synagogue.

[Jonathan Webber is now a social anthropologist and a significant figure in the community, deeply involved in the controversy about the future of Auschwitz. George Webber founded Jewish Book Week which Marilyn has been involved in.]

4. I remember Diana Saunders, yet another denizen of Bancroft Avenue, who taught me how to jive at the Synagogue Youth Club, to the music of Bill Haley.

[I cannot remember if this was before or after the Six-Five Special episode (1.F.ii.3). Probably after, or I wouldn't have been so embarrassed about dancing in public. I met Diana recently, she is now an advocate in New York. She cannot remember teaching me to jive. But if A. J. Ayer is right in the chapter on memory in his *The Problem of Knowledge* she will remember it one day. I have planted the seed of time and the grain will grow.]

5. I remember two pairs of friends, Hilary Sefton and Susan Elman, and Hilary Sefton and Elizabeth Cohen. I was in love with Hilary. She lived in Church Mount, the other end of the street from Martin Silk, and went to South Hampstead High School. I remember being shocked and amazed when I noticed during one lesson that her blouse was wet under the armpits. She must go to the toilet too, I reasoned. That day she was in school uniform: white blouse with a purse slung over it, and a blue skirt. She told me once that her father had a very soft skin. She said he was in buttons. I remember the first time her best friend Susan Elman, who also went to South Hampstead, wore stockings. She was wearing a blouse and a flouncy skirt. Susan, like so many others, lived in Bancroft Avenue. She was demure and pretty. Hilary was tall and attractive. Even though I loved Hilary, I never declared my love but I don't recall any anguish, either physical or mental. Hilary's other best friend, Elizabeth Cohen, lived in Winnington Road and was a bit of a mystery

although she was perfectly friendly – tall and attractive in the style of Hilary rather than Susan. She went to Henrietta Barnet.

[I have been told that Hilary now lives in Israel. For all I know she is a grandmother. If asked, she would certainly remember we were in the same class at Hebrew classes but she could well be surprised to learn that I loved her, unless my neo-Platonic crush (ah, the green paradise of childhood loves) on her was written all over my spotty face. Again, the figure of truth as polyhedron. I wonder if she has ever thought about me in the intervening years: perhaps she has read something of mine? Oh, the sheer contingency of life, preordained or not. Concerning toilets, I had three sisters and a mother and knew *they* went! So why should I have a thing about Hilary's body? Ah, I touch on this in my afterword, where I risk an uncharacteristic speculation. My mother met Susan Elman in Brent Cross recently. Susan teaches law at LSE and lives part of the time in Israel where her parents, friends of my parents from East End days, also live. As for her stockings, I *think* I remember that one or two other girls also made the transition the same week, but I might be mistaken. I wonder if the first pair of stockings was a 'reward' for the first monthly period? It's unlikely that friends were synchronised even if they went to the same school, after all it wasn't a boarding school. I am curious about Elizabeth Cohen, but not enough to do anything about it. Postscript: I met Susan at a talk given by my friend Eva Hoffman in Michael Joseph's bookshop recently. I didn't mention stockings.]

6. I remember Maxine Swann who lived in Holne Chase. She was the first girl I took out, but it wasn't solo: we went with another 'couple', Paul Rochman and his girlfriend Michele, one afternoon, to see *The Inn of the Sixth Happiness* at the Odeon, Temple Fortune. We knew that in the name of the film *Eighth* had been changed to *Sixth* because it sounded better. Not to our ears it didn't.

[We may have sat in the back row, because that was what you were supposed to do, but *trou de mémoire* department . . .]

7. I remember my first solo date, Rosalind Montague, whom I asked to go with me to *April Love* at the Ionic cinema in Golders Green. My father said she should pay for her own cinema ticket and that I should take her home, and that she should also pay for her own bus ticket. We had an ice-cream.

[I wonder if I paid for the ice-cream. I wonder where I met Rosalind for the first time: she was neither a synagogue friend, nor a street friend, nor a City of London Girls School friend. Perhaps a friend had taken her to the Synagogue Youth Club. There was nowhere else . . . unless, as is possible, she went to Queen's College, Harley Street, and we were introduced on the tube by a mutual friend. She was married for some years, I later learned from my sister Ruth, to an older school friend of mine, Graham Craig. A *Jewish Chronicle* article recently informed us that she deals in futures, that is, reads tea-leaves. Perhaps she dunks a madeleine before tracking the parabola of the future perfect.]

4

Schools outside 'The Suburb'

To carry on the feelings of childhood into the powers of manhood

COLERIDGE

(A)

TRANSPORT

1. I remember the 58 bus which came straight down Lyttelton Road and Falloden Way, unlike the 102 which turned right from the East Finchley end of Bishops Avenue on its way to Henly's Corner and Golders Green. My 58 arrived at Market Place or was supposed to arrive there at 8 o'clock.

[Later the 58 was abolished, 'just like that' (Tommy Cooper catchphrase). By then I had already realised that it was the bus number/name which was abolished, the buses themselves lived on under other numbers/names. But of course I never noted the registered number plates and so could not look out for former 58s. A brief thought on Henly's Corner, at the north-west boundary of the Suburb: the garage it was named after has been demolished, but for me – and doubtless for many other people – it will always be known as Henly's Corner, just as I still know the junction of the North Circular Road and East End Road, admittedly outside the Suburb, as Lamb's Corner. The Market Place bus stop has also been moved along a few yards. And where did the 58 begin? Archway?]

2. I remember sometimes going to City of London School via East Finchley tube station, sometimes via Golders Green. I waited at Market Place for the 102 bus in one direction and the 102 or 58 in the other, and took the first one to arrive. Sometimes I would walk to Golders Green, sometimes to East Finchley,

95

which was a little nearer on foot. There was a short route to East Finchley through side streets and alleyways. The quickest way to Golders Green was either via Hoop Lane, between the crematorium and the Jewish cemeteries, or via Heathgate and the Heath Extension to Rotherwick Road. I remember thinking that even though we lived approximately halfway between the two stations my identity was firmly that of a Golders Green station boy rather than an East Finchley station boy.

[What do I know from 'identity', certainly the hindsight description of a felt condition? Golders Green, being a terminus and a major shopping centre, was a more interesting station than East Finchley. Furthermore, I should explain that the Suburb is bisected by a main road with Market Place at its heart. We lived on the same side of Market Place, in the same kingdom, as Golders Green tube station – a strong geo-ontological pointer to a preference for Golders Green. More prosaically, the journey to Arnold House, my prep school, unlike the later journey to City of London School, *had* to involve Golders Green, since the school was in St John's Wood – which meant taking a second bus, the 2 or 13 from Golders Green; East Finchley was on the wrong branch of the Northern Line for that connection. Later, the inspector at East Finchley station did not look too closely at my Golders Green season ticket. Had he noticed would he have complained? Even when the cost was the same, it was forbidden, I believe, to commence a journey at the wrong station.]

3. I remember the days when the 102 bus ended and began its long journey from and to Chingford in Golders Green bus yard next to the Hippodrome theatre: thence it moved to the little annexe backing on to the station shops.

[This made no sense to my mind. For me, change was against nature and therefore incomprehensible if not actually bad. Whatever was was right. I did not know then that change had nothing to do with nature, for the signs and wonders of my human world were not supposed to change and hardly ever did. I failed, as privileged children must fail, 'to see in the need to differentiate between nature and culture . . . the echo and obsession of knowing ourselves to be mortal' (Octavio Paz).]

4. I remember, 'Penny half, please.'
[In today's money that fare amounts to less than a quarter of a new penny.]

5. I remember, 'Rose-red city half as Golders Green.'

6. I remember in the evening, on the bus home from Golders Green, I would sometimes ask a person – usually upstairs, I preferred being upstairs – if I could please borrow their evening paper to learn the cricket scores. Downstairs, you gave up your seat to one of the five standing passengers in a full bus, to an old lady that is.

[‘Old’: how did we define old? Probably a grandmother-type person, or was it any female around a certain age, say one’s mother’s age? On the tube too you gave up your seat. I did not actually buy an evening paper. There were three: ‘*Star*, *News* or *Standard*. *Star*, *News* or *Standard*’. Sometimes my father brought home an *Evening Standard*.]

7. I remember during the bus ride from St John’s Wood to Golders Green there was a clock stopped permanently at ten minutes to ten on a parade of shops after Finchley Road but before West End Lane.

[Never to go no more, indeed. Until it was removed.]

8. I remember a man older than my father getting on the bus at the request stop after Market Place, every morning. I felt superior to him because buses automatically stopped for me at Market Place, whereas you had to hail buses at request stops, and that particular request stop was nowhere, nothing. This man was short and wore a hat. He always smiled and said good-morning to me.

9. I remember the bus conductor’s wooden ticket holder and the row of wonderful coloured bus tickets which sometimes had to be replenished from a box kept in the luggage/pram compartment, and the ping when the ticket was punched in return for your money. I always added up the figures at the top of my ticket to see if they totalled 21. The other hope was that they were the same as the four figures of my SPEedwell phone number. The betrayal, the disappointment, when the conductor’s gadget was replaced by a new-fangled machine!

[And now the newfangled machine, the Gibson, is itself displayed on London Transport Museum posters as an example of old technology. Was 21 supposed to be lucky? Telephone 'numbers' were like addresses: apart from SPEedwell, I remember TUDor, CUNningham, PRImrose, ELGar, CITy, VIGilant, MONarch, ABBey.]

10. I remember on winter evenings, if I was downstairs, the brown screen behind the bus driver in his little compartment, and how homely the big red bus was, especially in the rain.

[I suppose I remember it as being homely because my tastebuds were imagining tea and toast and jam, or sponge cake, on arrival home about fifteen minutes later but I'm working on that. For the time being the gloss on the memory must remain in paren-hypo-thesis. But that particular memory of the (pre-Routemaster) bus is always associated with rain. Red London buses were part of being a Londoner, common currency, shared discourse. Abolition of municipal government of this great capital city, deregulation, privatisation: the Tories have a lot to answer for. We don't want a mayor, we want the GLC back.]

11. I remember tube season tickets and how they fitted into the small plastic holder attached to my diary. I liked my diary for that reason. Other people needed a separate holder for their season ticket.

[Every year my father was given several promotional diaries. He would pass on to me the diary which his club sent its members. That was the diary with the plastic holder attached.]

12. I remember my tube journey from Golders Green or East Finchley to City of London School at Blackfriars offered me a choice. I could change either at Bank for the District and Circle Line, or at Charing Cross/Strand for the same line in the other direction.

[At Bank (known as 'The Bank') you went from another station in the same building, Monument, whereas Charing Cross/Strand were really the same station in different buildings. Strand and Trafalgar Square stations have now been abolished and are known as Charing Cross, while Charing Cross is known as Embankment.]

13. I remember we, Ralph Ullmann and I, used to time how long the tube took from Hampstead to Golders Green which we knew was the longest on the

whole network. That distinction belonged to us, not to Richard Hyams, who always went to East Finchley, either he or we having changed at Camden Town. The world record was three minutes nine seconds. At one point you could see from the tube window an unfinished platform: there was to have been another stop between Hampstead and Golders Green, at the Bull and Bush pub. But it was never completed. Richard Hyams used to argue that Morden to East Finchley was the longest tunnel in the world, but he would wouldn't he? I argued that the honour belonged to the other branch, Morden to Golders Green.

[Morden to Golders Green – that is, Morden to Anthony's stop. This version of reflected glory – a very minor sin – is further proof that my identity was linked with Golders Green rather than with East Finchley.]

14. I remember we used to do homework on the tube – especially if it did not involve writing – like learning passages of Shakespeare or other poets by heart, or reading set books. One poem was 'The Listeners' by Walter de la Mare. ' "Is there anybody there?" said the Traveller,/Knocking on the moonlit door;/And his horse in the silence champed the grasses/ Of the forest's ferny floor./ And a bird flew up out of the turret,/Above the Traveller's head:/ . . . "Tell them I came, and no one answered,/That I kept my word," he said.'

['By heart' is an interesting idiom. What we were doing was learning 'by head' or 'by mouth'. However, in the case of 'The Listeners' 'by heart' seems right. I loved it, and still love it.]

(B)

PREP SCHOOL

(i) Teachers

1. I remember the women teachers at Arnold House were addressed as sir. My first teacher, Miss Spooner, used to powder her nose in class. Miss Bluett was Australian. Miss Hasenclever, who was *very* old, was known as Crabapple because of her wrinkles. One of them taught us embroidery. A piece I did survived for years.

[What conceivable rationale was there for the transvestic nomination? As for Miss Hasenclever, she is dead by now. But what I should write is: Miss Hasenclever will have died during the period between the 'event' (knowing her) and the correlative memory. The man who got on the bus at the request stop after Market Place, which is all I know of him and insufficient to identify him, will have died or is pushing a hundred in a home somewhere. The youngest grown-ups in these pages will have reached their seventies. Every act of memory, every retrieval, reorders, rewraps, reconstructs, reconfigures the entire collection in one's mind, even if it is merely a question of perspective, since I myself pass time – for time does not, of itself or in itself, pass. You can't allow yourself to pay too much attention: all those people living and dying. I wonder how many people play the game 'What was my father up to at the age I am now?' Whenever I play this game it induces humility, given one's own fallibility as a parent. One example: for a long time I thought my father advised me badly when I wanted to change subjects for a second time at Cambridge. I accepted his advice but was not well pleased. Indeed I was angry. He was 49. When I became 49 and was making my own mistakes I privately forgave him his fallibility, for he knew not, etc., etc. He was already dead, which was typically convenient of the built-in unfinished business between parents and children – convenient for me, I mean, as it meant I could avoid the embarrassment of telling him I forgave him. Much later, after further reflection concerning the university courses in question, I came to the conclusion he had been *right* in the first place! It follows that, with any luck, my own mistakes will be forgiven, and may not even be mistakes, some of them anyway. I'm not holding my breath, 'playing dead' as we used to say. I was delighted to find that in his great memory book, *La Boucle*, Jacques Roubaud too plays this game, which can also be reversed: what was I like at the age my son is now? I do play the game using my mother and daughter, but less so, although at one remove I can gain a perspective on my mother's relationship with my sisters: there is more to mind, and to art, than gender.]

2. I remember the headmaster George Smart's brother, John Yeo Smart. The former was very serious, the latter very funny. John Yeo finally got married – and moved to Wildwood Road in Hampstead Garden Suburb – but his brother never married. The school was in two houses in Loudon Road in St John's Wood. The school uniform, bright scarlet and green. Once in the headmaster's office I asked to be excused attendance at occasional Church services because I was Jewish and was not supposed to go to Church.

3. I remember 'Please, sir, may I be excused?' was the formula you used if you wanted to go to the toilet.

[It also answered to the name of lavatory or WC in my family. Loo was never used; in those far-off days it was an upper-class term.]

4. I remember the Latin teacher, Mr Gardner, with his military moustache. He would say to pupils who made a mistake – rarely me at that stage – 'The devil damn thee black, thou cream-faced loon!' The French teacher was Mr Oliver Uren but it was Mr George Smart who conducted our first French lesson: 'Madame Souris a une maison,' said the class in unison. There was a bad-tempered teacher I disliked, name of Langridge or Langrish. And Mr Smith, who occasionally beat boys with a gym slipper; he selected me for lunchtime football in the lower playground, an honour bestowed only on a few.

['Rarely me': the three years I spent at Arnold House were the only time I did really well in my entire academic career, including Cambridge, apart from my first year at City of London (knock-on effect from prep school) and the six months at the British Institute in Paris (see 4D). I did not know that Mr Gardner's curse was a quote from *Macbeth*, nor did I notice that translations of both meanings of our first French phrase fit nicely into two rhyming amphimacer couplets (name courtesy of Coleridge's poem on metre: dum di dum, dum di dum. No, not 'nor did I notice', rather 'nor could I have noticed', apart from the rhyme). Several years after leaving Arnold House I went occasionally with my father to the Partisan Coffee Bar in Carlisle Street where left-wingers used to hang out, and there we met . . . Mr Uren. He's not in the London telephone directory but perhaps he never was. I remember him as a bit of a dandy.]

5. I remember I spelt 'encyclopaedia' correctly when asked by a teacher. My classmate Stephen Potter pointed up to a set of encyclopaedias on top of a cupboard and said I had seen the spelling there, but I had not.

6. I remember an interview with the headmaster of Westminster School, where Arnold House schoolboys traditionally ended up. My father told me afterwards that the headmaster had said: 'You have a clever son, Mr Rudolf, but unfortunately our Jewish quota is full this year.'

[Which was why I went to City of London School (after an alderman, Sir Bernard Waley-Cohen, had signed the forms at his house in Highgate). It took far more Jewish boys than Westminster. I remember my friend Michael Duschinsky being sure that CLS had a quota; he thought this was disgraceful and started a campaign to prove its existence and make it public. He even wrote to the school historian. I think now and I think I even thought at the time that schools with a Christian foundation and constitution had a perfect right to discriminate positively in favour of their own religion. How many non-Jewish children go to Hasmonean or JFS? This is quite independent of arguments about state schools versus private schools, etc. I doubt I had the nerve to confront Michael, who was better at argument than I was. I also have a funny feeling that part of me liked losing arguments because I could then identify with the loser, the underdog, namely myself: identifying with the underdog is a good socialist principle. This could explain a long list of socialist or even Old Labour failures.]

(ii) Friends

1. I remember my best friends: Stephen Hunt, a sweet boy known as pussycat because he had a kind of crewcut we liked stroking, Colin Macleod, Alastair Macrae (whose father was a leading anaesthetist), Richard Scoular, and Wilson, possibly Andrew Wilson. Other friends were Billy Falk and David Assersohn,

David or Peter Kleeman (known as Kleeware), Alan and Bobby Lorenz, Robin Hirsch and 'Pooch' Webber. I visited Andrew's house, which was in the grounds of the church (presumably it was the vicarage) in Hamilton Terrace where his father was the vicar – possibly St Andrew's Church, since I remember that my friend and his dad's church had the same name. Was this coincidence or design? Richard Scoular lived near the school, in a big house one minute from Lords cricket ground. At one period some of us conversed in a secret language: Yurawus and norowo for yes and no, etc., etc., which Colin Macleod was brilliant at.

[Thirty-five years later I overheard my daughter using a structurally similar language: yevegev and novogov. If I drive past the church in Hamilton Terrace I'll be able to confirm that Andrew was his name: but rules are rules, the paragraph above must not be changed. A less flattering account of Stephen Hunt can be found in the autobiography of Robin Hirsch, now a theatre person in America. I once noticed on TV that Richard Scoular was a losing Tory candidate in a general election. It's hardly surprising he was a Tory – I must have been one of only a handful of socialists in the school, and of a slightly larger handful of Jewish boys. (Of the socialists, what percentage were Jewish? Of the Jews, what percentage were socialist?) Postscript: I could not resist driving down Hamilton Terrace. St Mark's Church . . . Sorry Mark! But, wherever you may be, do you remember Anthony Rudolf? Why should you? I, for one, have forgotten much of whatever I knew, including the names of most of the boys in our class. If I could come back, renew my days as of old, renew even one day in my life, one day in the life of Anton Kirillovich, fully remember it unto the last drop, why, describing it would take hundreds of pages. Utter futility! I forgive myself this grandiose fantasy. Borges in *Labyrinths*, Charles Péguy in *Clio*, Jacques Roubaud in *La Boucle* and Georges Perec in many essays deal with such dream stuff, the little life in *gros plan*.]

2. I remember that one year, instead of arranging a birthday party, my father took me and my two best school friends – Stephen Hunt and Colin Macleod – to the Farnborough Airshow. It was the year the test pilot John Derry crashed the sound barrier, and then died when something went wrong. But we sang songs on the way home, including 'Sucking Cider through a Straw'.

[Colin Macleod was clever, top of the class. Later he was to become a classics superstar at Oxford, before committing suicide by placing his head on a railway line: brooking no possible reprieve, unlike certain other techniques. On a later occasion his older brother Robert, then co-owner of the Owl Bookshop in Kentish Town and also ex-Arnold House, gave me a copy of Colin's poems.]

3. I remember other boys at the school, including Michael Pennington and the roly-poly son of [?the heir to] the Nizam of Hyderabad, Prince Mufkham Jah, known as Muffer, who went home in a Rolls-Royce. One day Muffer came into the gym during boxing and interrupted the proceedings with the announcement that the Tories were leading in the General Election – and everybody except me cheered. There was Gordon Rowland, whose parents were friends of my parents. I remember his friends Buckley-Sharp and Naylor-Smith, because their surnames were double barrelled, that is to say posh. Once I took a Green Line bus to Potters Bar on my own and visited Gordon Rowland's aunt. Tooth wore glasses and was good at maths; Michaelson was plump, and one or both of them went on to Highgate School. There was a boy called John Tavener who, when the music teacher was away, played the piano accompaniment for the hymn sung at assembly. Some boys, but not I, thought he was a cissy. James Loudon's mother was called Lady Prudence and they lived in the big house at the junction opposite Jack Straw's Castle by Whitestone Pond. Anthony Champion died during my first year. The headmaster made the announcement before French one morning. We all brought money for a funeral wreath.

[Michael Pennington was to become a well-known actor – he has hardly changed. In the face of the composer John Tavener I see the boy who played the piano all those years ago. The boxing instructor was called Reg or Jack Gutteridge. He was later to become a wrestling commentator on TV, name of Jacky Pallo. This was the 1951 election. The Green Line bus episode, apparently banal, bears comment: why on earth did I visit the aunt of a child of friends of parents of mine? As a person with his priorities in the scale of things I could not care less, as a writer in this context I am quite interested, but interested less in why I visited her than in why I remember the occasion. Maybe the bus is the key. Maybe it was the first of the tiny handful of times I took a Green Line bus, since how often did I need to visit the Home Counties? Compare again the case study of Jean's Teashop (2.A.23) in the ur-phenomenology of remembering.]

4. I remember being teased with 'Rudolph the Red-Nosed Reindeer'. I explained that my name was spelt with an 'f' but no one cared . . .

[. . . one effing iota, as it were.]

(iii) Food

1. I remember hating the school food. I always threw suet pudding on the floor when I thought no one was looking, because it made me feel sick. Macaroni and semolina made me feel sick. Custard made me feel sick.

(iv) Sport

1. I remember boxing in the annual tournament at Seymour Hall and the year I lost in the semi-final of my weight to Quentin Livingstone. He and I both burst into tears while waiting for the result. The two judges disagreed with each other; the casting vote of the referee went to Quentin. A great pea-souper fog, also known as smog, descended as we drove home. We abandoned our car by Rossmore Court in Saint John's Wood and took the bus to Golders Green. Imagine my curiosity and excitement when we transferred to the trolleybus which would take us to Henly's Corner and I saw the man with a flare walking in front of it.

[It occurs to me that if the trolleybus was going slowly enough to follow a man on foot why on earth did we not walk the quick way home instead of 'walking' in a trolleybus? Also, since it *was* a trolleybus this could mean that the buses, 102 and 58, were not running, which in turn means we would anyway have had to walk an equal distance from Henly's Corner, since the trolleybus did not turn right but went on at least to North Finchley, and probably to Barnet. Perhaps it was considered dangerous to health to walk in the smog. I should ask my mother about this. If an awareness of environmental pollution already existed, I hope the men with flares had some sort of filter breathing system to protect them: like a hanky. I think our car that day was a grey Vauxhall, the one which succeeded the little Standard.]

2. I remember walking in lines of three to the swimming pool in a basement below some shops in Finchley Road just before John Barnes' department store.

[I think we were not allowed to talk but I don't think we had to hold hands.

Are the remains of the swimming pool still there? Urban archaeology is fun. Check it out next time I'm passing. John Barnes itself is now Waitrose. The sainted firm of John Lewis took longer to abandon another good department store they owned, Jones Brothers in Holloway Road. They do not give a toss about local convenience, especially for the people without cars to go to Brent Cross in.]

3. I remember going in the coach to play cricket at the Indian gymkhana at Osterley and then at Cannon's Park. After cricket we were given orange squash and you could choose a jam doughnut or a bun with icing on it.

4. I remember once walking from the coach with my class or year to play soccer on the Heath Extension. The column of boys halted by the pillarbox in Welgarth Road. There I peed in my trousers I was so desperate. No one noticed, thank goodness.

[Each time I pass that pillarbox I muse how passion (in this case pission) remains stamped in lifeless things. I also reckon that had I moved to another city at some later date I'd have always retained a memory of that particular occasion, even without the visual booster I receive on occasional drives through the Suburb.]

5. I remember one sports day I was injured and took part in only one event, the hurdles. I came third and received a book token for seven and sixpence.

[That's a lot of prizes, three for each event. How were they financed? Out of the school fees, I suppose.]

(C)

CITY OF LONDON SCHOOL

(i) Teachers

1. I remember 'Reggie' Hatton, the form teacher of my first class Old Grammar, which was the top year of the junior school. Entering the classroom with other new boys on our first day I waved to Richard Hyams whom I already knew from Hebrew classes. I was put into Hale House, which was one of six, the others being Abbott, Beaufoy, Carpenter, Mortimer and Seeley. We were given a copy of the school rules. Mr Hatton was the gentlest and sweetest teacher I ever had. He taught us geography, always my worst subject after chemistry. I remember oxbow lakes. Oxbow lakes I understood. The headmaster of the junior school was Mr 'Biff' Vokins, a very tall man in a grey suit who taught us English and never never raised his voice. We read 'The Cricket Match' from *England, Their England* by A. G. MacDonell with him. I came top in Latin and French that year and third overall in the class. We learned Latin from *Paginae Primae*, written by a former headmaster, Dr F. R. Dale. I remember Kennedy's *'Eating' Primer* the following year in Old 2A: all covers had already been inked in.

[I was never to do so well again, to the dismay of my father. But perhaps I arrived at my natural level, just below the middle rather than at the top of the 'A' stream. In Old Grammar I had the advantage of going over stuff I'd already done at prep school. Biff had natural authority, only in part due to his great height. I cannot imagine he ever needed to biff *anybody*. I have the school rules somewhere and must try to find them. The little blue pamphlet ('Sub-prefects may give detentions. Prefects may cane' – two sentences I remember to this day) belongs in a time capsule of a vanished age. Even at that time the pamphlet's unmodernised late-Victorian tone did not fairly mirror what the school thought the school represented, and perhaps did represent. CLS was a place which wanted the best or the 'best' of both worlds in an Edwardian liberal sense. It exemplified a modernising traditionalism, traces of whose crisis can be tracked in the work of E. M. Forster, both his fiction – culminating in the Malabar Caves in *A Passage to India* – and non-fiction. That typically English centre still held sway in the minds of people like my father (a moderate conservative in his youth who became a radical liberal with Bevanite tinges), as did the Jewish centre represented by the United Synagogue. It has taken many decades for me to grasp the parallel. It would take a book to explore the idea. For the time being I'll say only that I am not in the least surprised that the boss of the United Synagogue, Jonathan Sacks, has head-aches, and well-publicised ones: his centre no longer holds, for the 'English gentleman of the Mosaic persuasion' is no more. If such a paragon had survived would he have approved of Barnet's *eruv* (in a phrase, the religious demarcation of an area as the symbolic extension of the home so that, for example, an orthodox Jewess can push a pram or wheelchair to synagogue on the Sabbath)? Or would he have seen it as an act of self-ghettoisation? Leaving aside the real problem for devout people which was addressed long ago by this device (a typically humanitarian Pharisee attempt to ease a burden), and leaving aside the psychology and sociology of Barnet Jews (for and against among the devout themselves, for and against among secular Jews, for and against among reform Jews) involved today, my feeling is that a great city like London, with its many minorities, can contain an *eruv* provided no one else's amenities (as opposed to susceptibilities) are damaged. Back to school: today the school's promotional literature has to be seen to be believed. But CLS is in the market place, the market place is in a jungle, there is no such thing as society, the atomisation of society (which does not exist) proceeds apace, and with it an increase in anomie. Postscript: I cannot see that New Labour has what it takes to solve these problems, but my son, a new (and New) Labour councillor in Barnet, disagrees with me . . .]

2. I remember the headmaster, Dr Arthur Willoughby Barton, a remote, respected but not loved Yorkshireman whom the boys rarely met in person before the sixth form. Once I asked him during sixth-form scripture, or divinity as it was called, if it was true what some people said, namely that god was made in man's image rather than the other way round. Not true, he said, and moved quickly on. His background, we knew, was science rather than classics and he had begun the latest round of modernisation of the school. Dr Barton had written two physics textbooks, on heat and on light, which we used. Once, standing by the porters' lodge on some errand or other, I saw by chance a boy running stiffly out of his study – having just been caned, perhaps for smoking in the rafters of the great hall.

[Dr Barton's science background was exceptional, perhaps unique, in an age when headmasters of public schools were from the humanities, many of them classicists. I met him only once after I left school, at a luncheon in University College London where I was the guest of a college lecturer in French, my friend Annette Lavers, now Professor. He and I caught each other's eye. I did not go up to him. I did not like him. I had been afraid of him. Yet I was wrong not to speak to him. My guess, possibly psychologistic, is that I regressed into being a schoolboy, safe in the knowledge he could do nothing about my lack of courtesy. In recent years I have met on several occasions my son's favourite teacher from his old comprehensive school whom he would invite over once every vacation when he was a university student. This teacher, as it happens, had been a student of one of the authors I have published, F. T. Prince.]

3. I remember Percy Copping who taught me Latin and English at different times. He wiggled or waggled his fingers in a funny way.

[Was this arthritis, I wonder now? Years later I discovered he was already the friend of the parents of an exact contemporary of mine, Audrey Jones, before she and I met at Cambridge. I still find this amazing, not so much because of the coincidence, which is a banal accident of London suburban geography, as that friends and teachers are supposed to belong to different worlds – hence too my amazement at meeting Oliver Uren in the Partisan. I know from the *Old Citizens* magazine that Percy is dead. Most of the other older teachers will have died by now.]

4. I remember Geoffrey Clarke or Clark who produced the school play and taught me English in the sixth form. He had a bulbous nose and a red face and was well known as a drinker. In the summer he would have lunch, perhaps with his friend Mr Harry Lee-Uff, in a pub rather than in the staff canteen: 'A beer and a sausage,' he told us. Geoffrey would light a fag the moment he left the class-room. While I was still at school I met him more than once at the Royal Court Theatre during the interval of a play. He had a wife called Margery and they had no children. Nobby Clark broadcast in the BBC World Service from Bush House once a week as 'Londoner'. I would try to impress him and my classmates with the names of authors I knew and whose books I implied I'd read. I remember him saying that someone called John Gross was the cleverest boy he had ever taught.

[Geoffrey was an effective teacher in spite of giving the impression, or perhaps in part *because* he made it quite clear, that teaching was not the be-all and end-all of his life: which was theatre. I would now hazard the guess that there was professional disappointment buried in his heart. He was, however, a natural showman and may well have enjoyed being a schoolmaster. His annual productions of the school play, performed across the road at the Guildhall School of Music and Drama, were justly famous. I still have some of my essays with his squiggles and comments – on A level set texts such as E. M. Forster's *Howards End* (a book which profoundly affected my world view) and *The Canterbury Tales* (a selection which probably excluded the rude bits) and *Vanity Fair* – but I resist the temptation to break the rules and check out the documentation. Mr Lee-Uff was as tall as 'Biff' Vokins. My impression is that men such as these served their entire careers in one school. Certainly Biff was already teaching in the thirties at CLS. All has changed, changed utterly, in the teaching profession.]

5. I remember the Reverend Ellingham and Mr Oakley, already old men and school legends in their own lunchtime. Mr G. Irwin Carruthers could be teased if you were clever. Dave Roberts once called out: 'Please, sir, it wasn't me who said it wasn't me.'

[Perhaps Mr Carruthers *allowed* himself to be teased if there was no malice and if, as I say, you made an effort. Doubtless there is a coefficient of self-confidence operating in this territory – or of aesthetics?]

6. I remember Mr J. M. C. Davidson who taught seven of us Russian to A level in two years: some, like myself, had changed from Greek, some had changed from German. My parents had been told by the school that I stood a better chance of getting into Oxbridge with modern languages than with classics. I had no option but to choose Russian. Mr Davidson, like others of his generation, had learned Russian in the RAF from old White Russians in exile. Once he was angry with me for showing more interest in the background music than in the words on a Russian record of Chekhov's *Three Sisters*. (*'Vi iz Moskvi?'*) We learned a Russian proverb: *Shchi da kasha pisha nasha* ('Cabbage soup and buckwheat, that's what we get to eat'). Russian was taught in the classroom next door to the staff common-room. Jimmy Davidson had a limp as a result of a rugby injury.

[I suppose I registered that he could not have been more than ten years older than us, but he was a grown-up and a teacher and as such a member of two other species. Ten years represents absolute quality rather than relative quantity when one is sixteen. If we were to meet in the street naturally I would recognise him; he would not recognise me. He was quite right to be angry over my lack of seriousness. An excellent teacher, he never seemed at ease in the classroom.]

7. I remember my third main sixth-form teacher, Pat Whitmore, who had a trench coat which we were sure had survived, like some of his physical gestures and slang usages, from Major Whitmore's army days in France. This flamboyant and colourful figure was doing a [? London University] PhD on the Minimes. He taught Camus with great enthusiasm and explained the allegory underlying *La Peste*. I enjoyed de Montherlant's *Le Maître de Santiago* but not *Le Cid* of Corneille. I went to a public library to look for, and found, a translation of de Montherlant's play. At the time I registered the name of the translator and was silently grateful to him. I remember Pat's expressions of frustration when we made stupid mistakes.

[I wonder if that frustration was symptomatic of a desire to be elsewhere, perhaps in a university (where he and several other teachers were certainly qualified to teach) – but this was before the great expansion in higher education and there must have been many dons *manqués* in schools. Anyway, why should the way he presented himself not be taken at face value? Or was there a mixture of the two? The third and likeliest possibility is that the expression of frustration was theatrical, and quite possibly he enjoyed what he was doing. I could also be projecting my own hangups on to this leading character in the school story which a version of one's schooldays is. The Minimes were a religious sect, founded in the same year as City of London School, 1440. The de Montherlant translator was Jonathan Griffin, later to become a close friend and colleague. The very first time I met Jonathan I told him about the translation crib. Mind you, and I tremble at the time-spans involved – which open what the novelist Christine Brooke-Rose in an inspired vowel-Spoonerism has called 'scope-gates' – I met him only eight years after the crib use of his translation. Camus, like Forster, was central to my thoughts for some time. Pat Whitmore's enthusiasm rubbed off on to me and led the way to Monsieur Gilbert Quénelle in Paris (4.D.i.5.]

8. I remember S. G. Ward who taught us Greek to O level. He was an entertaining, learned and inspiring schoolteacher. He had a mannerism of wiping his eyebrow with the back of his hand. I remember his impatience with philosophy, how he disparaged a book called 'believe it or not *The Meaning of Meaning*'. I continued for a while with post-O level Greek on a voluntary basis even though I was now in the Modern Sixth.

[Perhaps such impatience was ontologically necessary for him. It can be inferred he was a no-nonsense empiricist.]

9. I remember J. E. B. Marsh, Boggy, who taught us first-year Greek in class 3A. He would time us reciting the alphabet as quickly as possible. Singularities of Greek included the dual form and the aorist tense. Mr Marsh was also the form teacher and at the end of each term would read out the form order. Since each subject was marked out of a hundred you ended up with enormous scores.

[I did not realise at the time that if the marks had been scaled down by a factor of ten, or even five, as in other countries, someone who was, say, seven places ahead of me would have come out equal, ditto someone four places below. Many years later I saw JEBM, in dog collar, across a crowded room at the Royal Academy. The aorist was to come in useful later as a metaphor. But you will have to wait for my novel to see what I do with it. I have just timed myself reciting the alphabet – four and a half seconds. I vaguely recall that the world record, three and a half seconds, was held by Jonathan Barnes, who is now a distinguished classical philosopher. *Recitation of the Greek Alphabet in Three and a Half Seconds* would make a good title for a novel.]

10. I remember Steve, whom everyone was allowed to call by that name, rather than Mr Stevenson. And 'Nabo' Taylor and 'Froggy' Wynburne and 'Rocky' Cornish – a sweet man relatively easy to tease – and Monsieur le Mansois Field the walls of whose downstairs classroom (perhaps room 21) resembled a phonetics laboratory, and Charley Haynes, the sixth-form eco-nomics teacher, who was rumoured to be a Labour supporter.

[Field was very small and 'very French' in a stereotyped way, like Mossoo in which school story, Billy Bunter? I would love to have one of Field's wallcharts as a souvenir. Rudolf, you dork, you have all of them, for ever, in this very sentence. I think now of Rimbaud's poem 'Les voyelles' and tell myself that the boy genius and his dominie lover would have been amused by those charts. I think too of Mallarmé teaching English, and his wonderful mistakes. What would I give, etc. . . .]

11. I remember another very tall, very thin and very polite teacher, Dennis Moore, also rumoured to vote Labour, who always wore a waistcoat, taught us Latin and was our form master for two years. He wrote *'bene'* in his copperplate at the bottom of the postcard I had pre-addressed to myself, and which the school posted with our O level results. Some people got *'optime'*. I associate the principal parts of irregular verbs with his blackboard: *fero, ferre, tuli, latum* and the declension of irregular nouns, *vis* (pronounced wis), *vis*, *vim*, (wanting), (wanting), *vi*, and wondering why they did not behave properly.

[Like 'Biff', Dennis Moore had natural authority and never once raised his voice. He was less obviously a performer than Whitmore or Clark but all good schoolteachers surely project a persona; their authority and influence conflate those of an actor and a parent. As young adults and parents ourselves, maybe our role model (it occurs to me now for the first time) was a kind of composite figure made up of aspects of our parents and some of our teachers, and contained conscious and unconscious rejections and assimilations of the example set by those we observed at close quarters – and before we go to work how many adults outside the family and apart from teachers do we have the chance to observe at close quarters? Mind you, one can admire natural authority without achieving it oneself!]

12. I remember T. E. (Taggy) Manning, the master in charge of my favourite school sport, Eton Fives. One day in hall Michael Duschinsky told me Mr Manning would not be in that day because his father had died. I remember thinking, 'so he had a father'. I took a good look at him when he returned: he did not seem any different. Taggy had a strong West-Country burr.

['So he had a father': I suppose in my inflexible way I failed to translate the father into a language I understood, namely the grandfather of TEM's children.]

13. I remember that B. J. (Bunny) Ross, who taught us history in the third year, gave us a holiday project. I chose the coal industry. Michael Duschinsky chose the press. I worked very hard, writing to many organisations for brochures,

reading several books, etc. I ended the text with a photo of a pit pony and a large hoarding which proudly announced that the coal mines now belonged to the people. My father said I could ask his secretary Miss (Pauline) Cohen to type it up for me. My mother said I should buy her a present, a pair of nylon stockings. I asked Miss Cohen what size she wore, eight as I recall, and went to a shop by Moorgate station, near the office, to buy them. When my project was returned by Bunny I was delighted to receive 50 out of 50, and assumed rightly that he thought mine was the best. So far . . . so good. But he had not yet seen, wait for it, Michael's. Michael's was better than mine and therefore, wait for it, my clever friend received 55 out of 50. I was disappointed but I remember thinking it was kind of Bunny not to mark me down.

[It was indeed kind, but it also was good and caring pedagogy, as well as amusing everybody, even though once again and as usual Michael had surpassed me. I did not know Bunny well but I suspect he was a great eccentric. Yet another lifelong one-school teacher. Easy to forget from this late vantage point that the photograph involved quite recent events – the pits having been nationalised only seven years earlier. Presumably I told Pauline Cohen why I wanted to know her stocking size! Later she married an Irish Jew and moved to Dublin. To this day she sends my mother a Jewish New Year card every September.]

14. I remember a history teacher, Joe Hunt. On one occasion I was surprised when he told me there was a tradition of reading in my family – so why didn't I read more?

[This extraordinary question can only have been put to me after a parents' evening, at which my father would have had an anxious word with Joe Hunt about his offspring. Did my father actually use that phrase about tradition, or was it a gloss on the part of Mr Hunt? The memory was triggered very late in the revision of this book when a painter friend said to me after I complained of shortage of time: 'Write more, read less.']

15. I remember various science masters, Messrs Brown, Dyball, Chatwin and Dr Lance Kramer. Dr Kramer left to head the science department at Eton. He was a big gruff red-faced anxious medium-fused kindly man. But science was not my thing, except where I could pretend that physics was maths.

[A comment now on my use of the word 'anxious' (this comment represents the homologous point at several places in these memories): I mention in my afterword the problem (or problematic, if you prefer) of the lexicon. I would not have *thought* then of Dr Kramer as anxious, but I would have *felt* it. Perhaps I am trying to say that in the interests of laser-precision one would have to go through the book sometimes differentiating between 'I remember thinking that . . . ' and 'I remember feeling that . . . ' and 'I remember noticing that . . . '. Such precision is not required – on the best working principle for a writer, namely that the reader is of equal intelligence to him or her, not more, not less, but equal, and can infer the nuance where required.]

16. I remember being taught maths by a teacher who would say, in a broad Yorkshire accent, 'You silly baby,' or to the whole class, 'It's money for old rope.' He was Horace Brearley who had played cricket for Yorkshire second eleven and whose son Michael Brearley was one year ahead of me. Horace taught us that certain theorems in geometry could be proved in more than one way, and that one proof was by 'symmetry' – but he never allowed us to use it.

17. I remember French *lecteurs* and German *Lektors*. One of the latter was teased by boys in class Old 2A, who crept under the desks to a different part of the classroom.

18. I remember noticing that many masters wore the same suit every single day throughout the school year, and in some cases for more than one year.

(ii) Friends and Acquaintances

(1) Close Friends

1. I remember Warren Pantzer. I was jealous of him because he was good-looking and because he had a cardigan with a zip. He had a blue fountain pen, possibly a Conway Stewart. I copied his signature and his style of clothes, for example wearing a short-sleeved pullover under my shirt. Once, after games at Grove Park, I was returning on the train to Charing Cross with him, Jeffrey Mortner, Richard Hyams, Ralph Ullmann and, maybe, others. We were playing a game which involved lying on the luggage rack. Damage was done to the

compartment and to Jeff's knee, the latter serious enough for us to report the incident on arrival and call an ambulance. The ambulance driver said that one friend could accompany Jeff. Jeff called for Warren but I happened to be nearest to the ambulance, and went along. My memory jumps or skips or even hops to our house, with my father saying hello from upstairs to Mr Mortner.

[My father was not being anti-social by not coming downstairs, merely resting while sitting *shiva* for his mother – the week of mourning after her funeral. Mr Mortner wished him long life. The game itself was surely a beating offence in Dr Barton's book but I remember clearly that we were not beaten or even punished in a mild way. I must suppose that somehow the incident never reached the beak's ears or that we lied convincingly and successfully. Evidently I was driven home from the hospital, probably the Royal Free, by Jeff's dad.]

2.   I remember Graham Reid from Palmers Green who was not Jewish but who attended the parties and barmitzvahs of the Jewish circle. He was tall and thin, one of the few boys in long trousers in Old Grammar. He was also the junior-school soccer-team goalie.

3.   I remember Norman Bar, who lived in Greenhalgh Drive, very near me. We shared an obsession with the Goons. Going home on one occasion, upstairs on the 102 or 58 bus as it turned right at Henly's Corner, he said how weird it was that when we were babies there was a girl somewhere, also in nappies, whom we would marry one day.

[This is a nice one for reflecting on. I suppose he was right: it is weird. But it's not that weird, in fact it's fairly normal, after making allowances for age differences between spouses. More weird, perhaps, was to have had the thought. I hope it is not too glib to suggest the possibility that, like Hilary Sefton's armpits in 3.E.ii.5 (sorry, Hilary, I must buy you a drink in London or Jerusalem to make up for that revelation though, as in the Leonard Cohen song, it is about my mind and your body, so you are in the clear), it involved an unconscious sexual displacement. At any event I have never forgotten his thought and where he voiced it. I believe he is now a solicitor. Some of his clients must say much weirder things. Maybe James Joyce in *Portrait* was on to something similar: 'while his soul had passed from ecstasy to languor where had she been? Might it be, in the mysterious ways of spiritual life, that her soul at those same moments had been conscious of his homage?']

4. I remember Richard 'specs' Hyams whom I also knew from Hebrew classes because he lived in the Suburb. Basically he was a close school friend, not really a Suburb or synagogue friend. On one occasion I received an anonymous note telling me not to go home, so I went with him to his house in Bancroft Avenue, where we had tea. I phoned home and there turned out to be no reason not to go home, so I did. He used to bring sandwiches to school for lunch. Sometimes he gave me half because he never finished them. They were wrapped very neatly in greaseproof paper. His father was a milliner; he played golf and his professional was Bill Shankley at Potters Bar. One term or holiday our group organised visits to our fathers' places of work. Richard's was more interesting than my father's because it was a factory and not an office. On one of those expeditions we also visited the café owned by a retired Arsenal and Scotland footballer, that very tough wing-half Alex Forbes, at Ludgate Circus, just where Blackfriars Bridge begins, to get his autograph.

[I wonder why Richard was known as 'specs'. He was not the only person in the group who did not wear glasses, which would have been a reason to give him that name, like calling a tall person tich. Quick peep inside a barmitzvah present, despite the embargo on documentation (cf. Muriel Spark's *Curriculum Vitae*, for entertainment in respect of documentation in autobiography): Cecil Roth's *Short History of the Jewish People* (illustrated edition); it is signed 'Richard "specs" Hyams and Michael Duschinsky' (see below). Doubtless a booster. Clearly Richard had no objection to his nickname. I wonder where his father's factory was: off Oxford Street? In the East End? In Clerkenwell?]

5. I remember Ralph Ullmann. He was seriously religious. When we were in the sixth form and no longer had to wear a cap (CLS tradition was to throw them in the Thames on the last day of the summer term before entering the sixth form), he would put on a beret at Golders Green Station. I used to think how strange it was that his mother was so much older than mine. He came to my house regularly to play table tennis but would not eat anything – even though my mother told him that she kept a kosher house.

[At the time I had no idea there were levels of *kashrus* observance. Later I realised that since he had three older brothers and I had three younger sisters, it was normal, as they say in French, that our mothers would not be the same age. Only later, too, did I learn that there are half and quarter generations even within families. Part of my temporal identity was the belief, inscribed in nature, that there were children and there were grown-ups. Today I see CLS boys on the tube wearing skull caps. School caps have been abolished and Jews 'came out' in 1967, after the Six-Day War.]

6. I remember my best friend Michael Duschinsky, who adopted the name Pinto-Duschinsky in the sixth form, because he was being brought up by his great-aunt Brenda (née Pinto) Duschinsky, known to him and to me too as Auntie. Oranges were good for his dodgy skin condition and he would sometimes eat them in class (privy to his secret, I alone would smell them; smiling he would glance at me), but he was never discovered. Michael was excused cadet force because of his skin – what luck. His father was a rabbi who lived in South Africa, whereas his mother lived in Los Angeles. Both had remarried. He had a half sister, Grace, in Los Angeles, whom I met when she visited London. I remember someone holding her up at Auntie's house, aged about three, and everyone could see the musical notes patterned on her knickers. Once Michael and I went on the river and somehow got lost or ran out of money when we reached the shore. We phoned home from the police station, perhaps at Richmond or Brentford, where we played word games and drank tea until my father collected us. We ate buttered *matsos* in the car going home, and complained there was no salt on them. At the time of Suez Michael presented me in the school cloisters with an ultimatum about Labour's attitude to the crisis, which my father had to answer – since I was not up to the task – by the next day. Michael and his aunt lived in a big rambling house at 147 Walm Lane in Willesden, practically next door to the synagogue. They were not in fact members of that synagogue because his aunt, born a Pinto, was of course Sephardi, and belonged to the principal Sephardi synagogue after Bevis Marks, Lauderdale Road in Little Venice. Michael pronounced the Hebrew word for wine as *gefen* and not, as I did, *gofen*. He used to come close to the top of the class almost every term but was something of an awkward squad and occasionally inaccurate – not as effortlessly or smoothly geared to earning marks as the

three Bs: Jonathan Barnes, Michael Booth and my future ex-brother-in-law, Alan Bell, who always took the gold, silver and bronze. Michael was a Tory and we argued political issues a lot though he never embarrassed me, as others did, by asking what I was doing in a public school. I knew that he had been smuggled out of a ghetto in a basket of fruit and that his father had marched a lot of Jews into the hills away from the wicked Germans.

[I am sure now that Michael was partly attracted to me as a friend because I had parents who liked him a lot and who, I now realise, understood that this proud boy enjoyed and needed to participate in a more traditional family structure than his own, devoted as he and his wonderful aunt were to each other. Also, despite being jealous of his high position in the class, I never really resented his brilliance and, unlike some friends, could cope with his touchiness. Later we were best men at each other's weddings and have always kept in touch. I think we both find it difficult to discuss party politics – he is after all a Tory who has been actively involved at Central Office and is one of the world's leading academic experts on democratic constitutions and on political finance, but our basic dialogue will go on. We monitor telephonically our children's progress. The ghetto he was smuggled out of was Munkacs in Hungary. In a recent phonecall Michael told me that that very day was the fiftieth anniversary of his rescue. On certain aspects of the historiography of the Holocaust we are in agreement, as was obvious from his article recently on Kastner and Eichmann and the possibility of bartering Jews for lorries, as well as the imbroglio concerning Oxford and Flick, whose wealth in part came from employing Jews as slave labourers, and the financing of the Flick Chair in Jewish Studies. But his proper opposition to the Volkswagen historian Mommsen sometimes leads to unnecessarily over-enthusiastic support for Goldhagen's *Hitler's Willing Executioners*, although he might claim I have been influenced by what he would call a fashion to denigrate this celebrated thesis. A few specifics: if we ate *matsos* after getting lost, dollars to doughnuts or rather shekels to almond pyramids it was Passover; the tone of his voice in the cloisters that day implied an ultimatum, but who knows what sanctions he possessed; Jonathan Barnes is the older brother of Dan Kavanagh, also an Old Citizen and the first famous novelist to have attended CLS since K. Amis, who in turn was the first since Talbot Baines Reed, unless you include the former headmaster Edwin Abbott Abbott.]

7. I remember John Shrapnel who joined the school in the fifth or sixth form after his own school closed down. His desk was by the window. He immediately became the star actor in the school play and joined the National Youth Theatre. I used to meet him occasionally in the Two-I's Coffee Bar – where Tommy Steele had been discovered – in Old Compton Street after his rehearsals. I knew that his father was a famous journalist on the *Manchester Guardian*.

[After seeing him on stage occasionally and on television many times, I overcame my middle-aged resistance to change, and renewed contact with him. On the occasion of a book launch which I arranged for one of my authors, he kindly stepped in at the last minute as a replacement for Susannah York. He tells me that it was a common misconception that he joined from a London school which had closed down. He joined because his family moved to London from Manchester.]

(II) Friends and Acquaintances

1. I remember Dixon who had a red face and blond hair. One day the teacher said Dixon's father had died and he would not be in that day. When he came back to school I remember he looked just the same, just as Mr Manning did. Dixon left the school well before the sixth form.

[Either his family moved or they could no longer afford the school fees.]

2. I remember being amazed that Michael Brearley was in the same school as his father. Once Michael and I were standing next to each other in the urinals, peeing on a Monday while wearing our cadet-corps uniforms, mine RAF, his Royal Navy. During one senior house cricket match between Hale and Carpenter, having caught two batsmen at close quarters, one of them David Robbins, I dropped Mike on the boundary after he had skied the ball to me in the outfield, probably on purpose, having scored a typically huge number of runs. One holiday he and I were members of our school team in the annual Public Schools' Eton Fives tournament held at Highgate School and he came home for lunch with me, who lived nearby. My mother made us an omelette.

[How come I remember it was a Monday? OK, it's not a memory but an inference, since that was the day we would be wearing corps uniform. Wrong, not an inference, a shorthand explanatory tautology. Why have I always remembered this episode, after all he wasn't captain of England yet? Don't ask me, but he *was* already famous in school terms, and over the years there have been several boosters. For example, collecting my children from primary school one afternoon, I was confronted by a young boy who said disbelievingly: 'Nathaniel says you were at school with Mike Brearley.' In order to increase my son's playground cred and glory I replied: 'Yes, and I played cricket against him too.' To this day I regret not being able to dine out on a spectacular boundary catch sending England's future captain back to the pavilion.]

3. I remember Ronny Fuss and other boys who joined us in the fourth or fifth year when Mercers school closed down. He used to embarrass me about my spots. I would smear on some brown cream occasionally even when I wasn't at home, which must have looked funny. I thought you should never tease people about that kind of thing.

4. I remember Graham Craig and Paul Zec who were two years older than me and who accompanied me on the tube in my early days at the school – Graham lived at Henly's Corner, Paul in the main Finchley Road, close by Golders Green station. Graham Craig had a school summer blazer, which was optional. Paul Zec was very keen on jazz and was the son of a *Daily Mirror* journalist who wrote about showbiz. Their surname had been shortened. Once I had a packet of refreshers and ate them in such a way that my older friends would not notice I had not offered them one. But they did notice.

[Only today I saw Paul Zec's name in the *Guardian*, as author of an obituary of Lionel Grigson, whom I later knew at Cambridge. For the school uniform to include two different blazers was surely extravagant, even for a public school.]

5. I remember Alan Bell and his friend Alan Hunt with whom, along with Ronnie Hooberman, I remained friends after we left school. Alan Hunt *really* went out with girls when we were still at school and boasted about his exploits. I had no idea what he was talking about. Hunt liked inventing or repeating catchphrases, for example, 'I'm Kraus the mouse, I smack you left and right,' spoken in a German accent. The two Alans were naturally gifted in languages.

I remember too W. E. C. Hillman and Andy Entwhistle ('Andy 'whistle – Partick Thistle', a classic Alan Hunt rhyme). Andy was a diffident, unhappy boy. One day it was announced that he had committed suicide. The Edgware contingent included Anthony Ian Brown – and Martin Vegoda, who moved in a very precise way and was inordinately neat and had a crewcut quiff.

[Alan Hunt's exploits: he did things or said he did things I would have then thought only married grown-ups did, if I'd thought about it, which I didn't, except it must have registered or I wouldn't remember. And was he responsible for spreading the charming description of bogeys as 'Jim Crows' and the rhyme on the same theme: 'God made the little nigger boys/ he made them in the night/ he made them in a hurry/ and forgot to paint them white'? Only last year I was standing at a bus stop or in a tube station and saw a London Transport poster with a message signed by the regional manager, W. E. C. Hillman. Such are the reminders of our youth. Without that booster – *there can't be two W. E. C. Hillmans* – I might still have remembered him (see 8 below) but I might not have mentioned him, which is no reflection on him. It is more than a merely poetic fancy to suggest that we can change the past. The past, everything that was the case (as it were), is a limitless repertoire of virtual possibility which I and you can invent and reinvent, shape and reshape and A. J. Ayer is quite simply wrong to deny this in *The Problem of Knowledge* – and it is not only one's own life one can reinvent. If Warwick Hillman reads this I think it is fair to say that I will have changed his own past for ever. Not because I am important to him, exactly the opposite is the case. If I were important to him (as, say, I am to Michael P-D) I would *already* be part of his past (unless he reads the *Independent*, in which case he might have seen my name under one of the occasional obituaries I write for them). No, he has surely given as little thought to me as I gave to him until I saw the poster. Now he will look back on CLS and remember me, and perhaps even remember trivial incidents involving me which I have forgotten. Finally, on the subject of WECH, I reflect briefly that he may well have gone into London Transport straight after university, where we met occasionally. He made a life. Each one of the people I am no longer in touch with has made some kind of life. If I work hard I can remember things about each one of them: pausing in this parenthesis to *think the past* and seizing accidentally on Warwick has already reminded me of other boys (thus, a boy called Richard Knight, and specifically his name as pronounced by one teacher,

Boggy Marsh, with the 't' heavily emphasised, as if in an elocution lesson). Each one of them, if pushed, might remember something about me. Stop this flow at once lest I dash my head against the screen. I was fond of Andy Entwhistle and I am pleased I remember him. He did not live long enough to make an adult life let alone an adult death. Remembering the dead, in one reading, is their only immortality. Would I have remembered Andy had he lived? Postscript: even if there were two W. E. C. Hillmans (not impossible but unlikely), the booster mechanism remains the same and the rest of the argument is unaffected, but there is more pleasure in the text if there is only one WECH. Last thought: the brain stores and files millions of memories. Let us attempt to gain access to some of those files before Alzheimer's or death do their ineluctable work and separate our minds from our bodies.]

6. I remember R. M. Spinks, captain of the school, on my first day at morning assembly in the great hall. How old and important and senior he was. On that first day I remember thinking it was like being in a school story.

[He died last year.]

7. I remember André, my French-exchange 'friend'. He was a year younger than me. The organisation (one woman in Fellows Road, Swiss Cottage) said this did not matter because French children were more mature than English ones. But he wasn't. He was quite gloomy too. We spent a few days at their house in Le Vésinet outside Paris, and then went to Royan on the west coast where he and I lived separate lives. His young stepmother was sympathetic and encouraged me to go dancing.

[There hadn't been a divorce. His own mother had died. That would account for his gloominess.]

8. I remember many other boys, including Stephen Waddams who according to Mr Lewis 'ran like a greyhound' in the junior-school cross-country race, Howard 'Tub' Davis who always wanted to become a doctor, and Eric Roth whose father rode to work on a bicycle.

9. I remember Michael Apted, Brian Lapping, Peter Levene and Anthony Lester, older brother of Martin who is mentioned elsewhere.

[Now Peter is Sir Peter Levene, Lord Mayor of London 1998–9 and top businessman, and Anthony is Lord Lester of Herne Hill. Brian Lapping's name often appears on TV screens, ditto Michael Apted, who is also in movies. Easy to see why I 'remember' these four from schooldays without making an effort.]

(III) Girls, One in Particular

1. I remember Vivienne, Yvonne and Patricia, the three girls from City of London Girls School whom we met on the tube and in the street. Vivienne Lissauer lived in the Suburb in Ingram Avenue. Yvonne, I did not know where. Patricia Hammerson lived in a large house in Brondesbury Park. Her father had a property company in Park Lane: their office and home phone numbers all ended 6666. I thought she was beautiful. They were about to move to Bishops Avenue when her father died. The girls wore bowler hats with elastic under the chin and sensible brown shoes. One evening Tisha and I went to the flicks in Kilburn to see *Caesar and Cleopatra*. We both wore glasses so it was quite difficult to kiss, even on closed lips, and taking the glasses off meant we could not see the screen, which was the priority, so the kiss was abandoned with a laugh and without resentment. During supper at her house her mother would press a button under the table so the next course would be brought in. Mrs Hammerson had a chauffeur-secretary, Mr Farmer. She was a friend of Sophie Tucker. One evening I was introduced to a large man called Arnold Goodman in their sitting room. Here was the piano Patricia played so well. When I went to Paris (see 4D below) for six months after leaving school, I gave Patricia a three-volume set of Shakespeare in a fine binding, each one inscribed and signed in the italic hand I had taught myself. Just after I returned home from Paris in July, we went to Golders Green Hippodrome for a d'Oyly Carte production of my beloved Gilbert and Sullivan – and I pretended I had to make a phonecall to my parents in the interval, but really I needed to have a pee.

[I wonder what I wrote in those three volumes of Shakespeare – three versions of an encoded statement of unrequited love? I chose the same Oxford Shakespeare edition as the one I had received for my barmitzvah from my father's client, Mr Dell. Patricia replaced Hilary in my affections but, like Hilary, clearly did not reciprocate my feelings. Possibly neither of them knew what I felt. I'm not entirely sure. One thing is certain, it never occurred to me even to attempt to touch Patricia's breasts (which was/were, if a girl did not mind, the sole erogenous zone permitted in those days to boys who found French kissing insufficient, not that she and I did the one or the other thing in the time-span of this book: the episode at the cinema did not involve attempted lingual penetration), not because I did not dare or because I felt it was wrong or that she might say no, but because I was not ready even to think about it. There was no sexual anguish on my part. The first French kiss appropriately enough had to await Paris. I have no idea whether the friends who claimed they had touched a girl's breasts really had or not, but undoubtedly they had begun having sexual stirrings. For me, J. Arthur Rank connoted only himself, not a man striking a gong. Nothing happened below the neck, alone or in company, until I was over nineteen and at Cambridge but that, as they say, is another story. Funny thing, writing: I could not bring myself to tell Patricia I needed to visit the gents (*as you do*), and yet all the readers of this book, perhaps including her, now know about it, just as they know about the breasts it never occurred to me to touch (as she already knew, in the sense that it would not have occurred to her that it would not *not* have occurred to me). Ah well. But I loved her, even in her bowler hat and sensible shoes, standing on the platform at Blackfriars station, smiling sweetly and very unspoiled (considering she lived in Brondesbury Park), waiting for the tube to take us to Charing Cross, whence she would travel home on the Bakerloo Line to Willesden Green and I on the Northern Line to the other Green. All things considered, you might think that schooldays are a kind of dress rehearsal for being a grown-up: work, love, even death. But since one does not know this at the time the formulation is in fact wrong. But the thought is right. Enough already, there is theory enough in the Afterword.]

(iii) The Building

1. I remember the great hall, with its folding wooden seats which we banged on the last day of term, and the marble scrolls of honour on the wall bearing the names of Cambridge Wranglers, whatever that meant. The masters sat behind the headmaster on the platform. On prize days they wore their college gowns. Percy Copping, Lance Kramer and Dr Wray had particularly fine ones. I remember the marble stairs which led up to the hall from the main entrance. In

the term after A level, my last term at school, I would sit in the hall, preparing for Cambridge entrance, reading *The Brothers Karamazov* and other Russian texts in translation. The organ in hall was played by Doc Wray, the music master, whom I called Do Ré. One of the boys, Martin Neary, also played the organ. After the business part of morning assembly the Jewish boys would go to a classroom or two for Jewish prayers at which *Singers Prayerbook*, the mainstream orthodox text of the United Synagogue, was obligatory. Chess was played in the hall, one of nine sports at which I represented my house.

[Mention of separate Jewish prayers reminds me that during my entire school career there was only one incident I can recall involving what I, rightly or wrongly, identified as antisemitism on the part of a fellow pupil – whose name it would be morally wrong to mention even assuming I was right in my assessment (people change). We squared up for a fight in the playground and then stopped – or were stopped – by friends or by the bell. CLS or City (the two diminutives), even in those days, had a very high percentage of Jewish students. I think this was due to three factors: it was a day school; its geographical location was equidistant from all the suburbs where we tended to live; it had a relatively liberal and progressive attitude to education. Mention of prayers also reminds me that once I suggested we read the New Testament in order to broaden our education but Michael Duschinsky scotched that. The teenage experience of reading several Dostoevsky novels was so powerful that till now I have been reluctant to put him to the reread test. Martin Neary became a famous organist.]

2. I remember the library where School Society debates used to be held and where you could look at magazines. Word went round one day that the latest issue of *Encounter* had an article by Arthur Koestler about an Indian fakir who, reversing natural processes, could ingest through his arse and shit through his mouth. Word was right. One day I borrowed the Nonesuch *Whitman* which had an ochre cover. Jonathan Barnes was the librarian.

3. I remember the art room. I was a member of group four, the no-hopers. This also included Warren Pantzer. The group drew, endlessly, goalkeepers making diving saves and cartoon profiles of girls with long hair. Marilyn Monroe was considered the beauty of beauties.

[Pop artists, sort of. Diana Dors and Sabrina were provincial versions of Marilyn Monroe, the deservedly iconic ur-beauty of the western world in her day. The next icon, overlapping with Marilyn in the eyes of the world (which elected JFK as hands-on rep *vis-à-vis* both), was Jackie Kennedy, followed by I wonder who: E. Taylor? B. Bardot? G. Kelly? Skip to our time: Diana Windsor of course, although Madonna's influence on young girls was far greater. I was eventually to have three icons, or *belles dames sans merci*, of my own: Juliette Greco, Jeanne Moreau and Melina Mercouri. Recently I saw a later photo of Moreau which, to my discredit, shocked me. Not knowing Jeanne personally, I prefer to remember her for ever as the great actress and sultry beauty of *Les Amants*. As for Madonna, give me Annie Lennox any day. Once, in my twenties, I found myself sitting next to la Mercouri at Lipp in Paris: I didn't dare say hello. But we are straying out of the self-imposed confines, the Oy Veh Corral.]

4. I remember the music room. Again, I was among the no-hopers, singing out of tune.

[I recall Warren Pantzer again. I suspect that this memory could be a synaesthetic projection from the art room.]

5. I remember the porters' lodge opposite the library where William and Sidney and Gus did their work and where the real world occasionally impinged on pupils.

6. I remember the school second-hand textbook shop next door to the masters' common-room on the first floor.

[That was surely quite unusual and a good idea. Even in those days, even in a public school, some textbooks were hard to find, and this was a sensible economy. Sometimes you found you owned a book previously belonging to a school hero, whether academic or sporting.]

7. I remember the cloisters, all of whose walls were covered by noticeboards with announcements for various teams and meetings: the jazz club, the fives ladder, the stamp club and so on.

8. I remember the tuckshop off the cloisters where we bought reinforcements after school lunch. There was a hoisting contraption in that room which Talbot Baines Reed referred to in *The Three-Guinea Watch*.

9. I remember Mecca, the school canteen. The food was known as Mecca muck. It was self-service. At lunchtime we queued up for our food in two sittings and then sat anywhere, at long tables. I was astonished when I saw fish and chips on the menu the first time I went down for lunch. This was better than Arnold House: choice of main course and puddings voluntary! At mid-morning break you could get white coffee and a cheese or butter roll.

[Mecca were professional caterers. There were Mecca restaurants in London. Today I believe it survives 'purely' as Eric Morley's organisation.]

(iv) Activities

(I) *Sport*

1. I remember the playground where we used to play various sports before school and in the lunch-break – particularly football. Sometimes there was cricket coaching. Horace Brearley held forth on the virtues of a straight bat. Younger boys went in for 'pilling', that is, the target was your opponent's pills: i.e. testicles. 'Fainites' and 'pax' both signified desire for a truce on the part of someone about to lose.

2. I remember the gymnasium where once a term we were weighed and measured. Here we had weekly 'gym'. One year I was a Chinese volunteer for my house gymnastics team because we were short of qualified people. Here I fought my last boxing match, retiring hurt after my more successful prep-school career, with my dignity more battered than my face. Mr Johnny Lawrence, known as Sod Lawrence, and Mr Stan Richard were in charge.

3. I remember the swimming pool where we swam naked. Some boys, like Richard Hyams, could dive, and others – myself and Ralph Ullmann – couldn't. The coach, Mr Halliwell, had a heavy limp, and a son in the school. I thought uncircumcised cocks were seriously *weird*. Some boys entertained us with armpit farts.

[Talk about getting myself in a twist concerning the difference between – to adapt an old Yorkshire saying – the knickers of nature and the fur coat of culture: a lot of people are under the impression that the covenant is something to do with tax-exempt charity . . . At times I think we, the *bnei bris*, children of the covenant, put the 'bris' into 'hubris'. Perhaps that joke would have appealed to Matthew Arnold, but then again perhaps it wouldn't. I'm fairly sure 'cock' was the word used for 'penis'. 'Dick' and 'willy' had not arrived yet.]

4. I remember the Eton Fives courts in the playground. In the second or third year a few of us decided this was the winter sport we wanted to play, rather than rugby. We dashed down to the school-team players practising in the lunch-break and spoke to the captain, David Bignell, and others. Within a few days we were borrowing the school gloves and joining in the practice sessions. At some point we persuaded our parents we needed our own gloves. We went to Jack Hobbs' shop round the corner in Fleet Street where there were two kinds of glove on offer, not to mention the old man's autograph. Michael Duschinsky and Richard Hyams bought the thick yellow gloves (supposedly more power), Ralph Ullmann and I bought the thin grey ones (supposedly more control). We all eventually made the colts and second and first teams. I remember thinking that Fives was a brilliant way of developing both sides of your body because there is no backhand – you have to use both hands, turning your body all the time. We made trips to other schools, including Aldenham which my best non-school friend Paul Rochman attended, and where the toilets had no doors. The Public Schools' annual competition was held at Highgate School. Once or twice I played for the Old Boys before I was an old boy, and after the game at Uppingham went to a pub for the first time in my life, guided by old timers like Garrett and Ollis and Hawken. Fellow members of the school team included Stringer and Brearley, Hall and Bates. I indulged in a crafty piece of gamesmanship as house captain: by playing myself and my partner as second pair I was certain we would win all five games; at the same time, with luck, our second pair playing as first pair would win one or two games, whereas the other way round overall we would win fewer. I was right, and we did win the championship. The housemasters, Jack Wheeler and Percy Copping, noticed, even noted with public disapproval, how I had achieved

this. Courts three and four used to be open, but they were resurfaced and covered over while we were there. I received half colours for fives and resented not getting full colours. Because of our names, Michael Duschinsky and I, regular partners in school teams, were known as the Russian spies.

[Sometimes I dream fives, at night and in daytime reverie, its rhythms, its interactions, its shapes, although I have not played it for thirty years. I miss it and would like to play once more before I die, although even one game will not do my back any good. In a long sporting life, fives is second only to table tennis as the sport I have most enjoyed playing, just as table tennis is second to cricket as the sport I most enjoy watching. A bizarre detail about fives is, as I recall, that the pool of players was so small (some English public schools, one or two places in the Empire and one college in Switzerland) the best pair in the world (i.e. the winners of the Annual Public Schools' Championship) could be given a perfectly adequate practice game by any pair good enough to play for a school, e.g. Michael Duschinsky and me!]

5.   I remember junior-school soccer, although all but two of the season's games were rained off. We lost both games to Colet Court, the junior school of St Paul's. I was left back and lucky not to be left out. My best position was centre half, where I played for my house, and also for 'rest of the houses' against the house champions, Beaufoy, led by Warren Pantzer, a star. We won 6-3. That was my best game ever.

6.   I remember the time the same group of us who gave up rugby for fives gave up cricket for tennis. City of London School, being where it was, had no sports ground on its own premises. Major outdoor sports were played at Grove Park in south-east London. Tennis was played at Sydenham in south London under a coach called Captain Rogers. But a new master i/c tennis, Mr Justin, who lived in Parsifal Road NW6 sensibly changed this when it turned out that all the up and coming tennis players lived in north-west London (being mostly Jewish). I remember having much trouble with the techniques of tennis, although I loved it. My racket was too heavy. Once we played against Haberdashers'. Peter Stern, whom I knew socially outside school, was a member of their team. This confused me. I remember wondering if I would have been me had I had gone to Haberdashers' instead of to CLS. More prosaically, I wondered if I would have had the same thought had Peter gone

to CLS and me to Haberdashers', and we had ended up playing in the same game on the same day.

[Captain Rogers was a military captain (Indian army retired) rather than a tennis captain.]

7. I remember cricket and rugby and soccer and cross country and athletics at Grove Park. I did not possess cricket whites, only a bat too heavy for me. I played cricket in tennis shorts. I hated the putative pain I associated with rugby and high-jumping but I was a good sprinter and long-jumper, and I finished sixth in the junior cross-country race. There was a long walk to the station before the train journey to Charing Cross or Cannon Street, followed by the tube ride home. We used to 'crowd the window' at each stop, to give the impression of a full carriage and thus keep the public out so we could continue our games or our homework.

8. I remember cricket-nets practice at Gamages department store in Holborn where we bought our school uniform. Patsy Hendren bowled to us in the Gamages nets.

[So, with Mike Brearley, that makes two England and Middlesex players I have played against over the years.]

9. I remember older boys who were legendary for their sporting prowess, like the runner Barry Savory, who was a junior international.

[Twenty-five years later he became my osteopath. He did not recognise me, his junior, which is what we would expect.]

(II) Non-Sport

1. I remember the debating society, the School Society. We debated with each other and with other schools, including girls' schools. Once I flourished a tomato or orange on some debating pretext and ate it. I was reported by a prefect and ordered to attend a 'prefects' meeting', that is, a prefects' beating, for eating on the school premises. I know who reported me. I remember the prefect who beat me in a hundred-per-cent painless and desultory way was called Chris Foster, an amiable Australian. But I was angry that I had been reported for an 'offence' committed outside school hours. The same Chris

Foster, who was in the tennis team, told younger players where they could buy Fred Perry shirts at a ten-per-cent discount: Tim Webb's shop in Kings Cross.

[The School Society, as I discovered later, was modelled on the Oxbridge Unions. Michael Pinto-Duschinsky was, inevitably, a star performer.]

2. I remember a school holiday in Provence, conducted by Taggy Manning. I shared a hotel room in Arles with Hyams and Duschinsky. We visited interesting places like Aigues-Mortes, Les Alyscamps in Arles, Tarascon of Tartarin fame, Daudet's windmill, Les Baux, and the Camargue with its flamingos and wild horses. A strange man in the hotel kitchen was eating the guts of raw fish. We all sang 'Sur le pont . . . ' when we visited Avignon.

[Many years later I wrote a poem about this holiday. It was published in an Oxford magazine called *Carcanet* by an undergraduate with an exotic Mexican name, who lived at Pin Farm in South Hinksey, and who later served Robert Lowell a burnt omelette for lunch. Maybe the poem wants to be rescued. Maybe it should continue sleeping. Doubtless the poem served as a booster for the raw-fish memory. But if that memory was powerful enough to survive until the poem it could probably have managed very well on its own, thank you very much, without the help of the poem. Even if we were being ironic I concede it was naff to sing that song in Avignon. But if not then, when? And if not there, where?]

3. I remember a school holiday in the Soviet Union: a joint group from our school and Shrewsbury School visited Moscow and Leningrad, the first school group to visit that country, or so we were told. On the boat, the *Baltika*, I met a Finnish girl called Piko Elander who was too sophisticated to hang around the likes of me for long, and who looked elsewhere for company. The boat docked first at Helsinki, where I bought an EP record. In Moscow, near the Bolshoi theatre, we sold items of clothing on the black market. There was an old tea lady with her samovar in the 'hard class' on the train to Leningrad, where we visited the Winter Palace. Unfortunately the Hermitage was closed. I shared a cabin on the return journey with Paul Adamthwaite and others; there was no food on the first night. The next day we met a lively singer called Anne Taylor. When we reached England it was agreed that I would visit Shrewsbury for a reunion but when the time came my father would not let me go. I was angry but I did not complain.

[Those were early days for Russian studies. I was one of the first two hundred students in the country to take Russian A level. Anne Taylor turned up in Cambridge, a mate of the jazz musician Dave Gelly, and years later became a pop singer, Tracey Taylor.]

4. I remember the annual French and German sing-song in the great hall organised by Rocky Cornish. I remember singing 'Avec mes sabots' and 'Ma Normandie'.

5. I remember activities I did not participate in like the model-railway society and the CEWC, Council for Education in World Citizenship, and the stamp society. I remember there was a Jewish Society and an Israel Society, neither of which I attended – not surprising given the amount of time I spent at my synagogue. There was always something going on in my school.

6. I remember the Combined Cadet Force, Corps as it was known, which was compulsory. You spent the first year in the basic section. Sergeant-Major Cox was based in the armoury by the swimming-pool. We visited Rainham for target practice. After basic you joined one of the three services. I chose the RAF partly because it wasn't the army, partly because courses were offered in the weather and in rules of the air, useful knowledge outside the service context. My first flight was in an unpressurised plane. I was very sick and Michael Booth was sympathetic. When the civil-defence section began I jumped at the chance of joining it mainly because uniform was not required: solely by virtue of age I was appointed Senior Boy. I asked the lecturer awkward questions about nuclear bombs dropped on London and began sympathising with CND (see section 5E).

7. I remember visiting Puddle Dock on the Thames several times, once with my friend Dusty Miller, before it was rebuilt by the famous actor-manager, Bernard Miles. We found old clay pipes and, once, a dead sheep. I loved the river. My father explained that all Millers are known as Dusty, all Clarks as Nobby, all Whites as Chalkie.

[I still love my sweet river, my London too, despite its ungoverned filth, potholes and all. I am a real Londoner. Rephrase: I am a real north Londoner.

Rephrase: I am a real north-west Londoner. No, I am all three. To explore the ontological ramifications of the three descriptions, the psycho- and socio-geographical parameters of a child's identity, beyond the unwritten and/or unconscious modalities loitering between the lines of these pages, would entail another book: a work of loiterature, to take Alan Hollinghurst's inspired word out of context. Let me slip in here a word I invented to describe the writing of Maurice Blanchot and others: obliterature. Perhaps my destiny as a writer is to produce a work of obloiterature.]

8. I remember the knick-knack shop at Blackfriars tube station, where I could buy or look at diaries, stationery, pens, key-rings, wallets, etc. I adored all kinds of paper and leather goods, especially small ones.

9. I remember the Jazz Club of which Alan Bell and Dave Roberts were enthusiastic members. I voted for my American step-relative Ruth Olay as best female vocalist one year. She had recorded an LP but no one else had heard of her and so she only got one vote.

[She cut three more LPs and was backed by top musicians, including Red Norvo and Shelley Mann.]

10. I remember the general-knowledge quiz, which the entire school partici-pated in every year. As with my regular studies, I did very well in my first year, and only in my first year.

(D)

PARIS, 1961

(i) Quartier Latin

1. I remember taking the Métro every weekday to the British Institute, 7 rue de la Sorbonne, where I was studying French literature, language and theatre. Some days I walked from Métro Odéon, other days from Métro Saint-Michel. If you timed it badly, the automatic gates would shut in your face before you reached the platform.

2. I remember open platforms on the backs of buses, but I preferred the Métro.

3. I remember my student card, which entitled me to buy a very cheap lunch in several student restaurants. Jewish students could have a kosher lunch in the Foyer Israelite, in rue Médicis opposite the Luxembourg Gardens. The chips were brilliant. There was another student restaurant at Mabillon.

4. I remember the director of the institute, Professor Francis Scarfe, and Madame Peyrollaz, who taught us phonetics from a book she had written. We also used a language laboratory. She was very patient. I remember her explaining the two ways of pronouncing the word 'nation' – approximately as in 'bat' and 'bark', depending on your region. She would quote lines from plays on stage in Paris, including Claudel's *L'annonce faite à Marie*: 'Ne soyez pas triste, mère,' and, 'Il est dur de voir mon enfant me quitter.'
[The sentences presumably carried weight with Madame P on account of their vowels.]

5. I remember Gilbert Quénelle, a superb teacher with a wonderful line in dry humour. He always wore thick crape shoes. I wrote essays for him on different writers and topics: Camus, Malraux, Saint-Exupéry. He expected a certain formality, but was certainly not uptight. *Au contraire*.
[I *have* kept in touch with him over the years. He told me I was one of four students who had done this. I have had a certain involvement with French literature, a certain idea of France. His input was decisive. He had the

advantage over my most influential CLS teachers in that in Paris I considered myself a student rather than a schoolboy. The last time I saw him in his beautiful flat in rue Monsieur-le-Prince (with the original seventeenth-century mirrors and other features still in place) he discussed my translation of Balzac's *Le Chef d'oeuvre inconnu*, drawing my attention to aspects of comparative sentence structure. Bliss.]

6. I remember trying to keep up my Russian because after Paris I was to study Russian and French at Cambridge, assuming I got in. I had Russian lessons with Marina Lvoff from Meudon in exchange for teaching her English. We met once or twice a week in the lounge of the British Institute, where we read Russian texts together, including Dostoevsky's *Notes from Underground*.

7. I remember joining several student societies and obtaining tickets for different libraries and permission to audit Sorbonne lectures. I heard celebrities like Vladimir Jankélévitch and Madame Amado-Valensi.

8. I remember the bookstalls on the left bank *quais* and around the Palais Royal. I remember buying cheap editions of classics, cheap prints of Paris, and a dictionary of slang, but above all I loved browsing. It reminded me of Charing Cross Road.

9. I remember the weeklies: *Figaro littéraire*, *Arts*, *L'Expresse*. François Mauriac had a column called, 'Bloc-notes', on the back page of *L'Expresse*. I also read *Le Canard enchaîné* but I didn't have a good enough knowledge of French politics to understand the jokes.

10. I remember square-ruled notepaper.

(ii) The Arts and Social Life

1. I remember not wanting to waste a minute. I wanted to learn about painting and music and the performing arts. I went to exhibitions and plays and concerts. And films at the Champollion in the eponymous street, which showed classics, and the Cinemathèque in rue d'Ulm where you could see

three films on the trot. One evening Eisenstein's *Zabastovka* (*Strike*) was shown without subtitles. People were calling for interpretation but I did not have the courage to shout out in French the words I understood in Russian.

2. I remember Jean Vilar's Théâtre National Populaire, and seeing productions of French and foreign plays, including Brecht's *Arturo Ui* and O'Casey's *Red Roses for Me*. I felt somehow superior to French people in the audience during the O'Casey play because the original language of the play was *my* language too. I went to the Comédie-Française and to the Odéon and to a production of Claudel's *L'annonce faite à Marie* starring Danielle Delorme. I went to a performance of Pinter's *The Caretaker* in French, with only five people in the theatre. Concerts organised by Jeunesse Musicale took place at the TNP. Salle Pleyel had wonderful acoustics. I visited museums like the Cluny, the Jacquemart-André and the Carnavalet and an exhibition of Jacques Villon's paintings. I visited famous churches like Notre Dame. And the Madeleine.

[That last sentence is a late addition, recalled over a cup of tea today. Does it take the biscuit? The tea, I mean. I was not to meet Jonathan Griffin for another eight years, but in 1961 he had *already* returned to London after his Paris years, already met Claudel and Sartre, Manuel Rosenthal and Louis Kaufmann.]

3. I remember cafés in Boul' Mich' where the toilet in the basement was a hole in the ground, which I thought was weird and unEnglish but all right if you were male and all you wanted to do was pee. I met French friends, including Didier Drugeon, in bars in rue Soufflot and rue des Ecoles.

[Not sure I trust that 'unEnglish', but holes in the ground were clearly French and, unlike French mustard and French bread and French kissing, had never been exported to the UK. French windows, French letters and Beckett self-translation are another matter.]

4. I remember meeting some North African students whose political arguments against Israel I could not handle. I wrote to my father for help.

[I must try to find the letter he sent me. This was several years before the Six-Day War, and might modify my recollection earlier in these pages that he was a non-Zionist from 1948 until 1967.]

5. I met Claude Benoît in the lounge of the Institut. She bestowed on me my first French kiss – as I already knew tongues in each other's mouth were called – on the Pont Neuf.

6. I remember two other girls: Céline Hirigoyen from the Basque country who played the famous organ in Saint-Sulpice. I would go up to the organ loft and listen to her; and Danielle Gendron from Laval who had a huge beehive hairstyle and lived in a Catholic hostel in the *Quartier*, south of the Luxembourg. Sometimes I went with Céline or Danielle or Claude to a film or play or concert, but often I went alone, and I always went to exhibitions alone.

[Oh dear, I am sorely tempted to look through my collection of programmes. I resist. The documentation of nostalgia would flood a text already on the brink while pretending not to be. Man the floodgates!]

7. I remember a fellow-student, Jean-Claude, saying we should visit a *putain*, a whore, in Montmartre. I did think to myself that it would be *interesting* to see a breast and perhaps touch one, and how much would the whore charge for that, but I said no. He asked me about girls in England and what I had done with them but I changed the subject.

[I changed the subject because it was certainly clear, even to me, that I was supposed or assumed to have had some sexual experience already; since I was absolutely not turned on south of my mouth by anything, not even by the new experience of French kissing, I can only hazard the guess that I was protecting myself against possible destabilisation, being unready. I vaguely recall thinking that I was supposed to feel ashamed of my zero but I wasn't ashamed. And my French kissing was improving.]

8. I remember Claude Benoît introducing me to a restaurant which she said I would like because it was Russian: Gaudeamus, rue Pierre Sarrazin, the first street on the left after the bookseller Gibert as you walk down Boul' Mich' to the Seine. An old man played Russian tunes on the violin. She also introduced me to the *crêperie* on rue Monsieur-le-Prince and a favourite bistro of hers in rue de la Harpe. Claude was studying English at the Sorbonne and, indeed, 'looked' English rather than French. She was eight years older than me, but you couldn't tell.

[We have never lost touch. We even went out together later for a while. 'Jamais de la vie/on ne l'oubliera/la première fill' qu'on a pris' dans ses bras', as Brassens sang. The time in Paris hurried slowly by, and the kiss on the Pont Neuf was what it was, *tout simplement*. Hilary Sefton, yes; Patricia Hammerson, yes; but Claude Benoît was the first in the literal sense of Brassens' song, though clearly he is speaking about full lovemaking. That kiss on the Pont Neuf was itself a bridge, a new bridge in terms of human intimacy. There was no going back. But going forward, never mind down, is outside the time-span of this book. I remained *on* the bridge for many months yet. The kiss may have been a figure for what was to come later but, yes, it was what it was. Now it is the flesh made word.]

9. I remember keeping a small package in my pocket tied with a rubber band. It contained lists of everything I wanted to do and see. Every week I added new plays, etc., etc., to see, and removed old ones I'd missed or put them on another page. Once I lost my package. I remember remembering it might be in a classroom at the institute. I rushed back and Monsieur Quénelle handed it to me with amazement.

[My bizarre Filofax *avant la lettre* may have survived. I suspect it would supply useful documentation for a case study in the problematics of teenage control mechanisms. Mind you, even today I find that keeping lists is a handy way of pretending I am going to do things I have no intention of doing. Perhaps the package is bundled together with the letters I wrote my parents from Paris, more nostalgia, more crap, another book. Cor blimey, mate, take it easy. Barthes is good on lists in his superb 'autobiography'. Somewhere down the line Barthes led me on to Roubaud and Perec. The untimely death of this key intellectual influence meant that his transformation from theoretician into writer was frozen in mid-journey.]

10. I remember taking the train to Poitiers to visit my American cousin Ray Noveck, whose father was a civilian accountant in the US army. We visited the PX store. Ray drove us back to Paris in his old banger and because he was tired I took the wheel in the crowded city itself around Place de la Concorde – with no licence and virtually no driving experience.

[Dodgy or what.]

11. I remember that I would occasionally meet friends of my parents, including Pierre Bonasse whom they'd known in London during the war. Pierre was in reinsurance which meant, according to my father, that you insured insurance companies. He had a *very* fancy office, more elegant and less crowded than my father's. He was an expert on round churches. I went for supper a few times at his house, which surprised me because I thought everybody in Paris lived in a flat. The house was 11 rue de Verzy, off Avenue des Ternes. His wife's name was Moune.

[Many years later I asked my friend Edmond Jabès – the French poet I was beginning to translate – about a critic called Pierre Missac who had written beautifully about him and about Walter Benjamin in *Critique*. Ah, you should meet him, said Edmond. His real name is Pierre Bonasse. And so we renewed contact, and now I can say that I knew a second man who, it turned out, knew Walter Benjamin personally, the other one being that old *flâneur*, Edouard Roditi. I miss Pierre, he was in the superstar league of educated and cultivated *hommes d'affaires*, an emblem of what one most loves in France. It was either Bonasse or Roditi who was with Benjamin when he discovered the Parisian arcades. Cassim was Pierre's wife's pet name for him. Hence Missac. (Remembered and spotted at proof stage.)]

12. I remember visiting in La-Celle-Saint-Cloud Fanny and Reinhold Kahn, the in-laws of my parents' friends, Ralph and Edith Leigh. Professor Kahn was one of the world's leading anaesthetists. Fanny was a school doctor. I sat in on an English lesson in the school.

13. I remember when a slogan went up on all the walls and trees in the *Quartier*, 'Mettons-nous au vert.' It was the theme for a student ball I did attend. I remember the pissoir in Boul' Mich'. I remember the waffles on sale at the corner of rue des Ecoles and Boul' Mich'.

[There had been no point in staying on at school after taking the university entrance exams in December 1960. The decision – presumably taken in consultation with my parents – to spend six months in Paris reads, with hindsight, like an accident of destiny. Paris *is* a moveable feast and for the little I brought to it I received blessings many times over.]

(iii) 'Le Toit familial'

1. I remember the student hostel where I lived, Le Toit familial at 9 rue Guy Patin, Paris 10e, behind the Gare du Nord and the Lariboisière hospital. I even remember its phone number: TRUdaine 2548. I remember arriving from London at the Gare du Nord with my parents and a farewell, both weepy and stiff-upper-lip, on the same day.

2. I remember the director Monsieur Nathan Samuel and his wife. Le Toit was a hostel for Jewish students. There were fifty rooms, two boys to a room. About ninety of them were Sephardim from North Africa, on scholarships to study medicine, etc., four or five were from Israel, two or three from metropolitan France, and there was moi, 'le spécimen anglais', as I was affectionately called in the house magazine. I remember being as amazed by the North Africans as they were by me. As I had not yet visited Israel or the Maghreb, I had never met anyone from that background, and I was certainly the first non-Sephardi Jew who was not French any of them had met, and undoubtedly the first English person outside the movies, and yet they had to admit I was Jewish even if I did pronounce Hebrew in a funny way.

[Years later I disovered that Madame Samuel was the sister of André Neher, a theologian of the Holocaust. The Samuels and many of the students ended up in Israel.]

3. I remember you went to the basement for breakfast: huge bowls of coffee which I drank black because I hated the smell and taste of hot milk, bread hot from the baker, butter and jam. The only other meal provided was Friday night dinner after the informal Shabbat service. Once a month they served couscous, which I did not like very much.

4. I remember sharing a room for several months with Henri Béhar, whose family left Egypt after Suez and who, exceptionally for a Le Toit student, was studying commerce and management, not medicine or dentistry. He spoke perfect movie American, and went all the time to films. One morning he returned with a big smile on his face and a big bite on his neck but I was too polite to ask where it had come from. He wanted to visit England, especially

after I told him my friend John Shrapnel was a National Youth Theatre star. I tried to arrange for each to visit the other's country, but I failed.

[I knew nothing about love bites but perhaps I intuited something since the smile told me he was not in pain, and he volunteered no information.]

5. I remember other friends: Paul and Alain Sultan, Jean-Claude Krieff and André Tibi, Meyer Cohen (who gave me a photograph of a mime which I still have) and Henri Wahba who took me to the ballet to watch and meet his friend, a prima ballerina, Nina Viroubova. There was a real scare among my North African friends that General Salan might attempt a coup against de Gaulle: Jean-Claude even fled Paris. I phoned my father at his office, and at some point discovered that the British embassy in Paris had a list of all British citizens in France who might have to be flown home.

6. I remember André (Pepinos) Baranes who was incredibly handsome, six inches taller than the other students, and the role model nonpareil for his friends. He used to bring girls back to the house. I was present on one occasion when about ten or fifteen people gathered at his door and the shortest one, Tibi, looked through the keyhole and provided a running commentary. A few minutes later Pepinos and his lady friend came out. After they went downstairs one of the crowd, doubtless Tibi himself, said they hadn't done it because 'elle a ses règles'. I looked up the word in my dictionary and still did not really understand what it meant, even in English.

[This extraordinary scene, which Jean Vigo would have relished, is a period piece. It would be impossible today. Other manners, other times *quoi*. On further reflection I cannot believe that I knew *nothing* about menstruation. Perhaps 'not really understand' means that even if I had an abstract notion about monthly periods I hadn't the faintest idea what this had or had not to do with going to bed with a girl or, rather, not going to bed with a girl. All this was below the belt, and anything below the neck was beyond my *dasein* (as I wouldn't have said) for some time yet. 'Emotional anorexia' (the phrase of a friend) surely exaggerates the condition.]

7. I remember sharing a room for a time with an American pianist who used to wake up in the night, pee in the sink, and go back to bed. Finally I shared

briefly with a dapper Israeli cellist called Raphael Sommer. Rafi was the student of Paul Tortelier and was expected to get a first prize at the Conservatoire. He himself had students so that he could finance his studies. He went to bed about nine o'clock and got up very early to practise.

[Sommer now lives in London and has made an international career. I learned from a recent TV programme that he had survived the concentration camp of Theresienstadt. Late postscript: a leaflet has arrived for a concert at the South Bank on Saturday. No message inside but the handwriting on the envelope looks familiar.]

8. I remember the gramophone in the lounge, and listening to records of Geza Anda, Clara Haskil and Arthur Grumiaux. I played the upright piano there a few times. Once in a while one had to spend Saturday night on a camp bed in the office to let people in after midnight, the only night of the week this was permitted. One night I went to a concert given by a pianist friend from London, Carola Grindea, and her violinist, Joan Spencer.

[Apart from Dinu Lipatti, Andras Schiff and Marie-Joao Pires, Geza Anda and Clara Haskil remain my favourite pianists.]

9. I remember my desk in the bedroom and the row of books: Livre de Poche texts with the old garish covers: Bernanos, Verlaine, Malraux, Sartre, Mauriac, de Montherlant, Saint-Exupéry; blue and white Classiques Larousse, the 'teach yourself' *Que sais-je* series and the Castex and Surer manuals of French literature. I bought a one-volume encyclopaedia which I still have occasion to use: the Quillet-Flammarion *Dictionnaire usuel*. I had a dictionary, the Shorter Harrap, in which I crossed out my London address and wrote in the Paris one.

[I have continued the tradition of adding my latest address in this dictionary. My current address, going back to 1981, is the eleventh. This raises the kind of question Georges Perec adores asking of his readers. What he calls 'endotic' (as opposed to 'exotic') anthropological information. Well, how many places have you lived in? My eleven consist of: the parental home, Le Toit familial in Paris, three student rooms at Cambridge, a Chicago flat, a Notting Hill bedsitter, a Lewisham flat, a Belsize Park flat, an Upper Holloway house, a North Finchley flat. A whole essay could be written describing these addresses, and addressing the descriptions, some of which would not pass muster with an estate agent but all of which constitute a fiction of reality, reality which is magical, unlike realism.]

10. I remember receiving the news that I had got into Cambridge. My first reaction was joy. My second reaction was relief that I would not have to go to University College London, where I had my 'insurance' place to read Law, which always seemed like a bad idea, both because Dr Barton in my final report had assumed that this was where I would go, and also because I had no interest in the subject (as the man who interviewed me for a place understood perfectly well). My third reaction, slightly delayed, was anxiety because Cambridge would involve harder work than A levels had.

11. I remember dances in Le Toit. I would wear my yellow waistcoat. At one party I met Eva Rawicz. At another, Nadine Fichbine. They invited me to their homes. Eva was poor, Nadine rich. Michael Pinto-Duschinsky came over for a month's stay at Le Toit. We had an argument about Sartre which Michael was supposed to lose because I was the French expert. When he held his ground I told him to read the *Que sais-je* volume on existentialism. He did so but was not impressed. Essence, said Michael, *does* come before existence.

[Reminiscent of the episode when Michael presented me with an ultimatum for my father. Heaven knows what Oxford PPE studies made of Michael's philosophy. Probably refuted him with a kick in the shins.]

12. I remember some of the shops on the parade as you came out of Métro Barbès Rochechouart, which was even closer to our hostel than Gare du Nord: a barber, and a café; and a cinema on the corner of Boulevard Magenta. The café had old-fashioned flipper games and served sandwiches in French bread, cheese or ham or *rillettes*. The barber put his knife under a flame before trimming your sideburns. He was surprised when I told him no one took this health precaution in England.

13. I remember going home for a week in the middle of the six-month stay and visiting my Uncle Phil in Chatham, where he ran the Labour Exchange, to discuss careers. I returned to Paris on the train and felt good as I walked from the Gare du Nord to Le Toit.

[Postscript: the D'Oyly Carte incident mentioned earlier, which I said took place on my return from Paris at the end of June, might have taken place during this week's break.]

14. I remember the upstairs cafeteria just opposite the Gare du Nord, where we sometimes ate: everyone joked with Eliane, the pretty cashier. I remember the bread there, and the very strong mustard I smeared on it.

15. I remember the day term ended at the British Institute. Shortly afterwards Le Toit required residents to vacate their rooms for summer students. I made half-hearted efforts to find somewhere else to live. A Sorbonne friend, Désiré, offered to share his room at the lower end of rue Monsieur-le-Prince with me. I told myself it was too small. I was ready to go home.

16. I remember Henri Béhar following me to the Gare du Nord with some of my gear, including my unused tennis racket, when it was time for my final departure. I nearly missed the train.

17. I remember having Russian lessons in London that summer, in order to catch up some more before university. My teacher was Madame Tamara Alhasova Tomashchina, who lived in Notting Hill.

[On the axis of calendar time which does *not* structure this book, nothing follows except . . . the other day, during final revision of *The Arithmetic of Memory*, I visited the duty doctor for an infected finger. The receptionist handed me my notes to take in with me. I peeped into them and found a summary of major medical events in my history: two hernia operations (1983 and 1984), serious back trouble (1976) and, in 1961, when Uncle Len Russell was my doctor, depression. Depression in 1961? I have no recollection of this . . . A quick phonecall to my GP reveals a clerical error. It should have read 1963 (early in my second year at Cambridge), which is outside the parameters of this book.]

5

Home and Extended Family

All he did was to remember
Like the old and be honest like children

W. H. AUDEN (on Freud)

(A)

FAMILY

(i) Father

1. I remember my father's fountain-pens, especially a vast Swan, and his florid signature. I often tried to copy it, and sometimes based my own on it. How I loved that Swan!

[In the years since his death I find that his handwriting moves me more than any photo. It was very distinctive (with the personal flourish of one more accustomed to dictate to a secretary), but every handwriting one knows well is distinctive, is it not? I still remember the handwriting of some school friends. I am tempted to joke that my father's has a rarity value because he hand-wrote few letters and hardly any of *those* have survived, in the family at any rate. But of course, the reason I am moved is that the writing is *by* him, 'in his own hand', original, albeit 'Swan's Way'. Photos are merely *of* him. His voice on a tape-recording is somewhere between 'by' and 'of'. Perhaps *from*.]

2. I remember my father had a smart camera he never used, and a cheaper one which he did.

3. I remember my father's watch: an Omega. This watch, and its expanding bracelet, fascinated me.

[My friend Augustus Young has written an inventive poem about his late father's Omega watch.]

4. I remember my father's wedding ring. A simple gold ring worn on his left hand. He never removed it. Correction: I never saw him remove it.

[The day after he died my mother gave it to me saying he had wanted me to have it.]

5. I remember my father had yellow-stained fingers for many years, because he smoked a lot; indeed he was almost a chain-smoker. He smoked Players ('Please'). He often told me that when I was a toddler during the war I broke up a packet of hundred cigarettes into three hundred or was it four hundred small pieces, so he would have *more*: this was my idea of a present. Sometimes he smoked a pipe.

[Arnold and Elaine Feinstein remember the war but cannot say if there was a shortage of cigarettes. Raymond Mason remembers being issued with to-bacco *leaf* in the navy. Cynthia Maccoby remembers smoking behind the woodsheds at boarding school, while Hyam Maccoby reports that there seemed to be no shortage in the army. But even if there was no shortage, what I did was unhelpful. I meant well. Probably Piaget would have a developmental view of my conceptual apparatus. Perhaps that was the moment my father took up smoking a pipe in addition to cigarettes.]

6. I remember his shaving brush and shaving cream and Gillette blades.

7. I remember his office gear: two-piece suit, cufflinks, braces, armbands, suspenders, *no* tiepin, Homburg hat. One pair of his black shoes looked old and worn, especially around the little toe. This pair had been handmade, somewhere in St James. He never wore a stiff collar.

[He switched to a bowler after the time-span of this book so I am only allowed to mention it in the commentary. He rarely wore a waistcoat. Stiff collars: this had little to do with status in my opinion, because I distinctly remember people in almost all professional or other groups wearing them or not wearing them, presumably as they saw fit – unless it was to save money on the laundry bills. Perhaps it was genuinely optional, above or below a certain income level? The Spurs chairman wears a stiff collar these days: is Mr Sugar trying to tell us something? Nothing could persuade me into one, that's for sure. And how did the suspenders, unfastened to a girdle, stay up? Round the calf I suppose. Why did men bother? This is surely the most bizarre item of clothing in the history of menswear.]

8. I remember the drinks cabinet – part of the sideboard – in the dining room. My father always served the drinks to dinner-party visitors. Slow moving, and therefore replaced much less often than sherry or whisky, the bottles of crème de menthe and Bols advocaat were my favourites to look at. One liqueur was there for *years*.

9. I remember *The Times* crossword. I sat there beside him (do I remember sitting on his lap?) in charge of looking up quotations in the *Oxford Dictionary of Quotations*. My brain would race to solve anagrams – he would write the letters in a circle on the margin of the crossword. He always said he could tell when the puzzle-setter changed, and that if you really wanted to make progress you should check the paper next day to study clues you had failed to answer. He insisted we attempt all the across ones first even if we had lots of letters towards the down ones.

[Walking around the mental image, I remember the crossword partnership happened many times (presumably after work midweek or on a Saturday after lunch) but I see one picture only. Which proves there is more to memory than a visual image, and that such an image represents many occasions rather than re-presents a single one. I still *hear* the insistence on the proper order: what a lesson in self-denial, or deferred gratification if you prefer. The frustration! The torment! That dictionary of quotations is on my desk. A few quotations have unexpected or interesting pencilled ticks against them. 'Train up a child in the way he should go, and when he is old he will not depart from it,' from Proverbs; and Dr Johnson: 'Marriage has many pains, but celibacy has no pleasures.' Emerson: 'Words are also actions, and actions are a kind of words.' And Disraeli's definition of a sound Conservative government: 'Tory men and Whig measures' could tell me something about my father. The Proverbs quote reminds one of the Jesuits' notorious claim, of course, which in turn reminds me of Gerard Manley Hopkins' squib glossing Wordsworth: ' "The child is father to the man."/How can he be? The words are wild./ Suck any sense from that who can./ "The child is father to the man."/ No; what the poet did write ran,/ "The man is father to the child."/ "The child is father to the man!"/ How *can* he be? The words are wild.']

10. I remember my father taking me to Charing Cross Road and the second-hand bookshops. There was one called Panzetta on the left hand side going towards Trafalgar Square. Mr Panzetta allowed me to browse in the reserve stock in the basement. I remember meeting an older bookseller downstairs in Collet's.

[This older man may well have been Edgell Rickword whom I later admired as a poet and corresponded with.]

11. I remember my father's first office in Finsbury Pavement, Moorgate (wait a minute, perhaps that should read the first office I visited), and the second one (nicely ambiguous) in Balfour House, also in Moorgate. I loved the stamp used for embossing addresses you could hardly read onto paper, the typewriters, the boxes of pencils, the rubbers, the carbon paper, the mysterious files full of letters and balance sheets. I remember dark rooms, furnished with old desks. My father had a large ink-blotter book in which he signed his post on headed notepaper. His partner and number two was Mr John Jacob ('Jack') Nunes Vaz. Other members of staff included Mr Richards and Mr Hammerman, as well as my second cousins, Michael Trevor and Stanley Davis, who were articled clerks. Dr Mannes, who my father said had been a judge in Germany before the war, had an office there. My father's cousin Reg Forrester worked upstairs in the same building. My father's first secretary Mrs Sawyer – first as in office above – was followed by Miss Cohen, Pauline. I used to meet people called clients. Sometimes I went to the post office in South Place or walked round the corner to Sun Street where my father's brothers, Isidore and Leon, worked together as printers. There was a restaurant in Broad Street which my father said had been an official wartime one, serving cheap food. We went out to lunch a few times, to Strongwater's Jewish delicatessen in Aldersgate for example.

12. I remember my father had a client called J. Spreiregen, who owned Kangol berets; and another one called Manshaw which sold costume jewellery. And Wesley Tee, the publisher and printer of *Motor Sport*; and one client in

Margaret Street, north of Oxford Street, doubtless in the rag trade. The book I had with me that day was called *A Treasury of Jewish Folklore* edited by Nathan Ausubel, inscribed by Grandma and Grandpa Rudolf.

[The nature, particularly significant and interesting to the son, of the father's relationship with a large number of his many clients, emerged years later in the letters they wrote my mother after he died: 'He was like a father . . . ', thus Ted Hughes, among others. Interestingly enough, a few years later, the Poet Laureate, in a message sent to my sister for inclusion in my mother's eightieth-birthday book, was remembering my father as being 'like an uncle'. Ted Hughes died recently. 'Dig deep,' he told me in Devon. 'Dig those poems out.' *He* was a great digger.]

13. I remember my father standing for St Paul's ward of Finchley constituency in the borough of Barnet as a Labour candidate in the local elections. The photograph of him in the local papers had him smoking a pipe.

[A touch of the Harold Wilsons there, perhaps; Wilson smoked a pipe in public and cigars in private. My father's wedding ring can be seen in a framed print of the photo, the very ring I would one day wear on the fourth finger of my right hand, a future destined to return to the past on my death. If my son, who will eventually wear that ring, and who recently qualified as a barrister, becomes a Labour MP, he will have achieved the professional and political ambitions his grandfather at a certain age had for himself.]

14. I remember my father sometimes helped me with maths and history homework. Apart from *Eagle* he did not approve of comics. I was not allowed to open end-of-term reports brought home from school.

[I tremble to think how my young friend Rhianon or my daughter Naomi, even at 13, would have reacted to *Girl*, the counterpart to *Eagle*, if a copy had turned up. The middle classes appear to have taken the Reverend Marcus Morris's comics to their bosom in those days: thus, I discovered recently that Rhianon's mother was permitted to read *Girl*. Perhaps these comics represented an up-dating of Arthur Mee's *Children's Newspaper*, which presumably died the death because it was old-fashioned?]

15. I remember my father used to say that the captain always goes down with

his ship. He also used to say that broccoli was the poor man's asparagus. Sometimes we had one, sometimes the other.

[I believe I interpreted this to mean not that we were sometimes poor, sometimes rich, but that we were somewhere in the middle. I wrote a poem about this years later, triggered by Margaret Atwood's challenging suggestion that poets prefer round vegetables. When I told a painter I know about my poem she referred me to someone who, to my astonishment, she described as being obsessed with broccoli. This was Paul Coldwell. He supplied a lithograph to go with the poem and printed them in a limited edition. Several copies were sold and costs were covered.]

16. I remember my father teaching me a nonsense rhyme: Lala, chignychigny, roonypoony, pingpongpiny, alabalabusta, nigeroi.

17. I remember his wallet, and on one occasion a huge crisp new five-pound note.

18. I remember I used to press one cheek of my father, and he would either blow a raspberry or puff out his other cheek. And then I would reverse the process.

[This yields an interesting example of memory retrieval involving a third party, namely my son, but it is permitted under the rules because the other day, unknowingly, he triggered the memory by asking me, out of the blue, if I remembered when he used to press my cheek, etc., etc.]

19. I remember my father's club, the Eccentric Club in Ryder Street. Its clock went backwards. I was amused by one dish on the menu, my old favourite Welsh rarebit, which was served as a *dessert*.

[Later my father joined the Reform Club. Lunching with him there a few times (including a memorable occasion when he was zomboid with jet-lag, changing planes on his way from Los Angeles to Haifa where his latest grandchild was about to land), I sensed and experienced certain social insecurities on his (first-generation) part. I feel now I did not make enough effort in his lifetime to understand and make allowances for those insecurities (which had been educated out of me or replaced with different ones . . .) but this is par

.or the course, or the discourse, namely the classic unfinished business we all feel after a parent dies. The literature of fathers and sons, from Samuel Butler and Edmund Gosse and Matthew Arnold via Henry Roth and Joseph Roth and Philip Roth to Alan Sillitoe, Paul Auster and Blake Morrison, speaks to me. I did not appreciate my father's qualities to the extent his clients did. As I add this gloss at the age of 53, with all the awareness of personal failures and failings attendant upon re-enactment of all I have done and been as an adult (adulthood defined as beginning where this book leaves off), I play my game of thinking about my father when he too was 53 and what we were up to, and for some reason I think of Henry (this is the first time I have *ever* called him by his first name; he, unlike his brothers, never called their own father by his first name even in Grandfather's absence) on the phone to me in Chicago, where I was living in my own place at last, on New Year's Eve. I recall two grown-ups discussing politics – in particular the forthcoming General Election at which I would not be around to chauffeur our family friend Reg Freeson (by this point a junior member of the government) as he defended his seat in Willesden East on polling day. When I returned to London that June I wanted to move out of Middleway. He resisted strongly, much more strongly than my mother, and quite irrationally I thought, given that I had lived alone in Chicago. There was a necessary and appropriate conflict, a moment of truth. How I wish we could have had a retrospective conversation about my childhood. But those conversations never happen: it *is* necessarily so. There is a sense in which this book is a version of my side of that conversation. Now he lies in Bushey Jewish cemetery, less than a hundred yards from his friend Miron Grindea, a far shorter distance than in 'real' life. What was his last conscious thought before his stroke? What was his last memory: was it a replay of his first memory? I think the very last experience of life might be a vivid awareness of *light*, perhaps a recapitulation of the moment soon after birth when the eyes of your mother fix you in the deep of their gaze. Maybe this happens only if your death is planned, whether premeditated suicide or execution or in war – if (for example) you are Isaac Rosenberg, who *volunteered* (in one version) to return to a situation where death was certain, and died not more than a few days after writing his last poem, ending as it does: 'They see with living eyes/How long they have been dead.']

(ii) Mother

1. I remember my mother wearing twinsets. Like all other women, she wore stockings with seams which had sometimes to be straightened after you looked in the mirror over your shoulder; they were sometimes worn with garters, sometimes with suspenders. I remember her coping skilfully with the technology.

2. I remember her going to the shops with my little sister Ruth in a pushchair. On one occasion only I remember her wearing what she called slacks. She often wore lipstick, but less powder and other makeup than many women. She liked hats, sometimes buying them at Simone Mirman's shop.

[I knew about kilts and togas but they were foreign. As a good English boy, I could not understand why women sometimes wore trousers if men did not wear skirts. Clothes, my 'thinking' would have gone had I possessed the necessary conceptual apparatus, were essentialised signifiers. There was nothing arbitrary or conventional about clothes.]

3. I remember the wooden trolley which my mother wheeled in from the kitchen to the lounge when friends or relatives were being entertained. Tea was served in a pink china tea set she still has, with her brilliant meringues and pavlovas.

[I have this trolley now. It is a lovely piece of thirties' design: a wedding (1938) present perhaps?]

4. I remember the little tin where she kept her thimble and needles and a few buttons, and on which the wording and image gradually faded.

[I think she still has it, one of a handful of family objects out there in the world and surviving my childhood years, independent of memory and dependent on it, as intimate in its own way as my father's wedding ring: that tin, which had once (during the war probably) contained peppermints or tobacco, would be whisked out when a shirt button needed sewing on, a sock darning; it is a small icon or talisman, which reminds me how utterly strange it is to get older, to be outlived by objects we acquire or make and think we dominate. I have a thing ('Il s'agit bien de *cet* objet' – Bonnefoy) about the things I have. Rilke: 'What sleeps in us keeps awake inside the things.']

5. I remember my mother in the kitchen koshering meat and in particular koshering liver which being ultra-bloody required a special technique over a flame. She explained all the rules to me (e.g. bloodshot eggs must be thrown away) but, she said, you sometimes have a choice: for example, her father who was *very* religious waited six hours before eating meat after milk whereas my father's family, religious but less religious, waited three hours. She quite often baked biscuits and cakes, with yummy leftovers in the bowl. She had a much-thumbed Florence Greenberg cookery book. There were two sets of dishes – for milk and meat – and a further two sets for Passover.

[Choice: i.e. a custom relating to your degree of piety rather than a law.]

6. I remember her sitting in an armchair with her stockinged feet folded underneath her. She smoked cigarettes.

[I tell myself I have seen other women do this but never, in all my born years, have I seen a man with his feet folded thus.]

7. I remember my mother stuffing envelopes for the local Labour Party and that I sometimes went with her to put them through ward members' letterboxes.

[This can't have been too time-consuming in Hampstead Garden Suburb. The Liberals used to poll more than old Labour, but several Labour MPs lived in the area.]

8. I remember I had a tutor, Mr Hughes, to prepare me for common entrance. My mother would bring him up a cup of tea and two digestive biscuits, and a lump of sugar which he gave me. Miss Olive Hicks, 7 Hogarth Hill, was my elocution teacher.

[Was the sugar-lump intended for the horse of instruction?]

9. I remember when my mother started her own business, called 'Sew Easy', working from home. During and immediately after the war she ran the business side of a magazine called *Doctor* with my father. I enjoyed looking through back numbers.

10. I remember my mother used to tell me about her pre-war boss, Mr Rappaport. And she told me that I won second prize in a baby competition, judged by exiled King Zog of Albania, who was living in High Wycombe, near where we had been evacuated.

11. I remember my mother helping me rinse my spots in a washbasin with various solutions. She tried to make me feel better when I was upset after my father said my concern over spots was due to vanity.

[There was no solution, unfortunately.]

12. I remember my mother was brilliant at removing splinters with a needle from her grey tin. She would first heat the needle in a flame. I remember the smell and colour of iodine.

13. I remember my mother telling me about her extended stay in Denmark and Germany in 1937. She cycled alone, from Copenhagen to Berlin, in order to find out what was going on in Europe. She told me about the famous Folk High School near Copenhagen which she attended, and about left-wing politics in the 1930s.

[Given her good feelings about Denmark, she will have been pleased and perhaps even unsurprised some years after the war when it became known that Denmark had saved *all* its Jews.]

14. I remember, when we were bored during the holidays and plaguing her to suggest activities, she would quote her own mother: 'Clap your hands on your *tochus* [bottom] and shout bravo'. She often used Yiddish phrases: for example, *nakhascop* (joy-head) and *a mazal in d'beina* (good fortune in your bones) and *sheine meidela* (pretty girl).

[This memory enables me to muse on the huge gaps in between the lines of these paragraphs. We are talking about five and a half thousand days, the great majority of whose details have been forgotten, even though some of the memories are representative. On the other hand, quite a lot of names and places and events have been excluded solely for reasons of space. No that is wrong, they have been excluded for reasons of shape, in the aesthetic interests of the book. The book, as written, establishes its own continuities, by glossing

Aisngeh?

over many gaps, not explaining many options: e.g. in para ii.11, above, chosen because it is on my screen now, I remember the downstairs washbasin in the toilet not the upstairs one in the bathroom: this could mean upstairs was never the *locus*, or it could mean it might have been a *locus* but I just can't remember. So, when we were bored and my mother spoke her joke solution to the problem, what happened next? I do remember hating it when she said that, just as my own children did when I would say it to them. If it was say midday during the school holidays, no doubt my sister Ruth and I consoled ourselves that lunch would be ready in half an hour so let's just carry on with whatever we happen to be doing. If it was two in the afternoon, this was bad news, etc., etc. Somehow I lived my five and half thousand days, as we all do, until one day it was time to begin or you might say end the process of growing up. Please see the Afterword for a gloss on this life-long trauma.]

15. I remember my mother used to say that tall people should wear horizontal stripes, short people vertical ones. I saw the logic in that.

16. I remember my mother sometimes (but never my father) calling me Moishele, my 'Hebrew' name.

[The word Hebrew is in inverted commas because Moishele is the Yiddish-style diminutive of the real Hebrew name and word: Moshe. Moshe = Moses, Moshe also being short for my whole Hebrew first name, Moshe Leb, Moses the Lion. For the record my full name is Moshe Leb ben-Rehavia. Where did my father, Rehavia ben-Yosef get that first name? Certainly he was not named after the charming eponymous quarter in Jerusalem where I met the philosopher Samuel Hugo Bergmann long ago and held in my hand the school-leaving keepsake volume signed by his friend Kafka. It is a nominal mystery which can never be resolved. Rehavia is a seriously unimportant biblical figure, mentioned in Chronicles 1. Perhaps, says Hyam Maccoby, they couldn't think what to call him so opened the Bible and chose a name at random.]

18. I remember driving round with my mother to see her mother Rebeccah Russell (Rosenberg) at 45 Wessex Gardens in Golders Green. Sometimes she would pick up meat for both of them from Frohwein, their kosher butcher in Temple Fortune.

(iii) Parents

1. I remember asking my parents if I was adopted.

2. I remember evenings when different combinations of my parents' friends came over. I called them uncle or aunt. One evening 'Uncle' Joe Pole came upstairs to have a chat with me and say goodnight. I was present at lively arguments about politics or the arts. Everybody was Labour Party, except for one or two Communists and one Tory, Archibald Rowland, Uncle Rowley. His wife, Hilda, was German. The arts that this group of friends discussed were literature and theatre. The predominant tendency within Labour politics was Bevanite. Sadie and Harry Passer would be there. They too had children called Anthony and Ruth. Rose and Ruby (Reuben) Silk were more left wing than my parents and often in disagreement with them. Harriet and David Shackman had very similar views to my parents. Harriet was secretary to Harold Davies MP. Phoebe Pole, and Joe, were a generation older than my parents. Joe worked in film publicity and had personally known Charlie Chaplin. Phoebe had been a suffragette. I remember David (Uncle Doddie) and Dora Sigaloff especially well, because he was my dentist and I saw him outside our house. Bob and Kay Hilton too would sometimes be there, Bob being an opinionated and arrogant autodidact but also a charming, friendly and intelligent man. Reg and Minnie Forrester counted as family friends even though Reg was a cousin of my father. Archy (Uncle Penny) Pennington, and his exotic wife Erica, a tiny dark lady with a Viennese accent who wore daring dresses with a slit up the side and flourished a cigarette holder, often visited. I remember figuring that Penny was not Jewish because he spoke with a posh accent, as was not and did Uncle Rowley. Ralph and Edith Leigh lived in Cambridge and tended to come over on their own, ditto Harold and Florence Gearing, who also lived out of town. Alfred, of Alfred and Leonie Westbury, had a moustache, smoked a pipe and loved cricket. Rae Borovoy used to visit when home from America. She would come with her sister Phyllis and their old mother, my Grandmother Russell's East End friend, who was as short sighted as the cartoon character, Mr Magoo. And I met others, including Bernie and Maureen Rubin and Evelyn and Professor Dick Peer. Later there were younger friends too, glamorous couples, men about town with their beautiful wives: Peter and Denise Golding

and, in particular, Peter (who had grown up in the Suburb and been a very young pilot in the Battle of Britain) and Jean Davis, whom I called by their first names.

[I enjoyed these evenings (occasionally afternoons), which were probably Sundays now I come to think of it. No one could call me argumentative but I think some of the interactive techniques influenced the tyro publisher. Music and painting and cinema were less important than books and theatre, and featured much less often on the conversational agenda. The circle did go to exhibitions and attend films (more rarely concerts, never ballet or opera) but these did not engage their intellect or their passions. Passion was theatre. Passion was politics. Passion was books. Real uncles and aunts formed another circle. So, there were Anthony and his sisters. Circling around them were the parents, in a first circle or system. Around the parents, in a second circle or system, the uncles and aunts and grandparents; parents' friends in a third, and parents' other worlds figured as yet more circles. It is quite proper that the child's kingdom or universe should generate a cosmology. In an ideal 'world' (defined as one where I had mastered word-processing to the level manifested by Roubaud who builds cybernetic 'branchings' into the very structure of the cosmology of his great book) this book's cosmology – embracing all the possible circles of the kingdom (Emerson: 'The life of a man is a self-evolving circle,' and Laing and Cooper: 'A person's life unrolls itself in spirals') – would interlock with the figure of truth as polyhedron, and some kind of gestalt three-dimensional map of the kingdom would emerge. On second thoughts, it's just as well I have to forgo such a grandiose ambition. No such complications troubled Wittgenstein and his followers as they 'played solar systems' on Midsummer Common in Cambridge. Of the figures who were still alive when I wrote the previous paragraph, some have died during the writing of this book: Doddie, Bob, Reuben and Dick; two couples have vanished: the Goldings and the Rubins. Friends of one's parents who treated one when young with friendship and respect are very important people in the life of a future adult, perhaps equal to uncles and aunts and teachers. I salute them all. I salute too the son of Sadie and Harry: Tony Passer, who died in a car crash when he was eighteen. Sadie sometimes cries when she sees me because my presence is an additional reminder of the tragic loss of *their* Tony.]

3. I remember we hired a television for the Coronation and it stayed. That telly or the next one had a large magnifying screen in front of it. My parents and I would watch some programmes together, like *The Brains Trust* on BBC on Sunday afternoon and *Free Speech* on the new commercial TV, also on Sunday. I enjoyed the wholly political *Free Speech* more, with A. J. P. Taylor and Michael Foot confronting Bill Brown and Bob Boothby, whoever Bill Brown was. Jacob Bronowski and the poet Ruth Pitter were regulars on *The Brains Trust*. Norman Fisher was in the chair. We watched *The Groves* (Granny Grove: 'I'm faint from lack of nourishment') on Friday before supper, and the nature programmes of Armand and Michaela Denis. Once, during *What's My Line*, Gilbert Harding got angry when some benighted participant, on being asked if her job required expertise, said no, she worked on her own. My parents, especially my mother, liked to listen to and later, with TV, watch, the monarch's Christmas speech. Tony Hancock was a great favourite. Once while I was watching Chris Chataway and Gordon Pirie compete in a 5000 or 10,000 metres event my mother angrily switched off the TV because supper would be ruined if delayed any longer. My favourite television cowboy was the Cisco Kid whose sidekick, Pancho, used to say, 'Let's went.'

[BBC TV has been re-running thirty-four episodes of Hancock. And a mixed bunch they are too. His best work was on the radio.]

4. I remember my parents reading the Sunday newspapers in bed and I would plead to see the football or cricket scores on the back page of the *Observer* or *Sunday Times*, which were then single-section papers. For a time they took both. Harold Hobson and Kenneth Tynan wrote on theatre, Dilys Powell and C. A. Lejeune on film, Raymond Mortimer, Cyril Connolly and Philip Toynbee on books. Desmond Shawe-Taylor was the *Sunday Times* music critic. One Sunday morning I remember being puzzled that their bedroom door was locked.

5. I remember that during the week my father read *The Times* and my mother read the *News Chronicle* but each also looked at the other paper. John Camkin wrote on football for the *News Chronicle* and there were classified advertisements on the front page of *The Times*. I enjoyed reading these advertisments. They included Miss Oliver or Olivier of Wimpole Street, who advertised colonic irrigation. I thought it was something to do with agriculture

in the British Empire and that I would eventually learn about it in geography at school. I could not understand why Miss Oliver would administer it to you.

[The 'irrigation' memory is unmediated. It did not depend upon the booster supplied by the amazing revelation that Diana Windsor went in for it, as was regularly pointed out by journalists of the prince's party. Alf Garnett would have been appalled. Aldous Huxley and Mae West swore by the technique.]

6. I remember we took several weeklies: the *New Statesman*, *The Listener*, *Tribune*, the *Jewish Chronicle*, *Punch*.

[I think they were delivered along with the dailies and Sundays rather than picked up at Ellington's.]

7. I remember the books and the bookcases. There were many books by Graham Greene and Angus Wilson, L. P. Hartley and Aldous Huxley, Arthur Koestler and George Orwell. And my father would buy the latest volume in the famous sequences by Anthony Powell and C. P. Snow. There were books by Montague Slater and David Garnett, Scott Fitzgerald and Ernest Hemingway, François Mauriac and Jean-Paul Sartre, Alberto Moravia and Ignazio Silone. There were other novels, including several by Bernard Shaw – and translations of Stendhal, Tolstoy and Turgenev; there were Left Book Club books and books on political economy (e.g. Galbraith), plays by Shakespeare, Bernard Shaw, etc.; there were volumes in the Thinker's Library by Bertrand Russell, Lord Raglan, H. G. Wells (my father told me he once sat next to Wells on a bus and chatted with him) and other thinkers; there were anthologies of poetry, and one or two selections of individual poets: I remember Dylan Thomas and T. S. Eliot. Some of the books had attractive covers. Two books were signed by authors, Desmond Young and Nigel Morland, who had been clients of my father. And a number of books were signed by the donor, including separate gifts to my parents from their friend Ralph Leigh. My father was a sporadic collector of fine printing: he had several of the large and beautiful books from the Golden Cockerel Press. There were black and white Phaidon volumes (El Greco, Vélazquez, etc.) and biographies: Deutscher's *Trotsky* and Hesketh Pearson's *Hazlitt*, and Stephen Spender's autobiography, and Penguin monographs on painters, and several Nonesuch volumes, including Hazlitt's essays. There was Malinowski's *The Sexual Life of Savages,* with photographs of naked

bodies, and a book I found hidden in the hall cupboard by Van somebody on sex. One or two passages had been marked. There was Dr Spock. My father still owned a one-volume encyclopaedia signed 'Henry Rudolf' and dated 1927 which I guessed must have been a barmitzvah present, since he was 13 that year. All the Jewish prayerbooks (*machsors*) for high holidays and festivals were there, as was the *Encyclopaedia Britannica*. Alongside it were *Britannica* Year Books which my parents bought for three or four years only. There were belles-lettres: Logan Pearsall Smith (I never forgot one sentence from *Trivia*: 'Some people say that life's the thing, but I prefer reading'), and *The Unquiet Grave* by Palinurus which I knew was a pseudonym for Cyril Connolly. And literary criticism: Edmund Wilson and Lionel Trilling. I remember books by one author he said he would read when he retired . . .

[. . . a remembrance of things to come, perhaps. Life certainly *was* the thing, but reading was part of it – perhaps the most intense and powerful and real part of a childhood, when virtual reality, as it wasn't known, takes you over. *It is the life*, in the joke phrase of my late and dear friend Michel Couturier. What were Shaw's unreadable novels doing there? His plays were very important for my parents' generation. That would perhaps explain it. The edition of *War and Peace* was inscribed to me on the day of my birth 6 September 1942 by my uncle Leon Rudolf with the remark that he was sure I would not mind if my parents read it first. He died yesterday after making a speech at his Masonic lodge, apparently ending with one of his millions of jokes. Hands up *anybody* who bought the *Britannica* Year Books for more than three or four years? Those books with attractive covers: probably published by John Lehmann or André Deutsch, who commissioned excellent artists of the day. Even if my father had lived longer after his retirement than he did, I wonder if he would have got round to reading the books on the retirement shelf. Oh, happy days, browsing among books. Within that grove, my budding mind took itself for long walks. I'm still walking. *Oh, les beaux jours* . . .]

8. I remember on one occasion my mother trying to persuade my father to change his mind about a film he would not allow me to see, and failing, but mostly they agreed with each other in public concerning Ruth and me, although my mother would sometimes console me if I was upset about some paternal prohibition or other. I remember abiding by prohibitions.

[Of course as a parent I now know that the common front vis-à-vis the child did not necessarily indicate private agreement between pater and mater – as they weren't known – even if these days a common front is less common in public than it used to be. With my junior sisters, Mary and Annie, the parents were more relaxed, being older, wearier, wiser, better-off and, not least, having experienced the social revolution in *mores* which came too late for Philip Larkin and almost but not quite too late for myself.]

9. I remember my parents did not always present a common front in matters not directly involving their children, for example food. Thus, I knew that when they went out for dinner my father would eat anything, including positively forbidden foods such as pigs and oysters. My mother would eat non-kosher meat if the animal itself was not forbidden, e.g. chicken or lamb. My father would have preferred a less strict regime at home but he knew it was not possible.

[The home was Esther's kingdom, mother's kingdom or even queendom, and what she said went. But the situation in general goes back to Moses Mendelsohn's celebrated formulation about being a Jew at home (and in synagogue), and a citizen outside. This can be said to have worked until 1967, when the Six-Day War created or at least accelerated a trend: rejection of the middle way, and an increase in on the one hand integral Jews as pious or observant as their religious leaders, and on the other hand progressive Jews who followed leaders who did not expect and sometimes did not abide by full orthopraxis. The centre is not holding. The problem is slightly different in Israel, especially in Jerusalem. I have touched on these matters in other writings. If even as late as, say, 1973 you had told even Rabbi Lew that twenty years later there would be a demand for an *eruv* in Barnet he would have been amazed, and he would have understood the problems created by high-profile Jews in an area, Hampstead Garden Suburb, previously the domain of low-profile Jews blending in nicely with the natives, their tennis clubs, their institute, their teahouse, not going with them down the pub even *they* didn't go down because there weren't any. I noted on a rare visit recently to one of the constituent United Synagogues that the magnificent Hertz edition of the *Chumash* (Pentateuch) has been supplanted by the fundamentalist Art Scroll version. No wonder the Masorti and Reform movements are growing. The

Lubavitch movement has a lot to answer for, but its influence inside Jonathan Sacks's United Synagogue is symptomatic of a deeper *malaise* within the overall Jewish community, both specific (most pessimistically described as Hitler's posthumous victory) and common to all religious communities (secularisation). The old centre, the United Synagogue, no longer holds, but the crisis which began with the non-election of Louis Jacobs (unwilling founder of the Masorti movement, and 'timid hero' in the phrase of Reform rabbi and influential theologian Ignaz Maybaum) to the Chief Rabbinate in 1956 will deepen for many years, probably until the London Beth Din moderates its hard line on the things that matter most to ordinary people, e.g. conversion – not an imminent prospect.]

10. I remember one day in the old kitchen, while sitting at the enamel-topped table, my parents discussed the facts of life with me; none of us was embarrassed; I remember that clearly, although I can't remember what was said. The discussion may have taken place after the subject came up at school: in my first year at City of London the class asked Mr Vokins to tell us about it, which he did after all the parents had agreed. On another occasion, certainly a few years earlier, I announced to my mother that according to one friend his mother had said babies were born from the back whereas another friend's mother had said they were born from the front. With no real or even unreal understanding of female anatomy, I could not believe the second one was right even though I knew the first one was wrong. I had to know the answer.

[I cannot remember what my mother said but I suspect that given her later enlightened attitude she did the right thing or rather said something appropriate. Postscript thought: I wonder why we asked our English teacher and not our class teacher. Given my own future sense of the deep links between literature and sexuality, English was – with a narrative deduction in the future-perfect mode – appropriate. Maybe it was Mr Vokins' idea in the first place. Ah, that very speculation sends a tremor of recognition through whatever part of my brain engages in memory retrieval: because I now vaguely remember someone at the back of the room laughing at an ambiguous use of the word 'balls' in 'The Cricket Match' which we were reading in class. Perhaps that set the ball rolling.]

11. I remember sport was of no interest to my parents, although when we eventually got a TV they would watch tennis; and sometimes they played tennis. Sport was *my* passion, my *passion*.

12 I remember walks on Hampstead Heath, Box Hill and Leith Hill and outings to Hatfield House and Luton Hoo and Whipsnade. Quite often we went to Kenwood. I would kick a tennis ball around.

13. I remember my parents taking me to the theatre: Shakespeare at the Old Vic: Robert Helpmann, John Neville, Dorothy Tutin, possibly Glynis Johns as Juliet? We saw *A Resounding Tinkle* by N. F. Simpson and *Five-Finger Exercise* by Peter Shaffer at the Criterion and the Wesker trilogy at the Royal Court, as well as Bernard Kops's *The Hamlet of Stepney Green*. And Ionesco's *Rhinoceros*, John Arden's *Live Like Pigs*, Behan's *The Hostage* and of course in the East End *Fings Aint Wot They Used T'Be*. On one occasion Patricia Hammerson came with us to a charity preview of *West Side Story*. My parents went to *The Caretaker* at the Arts Theatre Club, but didn't take me with, maybe because I was too young to be a member.

[The Royal Court was the place to go. I knew from an early age that theatre mattered a lot to my parents. Theatre mattered to me too, but concerts ran it close. In recent years I have neglected theatre. Writing this book has brought back to me the magic of those evenings, and the animated discussions on the way home, and my mother being dropped outside the theatre when it was raining, because of her high-heeled shoes, leaving my father and me to walk a few blocks after parking the car. The experience of parental interaction, incarnated as the dialectics of non-rancorous disagreement, is one of the greatest losses to children brought up by separated parents even in the most carefully thought-through post-divorce scenarios. Recently my son and I went to the Royal Court to see the excellent new Sam Shepherd play, whose title I've forgotten, short-term memory situation situation or what . . . And who should be in the bar at the interval but Arnold Wesker. I told my son *and* Arnold how significant his trilogy had been for me, and in this very theatre, and how appropriate and meaningful this encounter was. On reflection I suspect I did go to *The Caretaker* but this memory may have been swamped by or conflated with the later Paris visit (see 4.D.ii.2).]

14. I remember my parents telling me I had been a good baby and an obedient child. If I was sat down somewhere, I would not move until I was moved. I also remember my parents telling me that I claimed my baby sister Ruth had attacked me with a fork.

[I suppose one could have a field-day reconciling my aggressive fork projection (projectile) and my passivity.]

(iv) Sisters

1. I remember my first sister Ruth as a baby and then as a toddler in a push-chair.

[I don't remember her in a pram, but I do remember Mary and Annie in prams, years later.]

2. I remember Ruth in the bath. I remember thinking girls were more compact than boys.

['Compact' is the only word I can find. You know what I mean. What a well-kept secret the clitoris is, surely the best kept anatomical secret of all.]

3. I remember Ruth's hair tied tightly back in two little pigtails with ribbons.

4. I remember Ruth not liking her other name, Vanessa, and my father saying how much he loved that name.

5. I remember persuading Ruth that our big old-fashioned radiogram which played 78s had a little man inside.

[Whose name was not Walter Benjamin. Connoisseurs of this key figure will pick up the allusion.]

6. I remember teasing Ruth that when she got married she might become Ruth Bottom whereas I would remain Anthony Rudolf.

[Both her husbands' surnames have begun with B, as it happens . . .]

7. I remember Ruth was friendly with our cousins Ruth Warwick and Angela Rudolf, by virtue of age and gender. I as the oldest child and indeed oldest

grandchild was without friends among the cousins.

[First grandchild, and male. A position of great honour and distinction in a Jewish family. Perhaps in all cultures. A preponderance of grown-ups, mainly female, probably leaves its trace. And along come the three sisters.]

8. I remember Ruth's blue polka-dot frock, and her vest called, for some reason, a gansey.

9. I remember Ruth taking part in a fancy-dress party at a hotel in Holland.

10. I remember my maternal grandmother being anxious because Ruth played a lot with Anthony (known simply as A which was pronounced like the 'a' in man) Goodeve from across the street – who was not Jewish.

11. I remember the arrivals of Mary and Annie. I remember knowing we were unusual, for virtually all my friends had only one sibling.

12. I remember not having very much to say to my two junior sisters.
   [I must point out that this changed later on.]

13. I remember lifting Annie up to touch the ceiling.

14. I remember them, like Ruth, being bathed.

15. I remember they had pets: hamsters, rabbits, tortoises and budgerigars. One of their tortoises was dead when we found him or her after hibernation at the bottom of the garden. Once I caught a budgy which had escaped from its cage. My mother told me I had had a pet when I was little, a dog called Plentymore (named by me after we missed a bus at Market Place), who died of distemper. I remember being told he was fed matchsticks to cure the distemper.
   [Matchsticks? Shum mishtake shurely.]

16. I remember my father calling Annie, whose full name was Anne Michele, by her 'Hebrew' name, Khayeleh, short for Khaya, life.
   [Mary, who rejoices in the name Mary Catherine Joy, was never called by her

Hebrew name Miriam, perhaps because it was an English name in its own right.]

17. I remember both of them reading the text traditionally read by the youngest person present on Passover, the *Ma-nishtanah*.

18. I remember Stanley Mussailloff, 'The Frankie Laine of Bombay', whom I met on the train returning from Paris. I brought him home, to sing for Mary and Annie. He had a sore throat but he sang for his supper.

19. I remember Kay Hayes from Ireland who helped my mother look after Mary and Annie after Lisa Butticaz, who was from Switzerland, had retired. Lisa whose English was not very good had lived in our house from the time I was born. She taught me how to cook Welsh rarebit, and once said that she liked all food except turnips. She told me she had had a fiancé when she was young but he had left her and after that she no longer trusted men. Her best friend was Lucy, who also lived across and down the road in Middleway. Lucy was short and hunch-backed.

[I have no way of knowing the extent of Lisa's influence on my attitudes and behaviour, especially in my earliest and unremembered years, and speculation falls outside the terms of this book. There were eight people at her funeral, including myself and my three sisters. I note that I describe Kay and Lisa above in such a way as to avoid using a descriptive word: maid? help? nanny? *Au pair* had not been invented or at any rate had not come into common use in Britain but *au pairs* don't stay for years and they are much younger.]

(v) Grandparents

1. I remember my maternal grandfather Meyer Russell (Rosenberg), known to us as Zeida Russell, who was very *frum* (ultra-orthodox), theologically anti-Zionist and had a beard. He had worked as a *shomer* (supervisor) in a kosher abattoir. I visited him in a ward in Edgware General Hospital before he died. He presided over traditional Passover *seders*, which I loved, at his house, 45 Wessex Gardens NW11. My grandmother Rebeccah Russell, née Winnick, was known as Bobba, corrupted by us to Bobby, Russell. I visited her in later years with my

mother, or with both parents, or on my own. One year she and I went on the tube to the London Palladium and saw Alma Cogan, whose songs included 'Love and Marriage' (' . . . go together like a horse and carriage. This I tell you, brother, you can't have one without the o–o–other'). There was an upright piano in her lounge at the front of the house, with the wedding photo on it of my mother's sister Fanny and her husband Jack. Upstairs, there was a smell of mothballs. Across the road there was a primary school, and next door lived a girl called Pat. A friend of my grandparents, the Reverend Freed, lived nearby. Bobba Russell drank lemon tea or black tea with a sugar lump between her teeth. She also took something called senna pods and she loved stewed apples, known as *compote*.

[They moved to Wessex Gardens during or after the war from the East End, where they had lived in Princelet Street, Steward Street, Wilkes Street, Hanbury Street and Fleur-de-Lis Street. My mother was born on the first floor of number 3 Wilkes Street (still there), a stone's throw from her father's synagogue, the Machzike Hadath on the corner of Brick Lane and Fournier Street (previously a Huguenot church now a mosque), and a few yards from the magnificent Hawksmoor church, Christchurch Spitalfields – monumentally remembered in wonderful recent paintings by Leon Kossoff. *Bobba*, the Yiddish for grandma, is of course the Russian word *baba*, old woman. I always wondered what the origin of *zeida* – meaning grandfather – was. On my last visit to Jerusalem I asked my friend Dov Noy, himself the *zeida* of Jewish folklore studies at the Hebrew University, and he said it is a corruption of *dyadya*, the Russian word for uncle, which, one assumes, is etymologically linked to *dedushka*, grandfather. I believe Rosenberg was changed to Russell from Rosenberg in the late nineteen thirties because it was thought indigenous antisemitism could be a problem. Also, if the Germans invaded it might not be a good idea to have a 'Jewish' name. Later I discovered that names like Rosenberg were Jewish only in Poland. In Germany, as we know, it was otherwise. As I wrote earlier (3.B.2) Zeida Russell died, ironically enough given his theological views, the day the state of Israel was declared. A further irony is that my grandfather had been a young associate (and next-door neighbour in Princelet Street) of that towering rabbinical figure, Rav Kook, who served at the Machzike Hadath synagogue only because the Great War found him in London and he could not leave. After the war he became the first Chief Rabbi of Palestine – Kook was a great scholar, a Zionist, a mystic and a poet, and he blessed the socialists who worked on the *kibbutzim* because they too were participating in the redemption of the land (which counterpoints nicely the religious imagery of my dear old friend, the 'poet-roadbuilder in Israel', Avraham Shlonsky). Of all the cousins only I am old enough to have the joy of remembering Zeida Russell properly, although Ruth has one vague memory of him. He himself had the joy of knowing me and Ruth and cousin Lorna in London – far away from his hometown in Poland, Lomza, which I visited with my mother and Aunt Fanny many years later.]

2. I remember Grandma Russell sometimes stayed at our house. When she was very old and ill and thin, staying in the bedroom which overlooked the garden and which had been mine before the loft was built, she used a children's pot for a bowel movement and asked me to remove it to the toilet.

3. I remember after she died her body lay at Aunt Fanny's house in Sutton prior to the funeral. I heard them knocking the nails into the coffin lid. I stood up and closed the door so that people would not hear this final salvo. Someone, perhaps an uncle, said I had done the right thing.

[An early published poem of mine tells this episode, which affected me strongly. Bobba Russell's death was my first death truly experienced as loss and involving mourning for I knew her better than I knew her husband, who died when I was only five; and I knew her better than my paternal grandmother, partly because Grandma Rudolf died two years earlier than her and partly because Bobba Russell lived close by and was supported by the daughter who lived nearby, my mother – who quite often took the grandchildren to see her. My mother has told me that although very traditional, Grandma Russell was not as religious as my grandfather, indeed there had been Bundist (Yiddish Socialist) tendencies in parts of her family in Wassilkow, near Bialystok.]

4. I remember my father's parents, Joseph Rudolf and Fanny Rudolf née Flashtig, known to me as Zeida Rudolf and Bobba 'dolf. This Bobba was a large woman, unlike Bobba Russell who was like a little bird. Bobba 'dolf had a funny ear because a piercing had gone wrong. She wore black shoes over swollen feet and often wore a hat. She spoke excellent cockney English, unlike

my other three grandparents. Grandma and Grandpa Rudolf lived in Manse Road in Stoke Newington and I loved visiting them. The route taken by our small car involved zig-zagging through very short streets at right angles, past some prefabs. One day my father said I should look at the trams as it was the last day they would be on the roads. My grandparents' house had small rooms on several floors. In the basement there were piles of comics belonging to my Uncle Leon who was now a printer, but who had been a comics publisher until D. C. Thomson of Dundee drove him out of the business by coming the heavy with W. H. Smith about this potential rival. On the ground floor there were piles of army-surplus clothes, which was my Zeida's business, supported by his son-in-law Uncle Sid Warwick. I watched TV in Manse Road on one occasion, perhaps for the first time: the Arsenal–Liverpool Cup Final in 1950 when Reg Lewis scored both goals. My grandparents liked soup ('zup') and sometimes gave me sixpence. The phone number at forty something Manse Road was CLIssold something. Joseph tended to defer to Fanny.

[Odd that in the same paragraph there are two memories which could be precisely dated if I did the research. Odder still would be if they turned out to have happened on the same date, but I have a feeling the trams stopped never to go no more on a Sunday and that they survived later than 1950. Watching television on a Saturday afternoon in their house is proof incarnate, *glatt* (very) kosher proof, that this grandfather was not as *frum* as the other one, who did not allow anything to be switched on, including the light. I believe, indeed, that the Russells used a *Shabbos goy* in the years before time-switches lightened their lives. But it is not impossible my Rudolf grandparents asked their son to switch on the television for me – after all *they* were not interested in football and would not have been watching in my absence! I wonder if there is a touch of hindsight about the final sentence in the above paragraph, influenced a little by my mother's occasional musings about her parents-in-law. No, I do remember that my grandfather was decidedly less forceful than his wife. I wonder what Grandma Rudolf would have thought of the body piercings of her great-granddaughters, my daughter and my niece, which are not restricted to their earlobes. Her non-broken English was due to her being brought here at two and attending the famous Jews' Free School in Bell Lane during the late 1890s. I found her entry in the surviving admissions book at JFS in Camden Town. All the other grandparents arrived here as young adults.]

5. I remember an argument one evening during supper between my two grandmothers – about my mother's gefilte fish. At issue was whether the fish tasted too sweet or not.

[This is absolutely and delightfully classic. For gefilte fish read perhaps daughter(-in-law). For taste, read perhaps ability to look after. Quite apart from the socio-culinary implications – the relative sweetness of the fish was cognate with the region or country of origin and with a particular pronunciation of Yiddish and Hebrew, etc. (more on this in Claudia Roden's superb new book) – what Bobba 'dolf may have been saying to her opposite number was: your daughter is not up to scratch; my son deserves the best gefilte fish, the best wife. Which is not a million miles from the Yiddish proverb my mother quoted me today apropos something else entirely: 'A mother says to her daughter what she can't say to her daughter-in-law.' I don't think my mother minded all that much. Such tension between *mechutanistas* was normal. How could a daughter-in-law mind what was normal?]

6. I remember after Grandma Rudolf died, Zeida moved in with his daughter Renee in Hendon, where he lived for many years until he removed to Waverley Manor near Henly's Corner (as was), a home for old Jews. As suggested above, he and his wife spoke Hebrew and Yiddish with a different accent from my other grandparents, their *mechutanim*.

[This last (and its female form in 5 above) is a Hebrew word which has no equivalent in English kinship terminology, though it does have in certain 'primitive' tribes, as I discovered when I wrote to one of my former anthropology teachers, Edmund Leach, about it. It means, phrasally, son/daughter-in-law's parents, that is my two sets of grandparents in their relationship to each other: grandparents-in-law, to coin a phrase. Zeida Rudolf pronounced 'amen' *oomayn*, a pronounciation which would have been familiar to fellow-Galizianers Joseph Roth, Bruno Schulz, Henry Roth and Sigmund Freud – but this sentence is a lapse into the later world of my personal and literary interest in East Galicia.]

7. I remember writing to Grandfather Rudolf when I lived in Paris, and one postcard to each pair of uncles and aunts.

[Joseph Rudolf lived till 99¾, the only grandparent to live well into my adulthood, and thus provide my children with the privilege of knowing and remembering a loved great-grandfather. His grandfather, whom he remembered, was born in 1797, so there will have been attested unbroken contact from the eighteenth century into the twenty-second century, assuming, optimistically, I myself will have become a great-grandfather somewhere along the line. Gaston Bachelard tells us that he was told his grandfather got lost in a certain wood and he, Gaston, has not forgotten this. It happened before he was born and therefore his oldest memories are more than a hundred years old. I understand his play. I too feel I have introjected my grandfather's memories and have a responsibility to pass them on. My close relationship with him, my taped discussions, my visits to his home town, etc., have been touched on in other books and will be elaborated later in a long postponed book which raises opposite problems to those faced by Dan Jacobson in his masterpiece of a grandfather book. If love can ever be uncomplicated (even such a pure love), then my love for him was that. Posthumously it became an originative love, generating thought. What shall the thought generate?]

8. I remember Yiddish spoken between the grandparents and among various older Jewish people. My parents spoke it when they wanted me not to understand something (as in 'time he went to bed; get him upstairs', etc.). There were all kinds of jocular, rude or affectionate terms. Older men would pinch your cheek and say 'little *lobus*' as in: 'The boy stood on the burning deck, his mother called him a *lobus*, because he wouldn't wash his neck and go to *shull* on *Shobbos*.' Grandma Russell called me a *bundit*, a Polish or Russian Yiddish word for *lobus*. I remember cheerful words like *pippik* or *puppik* for waist-dimple, and *tochus* for hinderlings, and *loch in kop* (hole in the head) and *maven* (an expert). *Oy veh is mir*, of course. A very common expression was *knena horro* (a Yiddish version of the Hebrew *ken ayin hara*, may no evil eye be upon you . . .) There were lots of words for the boy's thingy, but none for the girl's – but if we had thought about it at all we would have thought you didn't need a word for what it would have not occurred to us not to think wasn't there.

[That last remark has a touch of hindsight about it, and ought to be in this parenthesis. We confused presence and visibility. The problem didn't apply to God of course. Let us change the subject, whether anatomy or theology, though the literary critic and scholar Murray Baumgarten told me at the barmitzvah at the Liberal Jewish Synagogue of Seth Sinclair, son of our mutual friends Clive and Fran Sinclair, to read a novel by Rebeccah Goldstein called *The Mind-Body Problem*, which touches on these problems. I remember the Welsh-born cousin-in-law of my father, Sid Pearlman, saying *knena horro* affectionately at a family wedding – on seeing a guest (not the bride) with large and presumably well-proportioned breasts. The phrase means 'how enchanting, may no evil eye . . . ', but leaving the rest unsaid. One Yiddish word I do not recall hearing as a child was *epikoiros*. This is one for connoisseurs and non-Yiddish-speaking readers must figure out how and why a Greek word ended up in Yiddish, and what it means. Fran Sinclair has died and so has Sid Pearlman. Finally, *maven* as in 'Hyam Maccoby' (see the Acknowledgments). Doubtless he was a *lobus* when he was a lad, but an *epikoiros* he isn't.]

9. I remember asking my parents why my Grandfather Rudolf and my Grandmother Russell didn't marry each other after they were widowed.

[The answer presumably has something to do with gefilte fish.]

(vi) Other Members of the Family

1. I remember my father's brothers and sister, and their spouses. I remember Uncle Isidore and Aunt Ethel (née Goldberg) who was Welsh, or rather Welsh-born (Swansea), and their only child, Michael. Uncle Isidore played the piano, although he could not read music. He told me he had played on a troopship, with his fingers bandaged, for two thousand soldiers off the coast of Africa while he was in the Royal Engineers during the war, a sapper. He talked about 'Monty'. Isidore used to play table tennis with me and took me a couple of times to football matches at the Arsenal. On one occasion Leslie Compton was standing behind us and I asked him for his autograph. After the match Uncle Isidore brought me home and we made a cup of tea while waiting for my parents to return. I wanted to warm up the teapot but he said that was rubbish, and I wanted to add 'one for the pot', and he said that was rubbish too. I was impressed and rather shocked because those were my parents' techniques, which I 'naturally' copied. We had a photo of him in army uniform looking like me. There was something wrong with one of his fingers. When he and his

brother Leon worked together as printers he was the one who stayed in the Sun Street office while Leon went off to visit customers or future customers with the van driver, whose name was Alan.

2. I remember my father's and Isidore's younger brother, Uncle Leon, and his wife Freda (née Berlin) and their daughters Angela and Marion. One of the comics he used to publish from his father's house in Manse Road, before devoting himself to printing, contained a character, Police Constable Tanner, 'so called because he was worth six coppers'. The back page carried advertisements for lucky charms and toby jugs and packets of stamps. One of his editors had been Bob Monkhouse. Leon showed me a letter he received from Billy Bunter's creator, Frank Richards, and lent me a large compendium of Bunter stories. Leon and Freda gave me a present when I went to Paris to study at the British Institute, a book by Leonard Bernstein. They had an infant son who died. Leon's eyesight was dreadful; I visited him in Moorfields where he had an operation for a detatched retina and had to lie on his back for weeks. It was one of the earliest operations of its kind in Britain.

[Leon died last week at 73. My father died at 71. Thus, in the end, Leon overtook him. Once in W. H. Smiths I saw Monkhouse's autobiography but mention came there none of his pre-celebrity career as an editor.]

3. I remember my father's sister Renee, and her husband Sid Warwick, and their children Ruth, Dennis and Alan. The surname, changed from 'Warsaw' or 'Varik' and oh so very English, gave rise to occasional misunderstandings. 'Are you the Warwicks of . . . ?' At family weddings Sid's party piece was to dance the *kazatzkah*. After a war spent partly in Africa – he amazed me by saying soldiers took salt tablets there – he worked with my grandfather in army surplus and second-hand clothes, at first from Manse Road and then from a shop in Bethnal Green Road. Sid had a large number of sisters, one of whom was married to my father's cousin, Mark Goodyer.

[Renee too has died, at the age of 70, leaving Isidore the sole survivor of the children of Joseph and Fanny Rudolf. November 28 1998: Isidore too has died.]

4. I remember my mother's older sister Fanny and her husband, Dr Jack (Simon), and their two daughters Lorna and Marion. They alone of the uncles

and aunts did not live in north-west London. Fanny was a schoolteacher, ending up as a deputy head. Jack, as a doctor and former army psychiatrist, believed strongly in the placebo effect and (? therefore) always smoked a pipe. He read a lot of books, including science, mathematics and philosophy and occasionally fiction – James Joyce and, in particular, the novelist my father was waiting till his retirement to read. We would visit their house in Banstead, Surrey, for tea, and go for walks on the common.

5. I remember the oldest of my mother's three brothers (the two sisters came first), Phil and his wife Simmy (née Gedalla) and their children Rosalind and Margaret. He was a useful tennis player. There were photographs of him in army uniform in Africa. Aunt Simmy's family and his own had lived in the same house in Hanbury Street in the East End. He married, in Palestine, not the girl next door but the girl from the same house. Phil wrote two pamphlets on careers, including one on flying. Like my father he was a *Times* crossword addict. Once at school I phoned him up because I had all but finished an *Observer* crossword and needed his help.

6. I remember the next brother of my mother, Stanley, his wife Freda (née Holomstock) and their children Norman and Sylvia, Martin and Alan. Stanley trained as an accountant in my father's office before moving on. They were married at Golders Green Synagogue in Dunstan Road. My sister Ruth was a bridesmaid, and my mother always kept a framed photograph of myself taken there. At one time they lived in Ossulton Way: my father and I would pass their house on the way to Sam the barber. Stanley told me he was in the glasshouse when he was in the army . . . teaching the men who had been sent there.

[Stanley died recently, the first of my mother's siblings or in-laws to join my father in Bushey. That photograph is still in my mother's kitchen, the look in the boy's eye increasingly mysterious as I get older.]

7. I remember my mother's youngest brother, Len, his wife Margaret (née Govinda) and daughters Valerie and Alison. He used to race me and win when I was young, which I found confusing. His surgery was in Harlesden; it had previously been run by a Dr Hastings Banda. Len was my sisters' and my own doctor for a while. He had been Michael Duschinsky's doctor before Michael

and I knew each other. I remember one evening waiting at a bus stop in Ealing on my way home after supper at their house, and reading Balzac in English.

[Why was I confused when he raced me and won? Not because he didn't let me win, I suspect, but because grown-ups especially relatives were supposed to be sedentary, unless they were professional athletes like Derek Ibbotson or Gordon Pirie or Christopher Chataway.]

8. I remember other relatives of the generation of my grandparents, including Becky and Issy Davis, who lived in Adelina Buildings, Adelina Grove in the East End (where I went to the barmitzvah party of Stanley or Dennis Davis) and Eva and Harry Zeissel who had a grocery shop off Hampstead Road. Harry's teeth rattled. Great-Aunt Sarah Jacobs had a golden-wedding party. Great-Uncle Jonas Rudolf lived in Colindale. Great-Uncle Harry Flashtig lived in Brighton with a favourite of mine, his wife Auntie Dora.

[All the relatives of that generation without exception were on my father's side of the family. The uncles and aunts and other relatives of my mother who left Poland before the war (those who didn't leave were, of course, murdered in Treblinka, Maidanek or Auschwitz – Belzec took care of various Rudolfs) all went to America, including my Grandfather Meyer's first cousin, Israel Rosenberg, a prominent orthodox rabbi, who was part of a commission which visited President Roosevelt in 1942 to discuss Nazi war crimes. To the best of my knowledge they were either religious or Bundists. Unlike members of my father's family in Eastern Europe, none of them were Zionists, so none went to Palestine before the war.]

9. I remember my father's cousin Zygfryd Rudolf who visited us from Los Angeles. He wanted to go to Bloom's immediately for his favourite delicacy: calf's foot jelly, what he called *pcha*. My parents told me that when Zygfryd lived in England during the war they had been the only members of the family who got on well with him. He had a stepdaughter, Ruth Olay, the jazz singer, who visited London (see 4.c.IV.ii.9).

[Zygfryd Rudolf – whose sister was one of the *chalutzim* (pioneers) who settled on *kibbutzim* in the *Yishuv* (pre-state Israel) – belongs in my future 'grandfather book'. He interests me a lot. Zygfryd had been a decorated soldier in World War I. He was a ladies' man as a batchelor and remained a handsome dandy – with a centre parting like an aristocrat in a Christian Schad painting – till the end. He eventually married the widow woman (as Grandfather Rudolf would have said) of a famous Hollywood Reform rabbi who had known Bertrand Russell. To say that Rudi did not get on well with the widow's daughter, Ruth Olay, would be an understatement. Let us put this down to mutual culture shock. Rudi had very strong opinions on everything from politics to art forgeries, from the strength of vaginal muscles (demonstrated with his fist) to choosing suicide if all else fails. He showed me his filing system when I visited him in 1975 – everything was in meticulous order and he implied he had a weapon hidden away in case he had to kill himself. Driving me to the airport he suggested a visit to 'the best brothel in Los Angeles' (by 1975 he was a widower and over 80). Thinking quickly, I declined on the grounds that I might miss my plane. To spare his feelings (doubtless the treat was on him) I didn't say that trips to brothels, even the best ones, formed no part of my life. (At that time Rudi was fond of my wife in an epistolary way and would ask her to send him things like a particular hairbrush obtainable only in Burlington Arcade). I suggested he make the visit on his return from the airport, which he thought was a good idea. My daughter was conceived shortly after I returned! I assume you can get calf's foot jelly in Los Angeles, so the Bloom's version must have been particularly good. Zygfryd's other step-daughter Mira sent me his possessions after he died (pre-World War I Omega fob-watch, still working, medals, piece of shrapnel, passports, certificates, etc.). Born a few years before Joseph Roth in the same part of the Austro-Hungarian Empire, dear Rudi belongs in a book inspired by any of Roth's great books. Rudi is *echt*-Roth. In this paragraph, at least, Franz-Josef rules OK.]

10. I remember my Grandmother Russell's excitement when her nephew Charlie visited from America, the first personal contact with her family across the Atlantic since she left Bialystok.

[Charlie Winnick, born in Wassilkow near Bialystok, became a subway engineer in New York. Zygfryd Rudolf born in Stanislawow, was a chemical engineer. He studied chemistry in Vienna and Brno and practised in Los Angeles. A few years senior to Charlie Winnick, Rudi was my first relative to enter secular higher education.]

(B)

FAMILY HOLIDAYS

1. I remember a day in Brighton. I was windswept and wore a green gaberdine raincoat tightly tied at the waist. I ate an ice-cream cornet. The ice-cream was cylinder-shaped, came wrapped in thin card, and was hard as a rock. The choice was Walls or Lyons, strawberry or vanilla, cornet or wafer, nothing else. The buses were yellow.

[I also remember a photograph of me on this holiday. I am not eating one of those dreadful ice-creams in the photo and I am a hundred per cent certain that my memory of the day (a day-trip or part of a holiday?) would be the same if the photograph did not exist. Or would it? Perhaps I saw the photo several times over the years following that holiday, and it has served as a prompt, a booster, a mediating category. Tightly tied belt: this image is redolent of photographic mediation. But, the green is a kosher memory. How can I prove this? Answer: *the photograph is black and white.* I suppose it still aided and abetted the memory of green over the years. As for the yellow buses: because they were different from my red London ones, they were *wrong*, inherently *contra naturam*.]

2. I remember another holiday in Brighton, when we visited Great-Aunt Dora, by then a widow. A man in our guest-house told me that my name, Anthony, meant 'sweet insect'. I shocked Dora by telling her I supported North Korea during the Korean War. I supported North Korea because I thought they, like the Third Division North in football, were the underdogs.

[On the other hand, North London was superior to South London. Third Division South and Third Division North vanished from the soccer scene long ago, as have the players' positions on the field. Is nothing sacred, etc.?]

3. I remember a holiday on a small farm in a Hampshire village called Adversein. My bedside book was Thor Heyerdahl's *Kon-Tiki Expedition*. My sister Ruth rode a horse on the farm. We went for walks down country lanes, among flowers and hedges and trees.

[Long after writing the above paragraph I remembered a photograph of Ruth on a horse. Another test case of memory retrieval: I no longer have the Heyerdahl book which means I well and truly remember things about the holiday not in the photo, and the order of memories suggests that the book triggered the horse, but since I saw the photo during the intervening years (perhaps most recently twenty years ago) there was definitely a booster effect. Perhaps too – here I have to speculate because my short-term memory is out to lunch and won't be back for some time – while writing my memories down unsystematically I remembered the book among other books and later decided to place it in the holiday section rather than Anthony's books' section (I.E). *Wehr veis?*]

4. I remember a family holiday at Noel (Knoll?) House in Dorset. This hotel had a pirate ship in the garden.

5. I remember a holiday in France at a hotel in Cabourg called Le Chat botté. We came home on a car ferry called the *Invicta*. It was a rainy evening and we were hungry on arrival in Dover, but parking was difficult so we drove on to Camden Town and stopped for fish and chips by the tube station. An enormous trunk was strapped to a luggage rack on top of the car, containing evening dresses and stuff.

6. I remember a holiday in Denmark at Hotel Trouville in Hornbaeck where we met 'Uncle' Victor, who taught us a two-pack game of patience called Spider and the phrase *yash menel shtoch*. Victor Blumenthal was not married and worked for an international Jewish charity called HIAS. For many years we exchanged Jewish New Year cards. In Copenhagen we met Paul Thorsen who was an Esperantist and had been a Communist, and whom my mother had met before the war in the Folk High School in Denmark. At the statue of the Little Mermaid we chatted with an American Olympic sprinter called Reg Pearmain who gave me his autograph. The Danish for many thanks is *manger tak*. We visited Hans Christian Andersen's town Odense and one day we took the ferry from Elsinore to another country, Sweden – score it up – returning the same evening. The ferry docked in a small town with the same name as Elsinore, but translated into Swedish!

7. I remember two holidays in Holland, one with Ruth in tow, the other with Mary as well. The owner of the hotel at Nordwijk on the Zuyder Zee was Mr

Tuppenbaeck, who chain-smoked. I saw him striding along the beach with a lady, perhaps Mrs Tuppenbaeck. On both holidays we stayed in the annexe. I had a toy gun and shot a butterfly by accident. I went into a small shop to buy an English newspaper for the cricket scores. On the beach we met a boy from Petersfield or Peterborough and, by chance, friends of my parents called Robin Salinger (a man with a foreign accent) and Billie (a woman soldier) who, I was told, were *very* close friends but not married. This struck me as odd: the same sort of age as my parents, obviously a couple and *not married*??? We visited Amsterdam and the Rijksmuseum. I loved the intensity of colour in the trees painted by Ruysdael.

[Many years later I visited Nordwijk during the rest day of an interfaith conference in Amsterdam which Lionel Blue had suggested I attend, and found the hotel in ruins. I am a little worried that I have forgotten the name of the hotel, because I knew it when I went to that conference. My memory is going? If not out for lunch, where? For a walk? I wrote a poem about the re-remembered butterfly and sent it to my then poetry publisher Michael Schmidt but he did not like it, unlike the poem about Provence mentioned in another section. Here too is another example of the possible prompt or mediating category. To go through every single memory in this book and trace its history would entail a writing of several thousand pages (unless I were to distil the result, to weave it into a novel: 'our life is woven wind', as Matthew Arnold translated a Joubert aphorism). The last sentence in the memory paragraph above while true possibly conflates the two holidays. This is only a problem if I say it is. Robin was an ex-Viennese rake, a stockbroker, a card.]

8. I remember a holiday in Italy, in Viareggio on the Adriatic, which came as a surprise because I had only heard of the Mediterranean. I went down every day to Bagno Pestrini which may have belonged to the hotel. The hotel itself was called Hotel de la Ville. I received letters from Susan Leveson. One lunch or dinner, when an English couple at the next table made a terrible fuss about the food, my father gently explained to them that really they should not have come to Italy if they were going to consider whatever it was to be a problem. Another guest, Hymie Gumbiner, and his wife owned a delicatessen shop in Old Compton Street. I met three girls on the beach, one of whom was very pretty and called Miniella Calabretta: she was from Rome; another was called Nadia,

whose entire address was Torno, Lake Como, Italy. I corresponded for a while with both of them. One day my parents and Ruth and I drove to Florence and Pisa. A watermelon gave me stomach-ache. We visited the Uffizi and the large synagogue, where my parents spoke Yiddish with someone.

[I now realise I *cannot* remember if Mary and Annie, who were very young, were there or if they had stayed in London with Kay. My guess is that if they had been there I would have remembered, therefore they weren't, but I am not so certain of this as to be allowed to write above: I remember that my little sisters stayed at home. This is another good example of a process which could be repeated at many points in this book. Jacques Roubaud's magnificent and beautiful *La Boucle* investigates these processes with such intelligence, subtlety and sophistication, and generates such a multifaceted content from the dialectic between complex structure and complex subject matter that he makes the reader imagine he is working as hard as the writer himself surely did. But the effort is worth it. Georges Perec in an interview cheerfully admits that his volume of 'I remembers' is 'stuffed with mistakes' . . . Finally, it can be inferred from 'Yiddish' that the man in the synagogue was a visitor and not the caretaker who, on the assumption he was non-Milanese Italian and therefore Sephardi, would not know Yiddish (though he might know Ladino): not knowing Yiddish is a subject of some signficance in Primo Levi's work.]

(C)

JEWISH PRACTICE

(i) Festivals and Occasions

1. I remember Friday nights. My mother would light the candles and make the blessing for *Shabbos* with her hands over her eyes. The two *challa* breads were on the table. I liked Friday nights. I knew it signified something important but I liked Sunday lunch too for the roast beef, which we never had on Friday night. Friday-night supper, like Sunday lunch, was always in the dining-room. We never went out on Friday night.

[The rule is that I do not discuss the matter with anyone else who was there, so all I can say is that I am as certain as I can be that my father did not make the blessing over bread or over wine until after the period covered by this book, partly under pressure from Mary and Annie who were more religious than Ruth and myself, partly because my parents became more traditional over the years (reciprocal transgenerational influence there, I suspect). But the blessing over the candles, that had always been done. Friday night, mother's moment, turned the week around. It was a Jewish pivot. There is no doubt that the felt rhythm of the year for me was Judaic. Diasporic Judaism is about time not about space (which has implications for Jewish attitudes to art I shall write about one day). Christian festivals were known, but irrelevant. 'As certain as I can be' still allows a modicum or scintilla of doubt and I like to think my decision not to write a linear autobiographical narrative – which would surely fail to problematise the process of memory, a pompous and even euphemistic way of saying it would evade or even lie – is vindicated.]

2. I remember New Year, when my mother would begin the meal by bringing to the table apples and honey and a pomegranate. We knew that the pomegranate was supposed to have 613 seeds – the number of commandments incumbent on a Jewish believer.

[Or 614 if you agree with the theologian Emil Fackenheim's view that Jews do not have the freedom to choose whether to stay Jewish: 'No posthumous victories for Hitler.' But posthumous victories for Hitler come in a variety of forms. Thus, the use (abuse) of the Holocaust to justify immoral behaviour towards the Palestinians (see various speeches by the former Prime Minister of

Israel, Menachem Begin, for example) also counts as a posthumous victory for Hitler, in my book anyway. The Netanyahu government is only in power in Israel because of the assassination of Yitzhak Rabin; Benyamin Netanyahu's failure to disassociate himself from the fanatics helped create the atmosphere in which political murder could take place. Rabin had finally and with difficulty come to understand that Israel will only be 'at ease in Zion' when the Palestinians have freedom and self-respect; the *sine qua non* for that is a viable Palestinian state. Despite the new, and undoubtedly unstable, agreement brokered by President Clinton, it is quite clear that Mr Netanyahu has not been converted to a Rabin-like understanding of the future shape of a land containing two peoples both of whom are in the right, that he has not broken with his Revisionist father's extremist ideology. I am pessimistic concerning the prospects for a secure peace.]

3. I remember *Chanukah* when uncles would give you *gelt*, a shilling or half a crown, the amounts differing perhaps relative to their incomes. We would say the prayers and sing the hymn *maoz tsur*. There was a joke English version: '*Maoz tsur, yeshuosi*, the cat's in the cupboard and he can't see me.' I liked the story of *Chanukah*, how we fought so bravely against the Greeks, the miracle of the oil, etc. We had *dreidls*, the little tops with Hebrew letters on. And of course we had a *menorah*, lighting the candles with the special servant candle. We ate *latkes*.

[Today young people often call the *menorah* the *chanukiyah*. I suppose this is a modern Israeli word. Strictly speaking the *menorah* was a seven-branched candelabra, whereas the *Chanukah* celebration requires eight candles plus the servant candle. The four Hebrew characters on the *dreidl* were the initial letters – NGHP – of the words meaning literally 'a great miracle was here' (*nes gadol haya po*). Given that historically *Chanukah* involved a battle against assimilation it is ironic that, by calendar accident, it has become associated with Christmas. Mind you, the calendar accident was very convenient for assimilationists and New York department-store proprietors, some of whom were the same people, not to mention Holywood moguls.]

4. I remember *Purim*, and eating *homentashen* (Haman's ears) at home but I didn't like this sweet pastry filled with poppy seeds. I remember my mother making fancy-dress costumes for the synagogue party.

[Marina Warner recently told me that she was writing a book on food shaped like parts of the human body, so I mentioned Haman's ears to her. A few days later I checked this out with my *maven* who referred me to Evelyn Rose's well-known cookery book. My memory appears to have confused two different dishes: *homentashen* is Haman's purses. Haman's ears or *hojuelos de Haman* are sugared fritters.]

5. I remember *Pesach*, Passover, at my Bobba and Zeida Russell's house. I watched my grandfather preside over the *seder*; he would lean to one side in the manner of free Romans rather than enslaved Jews; I was called on to say the *manishtanah*; everybody told the story of the Exodus; my uncles gave me wine and I would be carried upstairs slightly tipsy to fall asleep on or under the *paranneh* – the huge eiderdown brought over from her small town by my grandmother – which I called the 'lump'. There were exercise books in this bedroom but they were not like school ones even though they were about schools. At Passover we used my *bobba*'s washboard for a game called 'nuts', using cobnuts. At home my mother cleared the house of the usual crockery and cutlery and brought down the Passover equipment from the loft. She cooked coconut pyramids at this time.

['As a little bit of musk fills an entire house, so the least influence of Judaism overflows all of one's life. Oh, what a strong aroma that is!' (Osip Mandelstam). *Seder* nights at 45 Wessex Gardens have been (I remember remembering them over the years), are and always will be among the most powerful memories of my childhood: which was what the rabbis intended, who instituted the festival in ancient times. What an extraordinary and inspirational archetype the Exodus has proven to be over the centuries. One of several negro spirituals with Old Testament themes, 'Let my people go' applies to the Kurds, the Gypsies, the Palestinians and so on. No person on earth – all inscribed in the book of the generations of Adam – is truly free, until all are free: I do believe this but I am no longer as confident as I used to be that we will overcome some day. I wonder what else grandmother brought with her from Russia or Poland – the name depending on whether you are talking about her small town Wassilkow near Bialystok then or now. I shall make an educated guess: candlesticks, samovar and *ketubah*, the wedding certificate which proved not only that you were married but also Jewish. As for those exercise books, I was to find out that they belonged to Uncle Stanley who had trained as a teacher before switching to accountancy. I wish I had kept one as a souvenir . . . absurd! What child knows that one day he shall be fascinated to look upon a relic? A final thought on memory boosters: I'm not sure why I should feel that a memory is less authentic if there have been boosters over the years. What if it's the most memorable things one remembers in the first place and that such memories deserve and (therefore?) get boosters? What if there was some truth in that infuriating remark my parents used to make when I'd express frustration on forgetting something: 'Don't worry, if it's that important you'll remember.' Certainly the Passover *seder* nights presided over by Meyer Russell have never left me and never will. Which is not to say that all abiding memories have such a deep personal significance.]

6. I remember *Succoth* but we did not build our own *succah* (tabernacle), at the back of the house. Ephraim next door used to invite me into theirs, and of course my *shull* had its own.]

(ii) My Barmitzvah Party

1. I remember my barmitzvah party, which was held at home not in a hall and to which all the uncles and aunts and all the great-uncles and aunts and certain other relatives were invited, as well as a few close friends of my parents. The caterer brought in special tables and chairs.

2. I remember Mr Taylor, the Sunday-school headmaster, appointed himself toast master. He had asked me if I wanted help with my speech but my father said I should write it all by myself. Dayan Dr Lew and his wife came, which was a great honour. But they did not eat anything.

[Perhaps they arrived after the meal; or they made a rule of not eating in the houses of congregants just in case there was a problem of *kashrut*.]

3. I remember various toasts – to the Queen, to Israel, to me and to my parents. The next day I had a party for my own friends: the food included left-overs from the grown-ups' party.

4. I remember some of my presents. There were two watches and two fountain-pens. There was a chess-set from the Forrester family, and Danby's edition of

the *Mishna* from Mr Taylor with his visiting-card inserted. There was a second *Mishna* which I took back to a Jewish bookshop and which was accepted even though, for some reason, the jacket was missing. There were books from my uncle Leon Rudolf and family: the *Oxford English Dictionary*, which I am sitting on now because the chair in front of the word processor into which I am typing a draft is too low, the *Oxford Classical Dictionary* and a book of Latin texts with facing translations. My uncle Phil Russell and family gave me a large atlas and Stanley Russell and family gave me a globe which lit up. Uncle Jack and family gave me my first camera, and Uncle Isidore and family gave me a pair of binoculars with my name engraved on them. Auntie Renee and family gave me a Parker 51, and the Leon Russells an anglepoise lamp. Someone gave me a pair of *tefilin*, the phylacteries worn on the forehead and arm by Jewish males after their barmitzvah. Bobba Russell gave me two leather-bound prayerbooks, and Zeida Rudolf gave me a three-guinea watch. This watch was luminous, the only light I could bear in my bedroom after the main light was switched off. I loved my luminous watch. I was given a briefcase, my first briefcase. It replaced the leather satchel I wore over my shoulder. Most boys wore their satchels over the shoulder, whereas most girls wore them on their backs. I was confused by the minority preferences. Surely nature intended the differentiation.

[I still have most of the presents described above and elsewhere in this book. One can tell that the uncles' and aunts' gifts were co-ordinated. I *think* the bookseller who took back my second Danby was Chimen Abramsky (recently retired as Professor of Hebrew from University College London), except he worked at (owned?) Shapiro Valentine in Wentworth Street in the East End and I went, I'm sure, to Jack Mazin's shop in Berwick Street. Perhaps I have perpetrated that *déformation professionelle* of remembrancers: conflation, for I certainly visited both shops at some point. Great-Uncle Zygfryd Rudolf, whom you have already met, was very early in the century given a pair of *tefilin* by his grandfather – who asked him after a year if he had been wearing them. Yes. Let me have a look, said the grandfather, my great-grandfather. Opening them, the old man took out a note of the realm and pocketed it. I too have never worn mine . . . *After* writing this section I came upon by accident the barmitzvah menu and toast list which everybody signed for me. I took it with me to my Aunt Renee's house where they were sitting *shiva* for her brother, my Uncle

Leon. One of the people present was Sid Pearlman who, with his wife Sibyl, had signed the card nearly forty years ago. As I was about to leave for a conference at University College London, for some reason he asked me if I knew someone called Philip Davis? Yes, I said, what a coincidence, *he* told me about the conference. Well, said Sid, I'm his great-uncle. Philip has written two fine books germane to my thinking: one on memory and writing and another on the experience of reading, but this is by the by, or the other way round.]

(D)

SUBURB PEOPLE, MAINLY MIDDLEWAY

(i) My Friends and Acquaintances

1. I remember when you went to a party you took a present and you said thank you for having me, just as you promised your mother you would.

2. I remember one year my father saying we wouldn't invite local friends to my birthday party because I saw them regularly anyway. I thought this was strange, and it was difficult to *explain*, for example to Ronny Green who lived up and across the road.

   [It *was* strange. Ronny later settled in Israel.]

3. I remember my street friends, who were mostly different from my school friends and my synagogue friends. Peter Goodeve was the older brother of Anthony and always played with our gang. They had a dog called Magee, gentle and slow moving, who slowed down even more if you said 'on account'. I loved Magee. The Goodeves were Canadian. Peter's father was a Sir, Sir Charles Goodeve. My father said Sir Charles received his knighthood because he had played an important part in winning the war at sea. One summer they had a paddling-pool in the garden and I didn't have a pair of swimming trunks. Sir Charles said I should wear a pair of underpants instead, but I wouldn't. Peter knew a lot about science and was good at making things. He had a bicycle. He was old enough to be eligible for National Service but did not do it for long. Nevil Shute was a friend of the Goodeve family and signed my copy of *No Highway*: 'Nevil Shute Norway'. Lady Goodeve was a pianist. I showed her my book of Tom Lehrer songs: she thought the music was terribly basic. I often played my Tom Lehrer record, a ten-inch LP, which we bought at a record shop in Hampstead.

   [Peter must have been born not later than 1938 given that he did National Service, which means he was at least four years older than me.]

4. I remember Pete Fremus at 28 Thornton Way where I watched television occasionally before we had our own. There was a weekly programme involving pilots: 'Black Ace calling station B, Black Ace calling station B'. Pete was from

Czechoslovakia. At one birthday party we had the ice-cream first followed by sandwiches followed by soup. His mother said that was how they did things in Czechoslovakia. Pete lived across the road from Peter Morton, and near Paul Blakeley who lived in Erskine Hill. Another friend, William Brotherston, lived in Hampstead Way but they moved to the West Country.

['That was how they do things': a likely story! Was Pete's mother playing a trick on us? Or is my memory playing a trick on me?]

5. I remember Ephraim Eder, and his sister Annette, who lived next door. He had ginger hair. Had our houses been semi-detached our bedrooms would have been adjacent during the period I slept above the garage. In any case we could communicate easily across the divide. The Eders were more religious than us and you could hear them sing *zemirot*, Sabbath hymns, every Saturday after lunch. His parents had a relative in America who sent them the LP of *My Fair Lady*. We used to play tennis in the street. When my Grandma Rudolf died his mother came into our house and covered the mirrors – which my mother then uncovered. Their dining-room, like our lounge, gave onto the garden, and their dining-room table was covered with glass. My mother's word for them was 'continental'.

['Continental' was neither a compliment nor an insult. It meant 'more excitable and less stiff-upper-lip than us'. A partial gloss on this would read their Jewishness as being more 'high-profile'.]

6. I remember Peter Rosenheim across the road. He was deaf and dumb *and* had tunnel vision; it was therefore difficult to attract his attention. His mother was a war widow. She told me that Peter was not born deaf but lost his hearing during an air-raid. Mrs Rosenheim went out to work. Peter and I were good friends, and continued seeing each other in the holidays after he was sent to boarding school. He had a dog called Bobby, who was much more aggressive than Magee, three doors up the road. Peter's younger sister Jill lent me her girls' school stories.

[Peter and I kept in touch for many years. I was his best man. I invited him and his wife and son to lunch when we lived in Belsize Park. His wife too was deaf and dumb. The little boy was their mouth and ears. Deeply moved, we watched them walk down the street as they left, each holding one of his hands.]

7. I remember other friends in Middleway: Everard de Westenholz up the street and Joanna Graham (Grabo) down the street. Down the street too, there were the Turner brothers and the Grodzinski brothers, and Michael Silman who had an older and younger sister. The younger one, Diana, had huge dark eyes. They seemed to become even larger after her mother died.

[Sometimes you know something about people's later lives: Michael Silman, for example, married my cousin Marion Rudolf and Diana and I kissed each other on a couple of occasions. But, overall, this book is, in part, a nominal reunion party of people who briefly crossed paths in the geo-historical accident of destiny we call childhood.]

8. I remember Linda, an older girl who lived a few doors down the street, and the Mytton sisters who lived up the street, next door Anne and Stewart Duncan. Across the road, between the Goodeves and the Greens, lived the Winstanleys and the Cooks: their children were more friendly with my sister Ruth, being of an age.

(ii) Family Acquaintances and Other Grown-Ups

1. I remember Ernest and Margery Kay who lived in Middleway. Ernest was editor of the *Evening News* and a close friend of Harold Wilson, up the road in Southway.

[His paper no longer exists. It was swallowed up by the *Evening Standard*. One of the Beverley Sisters moved into his house.]

2. I remember an old lady who lived a few doors down the road on our side. The children in the street disliked her. We would ring on her doorbell and run away.

['Wronging the ancientry'.]

3. I remember Mr Flint in Brunner Close who was an optician and tested my eyesight for the first time.

4. I remember Tony Mandelson who lived in Southway near Harold Wilson and whose wife's father was Herbert Morrison.

[He was a very nice man and worked for the *Jewish Chronicle*. His son is called Peter.]

5. I remember Mr Fairston, known to one and all as Fairy. He lived on the other side of Market Place in Gurney Drive.

6. I remember old Mr Burnaby immediately across the road and his wife (or sister). He would look out of his upstairs window and stare for hours on end, like a character in a story. I never rang on their doorbell.

[It was safely scary, as in a book. I reckon he was pushing a hundred in 1950.]

7. I remember a black family with an unruly but friendly child called Eugene who lived in Middleway for a while in a house supplied by the council. My parents disapproved of the racial prejudice expressed by various people in the street.

[Many years later, when my father became a magistrate, the conventional establishment side of his nature – which wanted to trust the police completely and initially did trust them – came into conflict both with his strong liberalism when it came to racial matters and with his ability to weigh up evidence. The latter two outvoted the former by two to one, which meant he was often outvoted two to one by two other magistrates sitting with him. My sisters and I were patronisingly proud of him.]

(E)

POLITICS AND POLITICIANS

1. I remember the Labour Party. Much time and energy went into it. My parents went to Labour Party ward or constituency meetings regularly. I remember asking my father if he supported Nye Bevan or Hugh Gaitskell, expecting him to say Bevan, and he said if he had to choose between them he was basically a Bevanite but he liked Harold Wilson because Wilson's position was halfway between the two in political terms.

[The Labour Party I am talking about is the late lamented Old Labour Party, not the new version which stands to the right of Helmut Kohl and Jacques Chirac, and is proud of it *noch*. I expected my father to say Bevan for that was where the emotions lay. His view of Harold Wilson, long before Wilson became Leader of the Opposition and then Prime Minister, may have been or may have become fairly common in the Parliamentary Labour Party, and eventually contributed to Harold Wilson's victory over George Brown after Gaitskell died. Perhaps my father was the first Wilsonite. Labour MPs clearly thought Harold could unite the party and therefore had a better chance of defeating the Tories. I myself remember a Penguin special by Wilson in the sixties based, I'm fairly sure, on an essay he had earlier written for the *Encyclopaedia Britannica* Year Book. This essay made much sense to me. I remembered it later when the *Guardian*'s Hugo Young, whom one always reads carefully, made an uncharacteristically unfair attack on Wilson's integrity. We lived, perhaps inevitably, in a constituency which never returned a Labour MP, though the idea of community embodied in Hampstead Garden Suburb was a socialist vision derived from William Morris and other non-Marxist inputs into the grand old party. As far as I'm concerned, the jury is out on Tony Blair. Hitherto this paragraph was written before the 1997 General Election: henceforth my mother does live in a Labour constituency! Around a year later the jury is still out. For the life of me and with the best anti-Tory will in the world I cannot see how the values to which Tony Blair swears allegiance square with the free-market economics he also espouses, Anthony Giddens notwithstanding.]

2. I remember asking my father, after I was criticised at school by Robert Davies for attending CLS even though I was a socialist, how to justify my

public-school education. He replied that in order to change the system social-ists needed to avail themselves of the best of what was on offer now.

['Best' raises many issues deserving of a more detailed reply than I can give. The education debate continues within the Labour Party – only one Tory has had any worthwhile contribution to make in recent years, namely George Walden. The sub-text of my father's remark was that the state system was inferior and would improve – thanks to a Labour Party which would contain more and more educated socialists – to a point where no one would want to use the public schools. The deeper sub-text involved the optimism of what one would now call an Old Labour mind-set.]

3. I remember my father was strongly in favour of the mixed economy, redistribution, greater equality, a universal welfare state based on a strong and expanding NHS, and that the way to achieve all this was through planning and progressive taxation policies. (I remember my mother failing to persuade Michael Duschinsky that a mixed economy was a good thing.) My father always said that indirect taxation in the form of purchase tax was iniquitous because it affected everybody equally. He went further and expressed support for the toughest possible taxation on inherited wealth. He supported the great liber-tarian causes of the day. He said he wanted reform, even radical reform. Needless to say, he hated left-wing and right-wing tyranny equally. He refused to go to Spain until democracy arrived. He explained to me that there was something called the National Interest which transcended party differences even in peacetime and which mostly tended to express itself in foreign policy.

[He was, as I said, Old Labour, but was he a socialist? As Professor Joad said on *The Brains Trust*, it all depends what you mean by a cow. While I sense an emotional attachment to the aspirations of Nye Bevan, I now realise he was intellectually persuaded by John Kenneth Galbraith's critique of capitalism ('private affluence and public squalor') and more influenced intellectually by Tony Crosland's revisionist thinking than he admitted at the time. I am happy that he outlived the Caudillo and was able to visit post-Franco Spain with my mother for her seventieth birthday. No comment on the National Interest beyond saying that I didn't understand his argument then and I know now that it cannot be sustained.]

4. I remember my first big political cause: capital punishment. I studied the

arguments, I read Camus and Koestler and others, I discussed the subject with friends and with my parents. I remember executions, including those of Ruth Ellis and Derek Bentley, and feeling physically funny when someone was to be hanged. There would be photographs in the paper and reports about all aspects of the process, due or not. Lord Chief Justice Goddard would wear a black wig.

[The whole country felt 'physically funny'. A lot of people got a charge, including Lord Goddard. In his case, apparently, the charge involved a discharge, and a dishonourable discharge at that. Talk about little death. But there were more important reasons to abolish hanging than the Lord Chief Justice's extra pair of trousers – as reported by Bernard Levin some years after the LCJ died. I remember the phrase 'the condemned man ate a hearty breakfast' but I suspect it comes from books.]

5. I remember meeting the Labour MP, Sidney Silverman, on the boat the *Baltika* during the school visit to Russia. He was short and had a grey beard. He and his wife talked about their son. I said: 'You mean your grandson.' But he didn't.

[I was a dickhead even if the word didn't exist then, but I don't suppose he was all that offended. Later he was to be the moving force behind the bill to outlaw capital punishment in 1964.]

6. I remember that my father knew several Labour members of parliament apart from Harold Wilson, including Stephen Swingler and Ian Mikardo and Harold Davies, and that he had known Phil Piratin, the last Communist MP to sit at Westminster. My father said he would have liked to stand for parliament in 1945 but that my mother was strongly opposed to it. He had also wanted to become a barrister, but for financial reasons it had not been possible.

[My understanding of parental disagreements has changed over the years. As a father yourself, you father your father, and you become more humble. You realise that it was not necessarily a right/wrong situation; you realise that they and their friends and relatives negotiated their ways across and around the manifold circle of a long marriage (in their generation long marriages were the norm), with their own trade-offs, some explicit, some implicit, some unconscious.]

7. I remember YANKS GET OUT OF GUATEMALA, on the bridge in York Way near Agar Grove.

8. I remember the great issue of German rearmament and how we (Finchley Labour Party) were opposed to it. I remember my father telling me about the good old days when Hampstead Labour Party was disaffiliated from the national party because of its support for popular-front-type politics in Italy (Nenni, etc.).

9. I remember political discussions during my time in Paris, mainly about the situation in Algeria, but also about Israel.

10. I remember attending part of the first or second Aldermaston March.
    [In later years I worried my head a great deal about the nuclear issue.]

(F)
SLOGANS AND ADVERTISEMENTS

1. I remember 'Dubon, Dubonne, Dubonnet' and 'Idris when I's dry' and 'Tizer the Appetiser'.

2. I remember a Heinz campaign on the tube, listing all 57 varieties over a period of months.

3. I remember Brylcreem advertisements, especially Denis Compton my summer hero, looking very handsome.

4. I remember Woodbines and Craven A.

5. I remember on commercial television 'Murraymints, Murraymints, too-good-to-hurry mints', sung by Eccles of *Goon Show* fame.
   [Was this Spike Milligan himself, or an actor/singer mimicking the goofy lad?]

6. I remember 'Get Gibbs SR'.
   [I *think*, hence the parenthesis, this was the very first commercial on UK TV.]

7. I remember 'Hoarse? Go suck a Zube.'

8. I remember Mr Cube, the campaign by Tate and Lyle against sugar nationalisation.

9. I remember 'Snap, crackle and pop' and the joke about the illegitimate rice crispy, 'Snap, crackle and no pop'.

10. I remember 'Wot, no sun?'
    [A Peter Simple catchphrase.]

11 I remember Lobby Lud, the *Evening Standard* publicity campaign. On the promenade in Blackpool: 'You are Lobby Lud and I claim ten shillings . . . '

[. . . or five pounds or whatever it was. *Bring back the ten-shilling note. Bring back the old money. Bring back, oh bring back, oh bring back the money to me.*]

12. I remember my father saying that one of the characteristics of a profession was that you were not allowed to advertise, and a good thing too.
   [Those were the days, my friend . . .]

(G)
FOOD AND MEALS

1. I remember my favourite snack: fried *wurst*, fried egg and chips.

2. I remember my other favourite snack, Welsh rarebit, with mustard and salt and pepper and tomato added to the cheese, and a little flour. Lisa would then spread it on toast and grill it. Then we added Worcester Sauce. I loved the colours on the label of the Lea and Perrins bottle. I remember people argued if the word was rabbit or rarebit. The tomato made it come out in red spots.

[I love the taste of Worcester Sauce and even as I type I am going into the kitchen to have a spoonful. To this day Welsh rarebit is favourite, but I add beer, and an egg for thickening rather than flour. Not a politically correct dish, cholesterol-wise. Dairy was once supposed to be good for you.]

3. I remember Vesop.

[A trademark of course. It was used for making gravy. I wonder if the 'Ve' signalled vegetable?]

4. I remember HP Sauce and OK Sauce.

[But not tomato ketchup. HP sauce was OK by my father but not HP agreements. If you couldn't afford it, don't buy it, he always said.]

5. I remember small sponge cakes. I slit them in half and added Robertson's jam, which had a golliwog on the label. I liked two kinds of Swiss roll – jam and chocolate: I mean chocolate cream in regular sponge, *not* chocolate sponge itself.

6. I remember loving spinach and hating Brussels sprouts.

7. I remember occasionally having a kipper for breakfast which I liked, and smoked haddock which I didn't.

8. I remember Cox's orange pippins which rattled. How I loved apples, including the little hard ones from our garden.

[Cox's no longer rattle, no longer taste so good. The world is going to the dogs.]

9. I remember chicken fat, *schmaltz*, smeared on bread. Yummy.

10. I remember when we had chicken my father always asked who wanted the parson's nose, but only *he* did. When we had roast beef he would sharpen the carving knife. His first job was to cut off a small fatty 'corner' for me, smaller than a gob-stopper.

11 I remember chicken soup, known as Jewish penicillin, which was great, but not the *kneidlach*, dumplings, known as atom bombs, which went with it. Sometimes my mother added *farfel* and *mandels*. Those I liked.

12 I remember quarter-pint bottles of milk.
   [But these may only have been available in schools.]

13. I remember cherryade and R. White's lemonade.

14. I remember my mother's chocolate-cornflake cookies.

15. I remember peanuts, also known as monkey nuts, and 'Moses in his cradle'.

16. I remember Smiths crisps, and the salt wrapped in blue paper.

17. I remember eat up your food because children in Africa don't get enough. And eat the old fruit before the new fruit.
   [Sometimes you thought you would never get a piece of new fruit!]

18. I remember *heimishe* pickles, herring (chopped and unchopped), *latkes*, chopped liver.

19. I remember the smell of fried fish filling the house, and cold fried fish to break the fast after Yom Kippur.

[The other day I bought some cold fried fish at Tesco's – marked down by fifty per cent because the sell-by date had been reached. Claudia Roden tells the story of the nineteenth-century origins of the English national dish: Portuguese-Jewish style of fish combined with chips as sold in Irish potato shops.]

(H)

OUR HOUSE AND GARDEN

1. I remember my address: Middleway, Hampstead Garden Suburb, Finchley, Middlesex, London NW11, England, Great Britain, Europe, world, universe, space, more space. Later we would add SWALK on the back of envelopes (i.e. sealed with a loving kiss).

[Perec and Joyce had similar addresses. As for mine, I'm not sure if 'UK' figured there before 'Europe'. But what was to change? What will have changed? What remains to be changed? Well, the postcode is longer these days; Middlesex no longer exists except as a cricket team and a university; Europe was a geographical not a political concept; space travel was in the future where, of course, 'everything, Josephine, will be all right' – Johnnie Ray. But, but, my mother still lives in that house, which is plenty, more than enough. 'Engrafted in the tenderness of thought' (Wordsworth), my mental picture of this house and 'its' memories would be oh so different had my parents moved, say, after my junior sisters were born. Perhaps my lost youth is WALK-sealed in this book.]

2. I remember the house had a name on the gate, Corrie. I hated this name. It had always been there.

[Inherited from the only previous owner, Miss Stubbs, unless it was built with the name.]

3. I remember the garage with two ancient rusty bikes my parents no longer rode and some bits and pieces which had belonged to Miss Stubbs. Near the ceiling was the box my father opened if a fuse needed mending.

4. I remember my father's first car, a little grey Standard with two doors and running-boards, THX 844. There was a crank for starting it in winter. The next two cars were Vauxhalls. I was allowed to change gear occasionally. I learned to drive in my mother's car, a Morris Minor, known to us jokingly in Yiddish as Moishe Kleine. My first driving instructor was a drunkard. My father's car had the AA badge at the front. Some friends' fathers' cars had RAC badges on the front but my father explained that he preferred the AA because the RAC

operated mainly in the north. I loved it when the AA man on his bike saluted you on spotting your badge. I always saluted back.

[The car should perhaps come under 'parents' since my mother also drove it before she had her own car but in fact I thought of it as my father's car, because it was usually not there when he wasn't. Sometimes, however, he did take the bus and tube to work. The joke is quite a good one in the context of name changes: many a little Jewish Morris would have been Moishe in the old country, and 'minor' has a nicely inappropriate public-school connotation.]

5. I remember the coal cupboard where Charringtons coal was delivered. It was needed for our kitchen boiler and for the fire in our lounge. Other people called their lounge the sitting-room or drawing-room or front room. I loved the fire in winter, and would stare at it for quite long periods.

6. I remember our kitchen when it had a boiler. Above the kitchen door was a panel telling you which bell was ringing. Our kitchen table had an enamel top, fading at the edges. There was a larder which was quite cold, but it disappeared when the kitchen was expanded, as did the coal cupboard. I remember sitting at the table and watching with resentment while my baby sister Ruth was fed the flesh of the tomato – leaving me with the pips and skin.

[The tomato episode is the famous, obligatory, official, kosher, earliest conscious memory or at least the one I have elected to be the earliest. I believe it *really* happened because the details are not the sort to have been handed down as a family story by the parents. Presumably there was a tomato shortage or a baby-food shortage – this must have happened in early 1946, a few months after the end of the war (Ruth was born in September 1945). Over the years I have often tried – unsuccessfully – to dig out an earlier memory, for two reasons: the first is patriotic: if I could remember the war it would be as though I had taken part in it. The second is competitive: I would possess a memory before the age of three which only a few people have or claim they have (thus Ruth and our grandfather). But note: I am talking about remembered memories. A subject rarely addressed is that of forgotten memories. Who knows, maybe when I was five or six I could remember things that happened when I was two but by now I have forgotten those memories. So, the correct description of the tomato story is: my earliest remembered memory. No! My remembered earliest memory. It is extraordinarily vivid. Is it possible not to have a vivid first memory? Is it possible not to have a first memory? Sad time stretches before and after, and a million forgotten memories dance unseen around my life – lost souls born unto death, appetent for redemption.]

7. I remember the downstairs toilet with a large wooden seat.

8. I remember the hall cupboard where we kept our coats. On the shelf we kept the blue-and-white Jewish National Fund Collection Box.

9. I remember the dining-room which was at the front of the house, where we ate meals on Friday night and at Sunday lunchtime. We had a green-fabric suite of armchairs, divan, pouffe and dining-room chairs, and a sideboard which matched the shelves around the divan. I remember being told that I had slept in one of the sideboard drawers under the stairs when there was an air-raid. The 'canteen' was kept in one of the drawers. It contained our best knives, forks and spoons. They lay there on velvet cloth, smooth to the touch like my mother's nylon stockings. The dining-room and lounge had separating doors. There was a bell push in the dining-room and in the lounge, and a soda syphon on the sideboard. I loved the 'bomb' which produced the sparkle for the water.
   ['Pouffe' is a charming word.]

10. I remember the lounge gave onto our garden with its rockery where we grew mint, and the apple tree which I shook for the small hard sharp-tasting green windfalls and which I climbed and sat in, and the lawn whose grass I cut with a manual lawnwmower with its basket on the end, and the hollow hedge right at the end where you could hide and, at least once, drop your pants and knickers and show each other the different bits. We had fireworks parties in the garden. Catherine wheels were boring. Rockets were the best. There was no hedge between our house and the Eder house next door. For some years we had a very tall and very old gardener, much cherished and respected by my mother, who would bring him a cup of tea. There was a baby grand piano in the lounge which apart from children practising was played on only by my Uncle Isidore, a saloon-bar pianist. My father kept his small collection of netsukes on the mantelpiece.

[I don't think the 'different bits' were considered rude, merely mechanical (ah, the innocent paradise of secret pleasures). Well then, who were you, own up; I can't remember but I am fairly sure there were two girls, my sister Ruth was one, and another boy. Own up, and you get a prize (no, not a commemorative peepshow in the hollow hedge). I have to confess that the detail of the basket on the lawnmower was triggered by mowing a friend's lawn the other morning. Technically the rule is that I remember or try to remember in an unmediated way, introspectively. But the rule, while a good discipline designed to prevent me foraging around for documentation or talking to family *mavens*, must not and cannot prevent outer stimuli from affecting me. After all, the outside world, the visible world, does exist or I'm a double Dutchman – a joke phrase of one of my honorary uncles. If I am told that the netsuke collection began later than summer 1961 my *terminus ad quem*, then my memory is temporally inaccurate, but not for that reason wrong *as such*. A memory is a memory, as Perec insists in *Je me souviens*. The lounge fire which I loved has already been mentioned in an earlier paragraph, triggered by a memory of the coal cupboard.]

11. I remember the upstairs bedrooms. Only my parents never changed their room. I slept in different rooms at different times. I liked best the bedroom giving onto the garden, with the string above the bed for switching the light on and off: I would push the string in the dark and let it swing back and hit the wall, then time my next push as perfectly as I could. I had an electric fire with a single bar. The fireplace was not used. Another bedroom, over the garage, had a little window, a mini-window, one pane, which opened. I remember sliding down the banisters.

12. I remember the Globe Wernicke bookcases around the house.
[These are rather beautiful. They do furnish a room, but they take up a lot of space. They presuppose a house not a flat, hardbacks not paperbacks. All the same I have one of them in my flat now, with plenty of paperbacks in it. Professor F. George Steiner (Oxford, Geneva and Edinburgh Festival) has written eloquently about reading and space.]

13. I remember in front of the house, at the end of the garage drive, Ruth and I and local friends would set up a stall and sell things to raise money for the

RSPCA, which was our pet charity. Our stock included bric-à-brac, c[...] cards, stamps, home-made ice-lollies, books, etc. Almost everybody [...] something. One who didn't was the ginger-haired woman who lived at the top of Middleway. She rejected us, we despised her.

[This paragraph presents an interesting taxonomical problem because it could be inserted in several places, and it is not alone in that of course. Where the event under description finds itself in the text does matter; what is not said by accident or design also matters. And the structure matters because, to adapt a phrase of Claude Lanzmann, the maker of one of the greatest works of our age, each fact contains the whole as well as being a selection from an enormous number of them. A constructed work is, in his phrase, 'a fiction of reality'.]

14. I remember when we received permission to convert the attic into two bedrooms and a playroom. We needed the space because we had acquired two new members of the family, my junior sisters, Mary and Annie. This was the first loft-conversion in the Suburb, and people came round to have a look. I moved into the attic: I had a fitted desk. In the playroom there was a large gramophone/tape-recorder/radio all in one, supposedly the first such triple centre. On one shelf there was a bound set of the the *New Statesman* dating from the 1930s. I enjoyed reading this, not least the advertisements. My father tried to keep all his theatre programmes. We had drawers full of photographs which I went through regularly. I loved looking at the men in plus-fours on youth-hostelling rambles, and my mother and her friends as flappers.

[It was typical of my father to resist buying a modern record-player for longer than most people, and then go over the top and buy a three-in-one monster. I remember other things in that loft which I am not including because 'at the end of the day' you can't include everything.]

15. I remember the pre-conversion attic which was reached by ladder, and above that the roof, and the excitement it engendered. I remember imagining the vertigo.

Afterword

Between the sentences of remembrance . . .

ELIAS CANETTI

1. I had been working on what I hoped was the final draft of my first novel. I wanted and needed it to lie fallow while I caught up with unfinished business elsewhere. Nor was I in a proper frame of mind to make a decision concerning a possible second novel: one look at my convoluted and illegible notes boosted my mental and emotional unreadiness. To kick-start a second volume would take months. But catching up with unfinished business was, fortunately, not a full-time job; there was time and space for other work. I had just finished reading Georges Perec's small book of 1978, *Je me souviens* ('I Remember'). Suddenly I knew what I could do, indeed, had to do. This would also solve the problem of what to offer my mother for her eightieth birthday. Such prompts from one's reading are often triggered by existing preoccupations. You are ready to be prompted. The device for generating memories which Perec used and which inspired me is one that he himself tells us was inspired by Joe Brainard's fascinating sequence *I Remember* (1975), which I was not able to get hold of until after I had made the first draft of my book. Perec too begins each numbered memory, 479 of them, with the refrain *I remember* . . . . They are personal memories but not of his feelings or attitudes or even behaviour. They are plucked from what was, in the writing, to become a quasi-mythic territory embodying aspects of the social world he experienced between his tenth and twenty-fifth years (1946–1961): names of best-selling novels, names of politicians, slogans, brief allusions to scandals, sports heroes, radio programmes, etc. If some of them are 'objectively wrong', he tells us, it does not matter.

206

2. Coincidentally my own book covers the same period as Perec's – from my first memory in early 1946 till summer 1961 – but in my case the age-span covered is from three and a half till nearly nineteen. And I am doing something different, something more structurally complex than Perec's least complex book, something which brings my book a little closer to his friend Jacques Roubaud's orchestrated and deeply *processed* archaeology of memory, *La Boucle* (1993). I would not be so immodest or stupid as to suggest that if you crossed these two marvellous French texts – at opposite poles of the writerly spectrum – you would end up with my book. Let us say that I have taken my bearings from both writers and ended up, for better or for worse, with something of my own.

3. I started writing my memories in a notebook I was carrying around with me everywhere. My shoulder-bag contained – in addition to the usual bric-à-brac – the two books mentioned earlier: *Je me souviens* and *La Boucle*, the former as a talisman, the latter to dip into and generate meditation, both books *bons à penser*, as Lévi-Strauss wrote of totems, good to think with. Unlike Perec's, my own memories, after the initial outpouring, began falling into categories and sub-categories: 'rememberable things' (in Wordsworth's phrase), generated each other, triggered each other 'by chance collisions and quaint accidents'. But I want to emphasise that I did not start with the book's taxonomy as tabulated on the contents page. On the contrary, the taxonomy arose out of the memories. After the two phases just mentioned, I willed myself to remember, to fill some of the many gaps (Wordsworth's 'days/disown'd by memory'), apparent or not, on my continuum, a continuum which covers around five and a half thousand days. Involuntary memory? Voluntary memory? Perhaps this opposition simplifies the phenomenology of anamnesis.

4. Carefully caught regrets and other explicit emotions are reserved for the parenthetical commentary, along with analysis, speculation and what Roubaud calls 'fictive deductions', though hardly at all what he calls elsewhere 'narrative deductions'. Let us not forget that the matrix, the seedbed, of the rest of one's life, of one's future adulthood, covers the mere five and a half thousand days mentioned previously, if the period is defined as beginning with one's first memory and ending just before departure for university. Again

unlike Perec, I am trying, by means of the juxtaposition between the emanatory memories and the conscious commentary, to establish my identity in terms of space and time, by offering for inspection various areas of my life as a boy, as a suburban Jewish schoolboy. I suppose I have tried to write the geography and history of my kingdom. I hope the reader will find this book an interestingly structured and carefully ordered taxonomy of things, persons, places and behaviours seen again, re-presented.

5. The sections and sub-sections of the book are analytical in the quotidian meaning of the word. Yoked together as a book, they form a kind of synthesis, with the connecting bits left out, albeit touched on in this afterword. The total picture can be found in the table of contents, though this bears as much relationship to the reality on the ground as the London Underground map does to London; the same might be said of Walter Benjamin's unwritten bio-graph of Berlin and lost (what would we give . . .) bio-graph of Paris, to coin a word he himself nearly coins in his superb *A Berlin Chronicle* (1932). The Themes/Motifs section of my book interacts structurally and conceptually with the framework adumbrated in the table of contents. Drawing both on the commentaries [found in square brackets] and on the texts, it amounts to a second set of contents (? discontents).

6. By now it will be obvious that I am emphatically not in the business of writing a traditional autobiography. Above all I am not concerned to tell an inner narrative of awakening or development or phantasy such as therapeutic and/or introspective hindsight can yield. I believe in the possibility of such a narrative but it does not belong here and would have to be constructed along different lines, most likely in the form of a novel (as Walter Benjamin well understood), a project whose realisation would have to embody the 'infinite dispositions and possibilities' (if I may quote a text I wrote years ago) of childhood, its deep content and meaning rather than its forms and structures. Meanwhile, if readers want to understand the pattern in the carpet, the only solution is to turn it upside down. As Ben-Bag Bag says of the *Torah* in the *Ethics of the Fathers*, one of my favourite post-biblical pre-modern works of Jewish literature, 'turn it over again, and contemplate it, and wax grey and old over it', or is that Joyce instructing us to read *Finnegans Wake*? I am trying to tell you that

unintended meanings are floating around this text, looking for an interpreter. Furthermore, my forgotten memories, lost souls, are entitled to a mention, unremarked beneath the visiting moon – for Mnemosyne herself sometimes bathes in Lethe – so I mention them again, a second time: are they still there, he said? This he, boat against the current, borne back ceaselessly into the past.

7. Walter Benjamin writes: ' . . . indispensable is the cautious probing of the spade in the dark loam, and it is to cheat oneself of the richest prize to preserve as a record merely the inventory of one's discoveries, and not this dark joy of the place of the finding itself. Fruitless searching is as much a part of this as succeeding, and consequently remembrance must not proceed in the manner of a narrative.' Childhood is an image, a collection of images, a construction, a fiction of reality – before we even start to write it down. The writing of it yields a metafiction, a fable, perhaps a fetish. The holes in memory cannot be plugged – which is good. They allow the swimmer, the digger, to breath, to move around, to *see* that his re-creation is good. If Mandelstam was right to say that 'memory loves to go hunting in the dark', nevertheless 'light shines best in darkness' (Meister Eckhardt).

8. This book of lived childhood is an offering, a keepsake, a family album. I am concerned to *show*. There is no overt agenda of enchantment, no covert agenda of disenchantment. Even in extreme cases of desperate hurt or unalloyed happiness the inner narrative of family life never entirely coincides with or totally disconnects from the outer. Most people find themselves somewhere on the spectrum between the two extremes and can make, if they wish, the imaginative leap involved in looking back upon their kingdom. Sometimes omens can be found, but I am not talking about second sight, which we are surely grateful we lack, just trying to avoid double vision!

9. If all parents get it wrong sometimes, as they do, as yours did, as mine did, as I have done in my life as a father, most of them did not do it on purpose, and most of them even got some things right. If we do not find an accommodation with living parents in our mid-life, if we cannot bring ourselves to reconcile our inner and outer narratives, or depth and surface narratives, our true and false selves, we could be eaten away for the rest of our lives. This book tells my

'remembrances of days foregone' (Shakespeare), my memories of things past – to adapt a phrase of the bard which has become very famous in this century – as truthfully as the rule or, rather, principle permits, namely no recourse to documents or to other people. But I am keenly aware that the very process of writing, the very writing of process, shapes, not distorts, the things I remember, 'all/the past lapping them like a/cloak of chaos', as that lord of utterance, Thom Gunn, writes in his beautiful poem on past makers, 'My Sad Captains'.

10. Many of the recollections undoubtedly represent, elide, conflate, hundreds of similar ones, and many more, some of them certainly quite important, have slipped through the net or been missed by the spade, for ever. Regret at the inevitability of selection, due in part to the ageing process in brain and mind (conscious and unconscious), is another way of acknowledging that the total recovery of the past on the page is necessarily doomed to failure. But if I was obsessive enough to want to list *everything* I would of course be in the position of Borges' College of Cartographers in *Dreamtigers* whose 'map of the Empire . . . had the size of the Empire itself', and end up listing nothing – as well as listing heavily, like a fishing-boat in a storm.

11. The recollections are virtually never dated, for the same reason that the text is not continuous: linear narrative would impose a straitjacket on the body of the work, a body where the dimensions of time and space, as they intersect in the mind of a fifty-something year old with all the usual baggage in his hump, merge in the womb of writing to yield tropisms, epiphanies, probes, presences, soundings, discrete series. 'They remind me, distant now.' (Gunn's sad captains again). I hope they will remind you. I hope the publisher will eventually authorise a second edition with a postscript which could incorporate the reactions of people named in the book (or, for that matter, anybody else) whose different takes on what is described demands that they write to me or, in a rather appropriate phrase, make representations. I could add information from the documentation I have not consulted. Perhaps blank pages could be included, as in Perec's book, for people to add their own series of *I Remember*. Let none of us be deterred by the conclusion of Robert Lowell's marvellous poem on Hawthorne, whose 'disturbed eyes rise,/furtive, foiled, dissatisfied/from meditation on the true/and insignificant'.

12. I have learned something from writing what I call above 'the geography and history of my kingdom': namely that my identity (apparently immutable during the book's time-span), or the sense of self which (dis)integrates all one's sub-personalities, involved the experience of sacred space and mythic time. I have discovered that for me these could only be delineated in a discontinuous form, juxtaposing self-sufficient memories: only in between the memories, out of sight like an underground river, does the lived time of childhood continue to flow: thus it is not-written. I think I have become honest enough with myself to admit that 'the usual baggage in his hump' contains compartments from the unconscious known as hidden agendas, unacknowledged traumas, ignorant armies clashing by night, etc., but those are the business of other books, other encounters, other scripts. If 'I' emerges – to choose three epithets at random – as competitive or narcissistic or goody-goody, then 1) so be it, 2) so what? For I am concerned with forms and structures rather than with their subjective correlatives. Of course I am 'only human': sometimes in the commentary I slip in a suggestion, a manipulation, the simple loop becomes a Moebius strip, completely by accident of course: *Honi soit qui mal y pense*. Occasionally sentences which should be in the commentary end up in the memory paragraphs themselves, and the other way round. But I try to abide by the rule: *'it' had to be remembered. Where there was mediation (documentary or personal), own up.*

13. Into which sub-section 'it' fits might sometimes be problematic: taxonomy as practised in a work is an art not a science, and remains philosophically problematic, though possibly only for philosophers. Where I notice a problem I say so. One cannot will things to cohere ('we have too many things and not enough forms', writes Flaubert, quoted by Derrida). Coherence only happens, or appears to happen, in treatises, novels, autobiographies. I think it is interesting that some of the memories, unlike an exasperated parent, turn up in two (sometimes more) places at once. Many more, if not all of them, interrelate or could be made to interrelate but I have abandoned a complex system of hyper-textual cross-referencing, such as Roubaud might have attempted.

14. I am supposed to be an adult now. The longer we live the more our actions

are endowed with consequences – and we have to assume responsibility – for other people. Growing up involves learning about this. Good parents, even 'good enough' parents, first seek to mitigate; if that does not fit the circumstances, then they must do their best to educate their offspring about the consequences of actions, including words. One aspect of morality consists in knowing the difference between what is *other* and what is *wrong*. But it's not just a question of 'us' and 'them', or even of 'them' being other rather than wrong. Categories overlap. Concentric circles overlap, as it were. Community is a complex idea, not the less important for being fashionable in centrist political circles. We is now we, now I and I. An I for a thou.

15. I don't know, perhaps at my age I am feeling fragile – in the last year three friends only a few years older than myself have died – and consequently I want to firm up my foundations for the building which must be repaired, so it may continue to be a safe house where my grown-up children can touch base when they want, for the loved friends whom I neglect because I have been trying to write books on the margins of a salaried job, for the books themselves, for my secondary activities (such as translation and publishing), for my mother and sisters and their families, for politics (the building of a safe house to contain all the individual safe houses), and for other commitments. I need to develop a greater awareness of the beauty of the threatened world outside, as well as of the beauty the safe house itself can generate: beauty which consoles and which makes one happy sometimes, beauty whose time is idealised by one possible escape from words, namely music, and whose space is idealised by another possible escape from words, namely paintings. But for my unreconstructed house to remain standing I have had to recover in the form – however fragmented – of an outer telling as many of my remembered experiences as I could, in order that the eventual inner telling of my experienced memories shall make more sense as I dig deeper into what I may sometimes want to forget.

16. Nobody returns to childhood in total innocence. If you could you would still be a child and your real childhood innocence, in the sense I have implied earlier, would be devalued. I have tried to taste and see and, indeed, use all my senses to accomplish the job of work I set myself, so that the unavoidable

212

power and counterweight of words, my own and other people's, could be drawn on safely as resource, rather than drag me down in a quicksand of received opinion, doctrine or image. Jacques Roubaud's great book has now become a source of reverie, though all non-utilitarian reading involves reverie to some extent. What matters is that Roubaud's work, like Perec's, is *there*. The presence of these two books in my hump and in my literal shoulder-bag, forces me to test my approach – more elaborate and elaborated than *Je me souviens* and, *au contraire*, less elaborate and elaborated than *La Boucle*. The two French books interrogate each other to good effect, just as their authors must have done 'in real life'. And in the three or four months since I wrote down the first of these memories, the two books have been interrogating me and my book – whether on the unspeakable Northern Line or in the now defunct Squires Lane Baths or waiting for a delayed friend in the then unreconstructed Lord Palmerston pub. I who have spent so much time trying to make sense of other people's memories, and other people's memories of other people, had best make the best possible sense of my own, even the embarrassing ones. And so, given that one cannot unlearn one's reading of the literature of memory even if one wanted to, I have gone to school with Perec and Roubaud and others – for whom Walter Benjamin shall stand as the supreme exemplar.

17. Memory, I have learned, does not reconstitute itself in a linear way. Why should it? Biological time may be linear. That's boring, a do-it-yourself zero-sum game. But the experience of life, the life of experience, is anything but. And so is the remembering, or in its commemorative intensity the remembrancing. Besides, disjunction is built in, otherwise by analogy it would be sensible to translate Racine or Ronsard into the English of their own day. This would not work, although – to pursue the analogy – one might aspire to a rule that the translator's *lexicon* be restricted to the appropriate quondam English. Figuratively speaking, one must try to remember in a *lexically* appropriate way, and non-judgmentally, what and how the child saw, penny plain and *as if* innocent of adult modes of self-knowledge, and unmediated by one's favourite village explainers (Norman O. Brown, Charles Péguy, the prose Rilke, etc.), reserving the twopenny coloured stuff for the parenthetical commentary: the use of language should befit my present station, not all that far from the two stops on the Northern Line my junior self hesitated between: to be an East

Finchley boy was *very* different from being a Golders Green boy. As you know (see 4.A.2), I tried both.

18. What then is this or any grown child up to when writing – which is the most intense version of reading – his lived experience? One description would be: he is translating the child and youth he once was (and the child's and youth's self-tellings) into a language appropriate to his own station in life, that is: a grown child, also known as a grown-up. In this language you learn to make sense of the accidents of your geo-historical destiny because the kingdom of childhood, with its sacred space and mythic time (both irreparable as gestalts), have been internalised, even as the once and future conflation (nature and culture) are separated out (see 4.A.3 and 4.C.iv.I.3). Without such a transla-tion or transformation you will invade the space and time of your loved ones, with dire consequences for all of you. A grown-up is, or rather, should be, focused and centred in his or her aloneness, his or her mortality, his or her individuation, and secure in this self-knowledge, reach out to others, to thou and thou and thou, and be reached out to in return. It is true that children too are lonely, 'lonely as a cloud' or 'as mirrors are lonely', but for long periods the loneliness forgets itself in tasks and consolations which counter rather than reinforce the loneliness: the necessary and the contingent are conflated. Like grown-ups indeed. But the children will be grown up one day. And that makes all the difference, for they have miles to go before they sleep. Before they sleep.

19). Memory often involves seeing (Jacques Roubaud plays on the words *voir/ savoir*) and seeing is said to be believing. When I say in the commentaries, as I sometimes do, that I only *think* I remember something or I *know* it happened but I can't actually *remember* it, what I mean is I have not been able to summon it up on line, whether visual or aural: digging the [cool web]site of memory sometimes yields nothing. How could some important memories have failed to make their presence known to the archaeologist in the employ of his own personal heritage department? No matter! By definition, no matter. As for the league table or hit parade or class list of unearthed, that is, *earthed* memories, readers can infer what they like. Despite Joubert's proper warning to those who would be memorious – 'A man should not express himself as he feels, but as he remembers' – one's obligation is to *think memory*, to *feel memory* (in the commentaries and texts respectively). The writer's job as a gardener is to stop the watch for the brief encounter with time and replant his memory in the proper place, 'winnowed from failures' and rerooted or rerouted with their own 'disinterested hard energy', to quote and quote again from Gunn's exemplary poem. Memory, like tradition, shall be remade, to the best of one's ability ('I cannot resilver the smudged plate', Lowell again in 'Hawthorne'). 'Between the sentences of remembrance,' wrote Canetti, 'the neglected life makes itself felt and you find yourself richer by all that you've lost.' Oh, marvellous tremor of time . . . Oh, Jerusalem . . .

20. During the time this book has taken to compose, I have sometimes felt I was living a waking dream – for remembering and predicting are to awakenness what dreaming is to sleep ('It's memories that I'm stealing,' sings Tom Waits, 'But you're innocent when you dream'). If we could map our life in some way, might it not resemble a musical score? I think of my own coalition of sub-personalities, now the son, now the father, now the lover, now the salaried worker, now the writer, now the Londoner, now the friend, now 'the ticket man at Fulham Broadway Station'. However, even though these sub-personalities could be said to move horizontally, in a linear way, and could be represented along parallel lines like musical instruments in a score, in fact they interact with each other, as it were vertically, like the instruments working together during an actual orchestral performance, all the time by 'virtue' of the mind's workings, of memory and prediction, of the unpredictability of third parties, of contingency and of coincidence. Horizontal *and* vertical images are there for the taking. (After writing this I came across a passage in Charles Reznikoff's letters where he describes poetry as vertical and prose as horizontal.)

21. Needless to say, by telling the story of people I have not seen for years I could be bringing an eternally forgotten past on their part into an unexpected present. Take for instance the memory of the clammy armpit (3.E.ii.5). The episode happened but it certainly did not exist for the girl as a signifying truth: after all, it was her body touched by my mind. But the episode, like the one about the nappy (4.C.ii.I.3), now helps to explain something I was not aware of when I followed my earliest instinct that this book should end in the summer before I went to university: those episodes hint a latency, and hence a future, a

no-going-back, whose beginnings were to be found or will be found in the Cambridge years. I am talking about two discoveries I was to make in Cambridge, a city I love and hate: sexuality, the expression or awareness of sex outside the unconscious mind; and writing, the reconfiguration of past inner experience in order to make sense of present inner experience with the inevitable result that you reconfigure future inner experience: a tense experience, you might say. For surely in the entirety of my text as written we find the signs and wonders of *virginal* love, its purity, its power, and its unconscious terrors. For clammy armpit read, perhaps, another clammy place, desired and feared, and once achieved, never glad confident morning again. (The concept of latency explains why this reading does not contradict my repeated and truthful statement that I had no sexual anguish during the period covered by this book.) For virginal love, read virginal life, a life unencumbered by the need to reword it, that is rework it, a life where absence is for the future perfect, marvellous shortcoming of time, indeed.

22. I think this book is the story of virginal life. When at long last I became sexually aware at university it was not only innocence of the body that I lost. For when I discovered writing, I lost my innocence of mind. And the totalising unity of childhood was gone for ever, twice over. This is the reason why my book has to end before Cambridge, where twice over I became self-conscious, that is conscious of self – through writing and through sexuality. Can what is lost be found again? All life, and the afterlife called writing, poses that question insistently. If we ask the right questions we can live without the answers. We have no choice anyway. But we can be forgiven for looking back to the mythic time when, and the sacred space where, someone, we thought, knew the answers. But not knowing the answers ourselves, we finally become our own parents by sussing one thing, the deepest secret of all in our long forgotten past (just as virginity was our future's deepest secret): *they did not know the answers either.* Nor did our teachers. (What the God I believed in – my 'Sea of Faith' is no longer 'at the full' – did or did not know is beyond the scope of this book.) If our parents did not know all the answers, it follows they must have had feelings. Forgive and do not forget. Forgive and remember. And then, maybe, our children will forgive and not forget us. Forgive and remember us. This is the meaning of the Fifth Commandment.

23. It is thirty-five years, half three score and ten, since the last memory recorded in this book, but only if I privilege linear time. Remember your childhood, to keep it holy, and the work will not have been in vain. How long shall the world last? As many years after I die as there were years before I was born (if upon this 'darkling plain' we repair what we have done to the planet). Your world is still there, my world is still there, as you turn your brain round, as I turn my brain round. Memories look back and forth. As Roubaud insists, the future is the future perfect. Compare Laing and Cooper's: 'Our roles are always *future* structures.' In life, what will be translates into what is; what is, as it happens, translates into what was. Mind translates the process into what will have been. Each memory is a memory of a quondam future perfect. Each memory of the same event is an intervention in the flow, but each is unique for you do not step into the same river twice.

24. Memory is the afterlife. The memories I write down (without reference to archive material which mostly never existed or no longer exists: my archives, not by accident, not by coincidence, began in Cambridge) are the afterlife of the afterlife. Reading them is the afterlife of the afterlife of the afterlife. There comes a point when you must close the book, stop writing and stop reading, stop recycling memory as paper, paper as memory, and live your life – a phrase which is surely the ultimate in self-reflexive tautological cognate accusatives, but you are *that* you are – with such intensity that you do not notice the mirror ahead of you as, striding into the future, your whole past unfolds before your eyes in an infinite regression. This very sentence on my screen, as I type it, will soon have been, will vanish, saved into the memory of a machine. When I think about this book I sometimes free float, free associate, free fall, walk my lost possessions around my head, and every time one image returns: I own this image/belongs to me for ever.

   I am lying in bed in the room above the kitchen, the room giving on to the garden. It is completely dark. I am pushing the string which when pulled switches the light on (or off); I push it forward, hard enough for it to reach the ceiling, and let it pass me till it hits the wall behind my head and then, with perfect timing, push it forward as it returns. On and on, on and on, until I fall asleep, cross the frontier, unguarded, into a land of dreams.

Woodside Park, 1994/1998

Note. Of the theoretical raps or riffs included in the body of the book, the following five are particularly salient to the Afterword:

    1.D.5 (Segue of Family)

    2.A.5 (Rudolf's Law)

    2.A.12 (Ontological Isomorphs)

    3.B.1 (Truth as Polyhedron)

    5.A.ii.2 (Essentialised Signifiers).

Themes / Motifs

The problems are solved, not by giving new information, but by arranging what we have always known

WITTGENSTEIN

. . . the theme is structure, the infinitesimals of universal structure, their reality, its reality

LAURA (RIDING) JACKSON

That which we call progress of the human mind . . . has never consisted of, and never will consist of, more than a correction of outlines and classifications, a regrouping of elements, a definition of affiliations, and a discovery of new resources within an entity which   is both closed and self-complementary

CLAUDE LÉVI-STRAUSS

NOTE Each theme or motif will be found by the reader in the numbered paragraph it refers to – the number referring both to the relevant text *and* its square-bracketed commentary, if it has one. The key word may not actually be in the text.

The main purpose of this section of the book is to signpost aspects of my memories or the parenthetical discussion of them, sometimes because this reinforces points made in the Afterword. The themes and motifs of the Afterword do not lend themselves to being listed here.

HISTORY (SOCIAL AND OTHER)

English (National) 1.E.14, 2.A.12, 2.B.7, 2.C.ii.6, 4.C.i.1, 5.A.iii.9, 5.A.v.1

English (Local) 2.B.13

Jewish 3.B.2, 3.B.3, 3.B.4, 3.C.5, 3.D.6, 4.C.ii.I.6, 5.A.iii.9, 5.A.vi.8, 5.C.i.3, 5.C.i.5

Theory 3.B.1 (Truth as Polyhedron)

ANTHONY'S 'IDENTITY'

Age 1.D.1, 2.A.5, 4.A.6, 4.C.ii.I.5, 5.A.iv.7

Family 1.C.11, 1.D.5 (Segue of Family), 1.J.3, 4.B.i.1, 4.c.ii.I.6

Geo-Ontological/Ontological (The Kingdom) 4.A.2, 5.A.iii.2

Geo-Historical 5.D.i.7

Nature/Culture 4.A.3, 4.C.iv.I.3, 5.A.ii.2 (Essentialised Signifiers)

Own Writing 1.A.4, 1.C.2, 1.I.6,

2.A.12, 2.A.16, 4.C.i.15, 4.C.iv.II.7, 4.D.iii.9, 5.A.i.15

Paris, Blessed by 4.D.ii.12

Psycho-Ontological 4.C.iv.I.6 *[handwritten: 128]*

Religion 3.C.8

Socio-Geographical 4.C.iv.II.7, 4.D.iii.9

Sexual Zero 4.D.ii.7, 4.D.iii.6

Sibling 5.A.i.12, 5.A.iv.7

Underdog 1.I.5, 1.J.4, 4.B.i.6, 5.B.2

ANTHONY'S ATTRIBUTES (SELECTED)

Nerd, not a 1.B.6

Feet compared to a right-angled triangle 1.B.8

Birthmark compared to coffee-stain 1.C.1

In the dark 1.D.3

Reader of girls' stories 1.E.4

Reader by torchlight 1.E.19

Platonic love 1.F.ii.13, 1.F.ii.15, 3.E.ii.5

British 1.G.11

Hero Worshipper 1.I.1, 1.I.3

Dreamer 1.I.2, 4.C.iv.I.4

Tony/Anthony 2.A.11

World-record holder 2.B.10, 4.A.13

Sex-change 2.C.ii.2

Tuneless voice 3.A.8

Competitive 3.B.6

Sinner 3.C.6

Rebel 3.E.i.3

Spotty 3.E.i.5, 4.C.ii.II.3, 5.A.ii.11

Moishele 5.A.ii.16

Academic career 4.B.i.4

Socialist 4.B.ii.1, 5.E.1

Sibling 4.C.ii.I.5, 5.A.i.12

Resistant to change 4.C.ii.I.7

LANGUAGE/LITERATURE

MEMORY

PSYCHOLOGISING (METONYMY, SORT OF)

136

POLITICS

RELIGION

STRUCTURE OF BOOK

Annotated Bibliography

Place of publication London, unless otherwise stated or obvious.

Abse, Dannie, *Ash on a Young Man's Sleeve*, Hutchinson, 1954

Adams, Henry, *The Education of Henry Adams*, Houghton Mifflin, Boston 1961
['From cradle to grave this problem of running order through chaos, direction through space, discipline through freedom, unity through multiplicity, has always been, and must always be, the task of education, as it is the moral of religion, philosophy, science, art, politics and economy; but a boy's will is his life, and he dies when it is broken, as the colt dies in harness, taking a new nature in becoming tame']

Agnon, S. Y., *A Dwelling Place of My People*, Scottish Academic Press, Edinburgh 1983

Alain-Fournier, *Le Grand Meaulnes*, Livre de Poche, Paris 1963

[Alain-Fournier], *The Quest of Alain-Fournier* (by Robert Gibson), Hamish Hamilton, 1953

Apple, Max, *Roommates: My Grandfather's Story*, Little Brown, 1994

Arnold, Matthew, *The Oxford Arnold* (ed. Miriam Allott and Robert H. Super, Oxford University Press, 1986

Auden, W. H., *Collected Shorter Poems*, Faber & Faber, 1957

Auster, Paul, *The Invention of Solitude*, Sun, New York 1982

Ayer, A. J., *The Problem of Knowledge*, Penguin, 1964

Babel, Isaac, *1920 Diary*, Yale University Press, 1995

Bachelard, Gaston, *La Poétique de l'espace*, Presses Universitaires de la France, 1957

—— *La Poétique de la rêverie*, Presses Universitaires de la France, 1961

Bailey, Paul, *An Immaculate Mistake: Scenes from Childhood and Beyond*, Bloomsbury, 1990

Balzac, Honoré de, *Gillette* or *The Unknown Masterpiece* (ed./tr. Anthony Rudolf), Menard, 1988

Barthes, Roland, *Le Plaisir du texte*, Le Seuil, Paris 1973
— *Roland Barthes*, Le Seuil, 1975
  [In an unpublished MA thesis for London University Karen Bowen has written interestingly on this book and on Robbe-Grillet (see below)]
— *La Chambre claire*, Gallimard/Le Seuil, 1980
— *Incidents*, Le Seuil, 1987
Baudelaire, Charles, *The Complete Verse* (bilingual edition with prose translation by Francis Scarfe), Anvil Press, 1986
  ['The curtain had risen: I waited and waited' – my translation]
Beckett, Samuel, *The Complete Short Prose* 1929–1989, Grove Press, New York 1995
Benjamin, Walter, *Illuminations*, Fontana, 1973
— *One-Way Street*, NLB, 1979
  [contains *A Berlin Chronicle* and *Naples*]
[Benjamin, Walter], *Walter Benjamin for Children: An Essay on his Radio Years* (by Jeffrey Mehlman), Chicago University Press, 1993
[Benjamin, Walter], *Walter Benjamin for Beginners* (by Howard Caygill and others), Icon Books, 1998
[Benjamin, Walter], *Walter Benjamin or Towards a Revolutionary Criticism* (by Terry Eagleton), Verso, 1981
Black, Gerry, *JFS: The History of the Jews' Free School, London, since 1732*, Tymsder Press, 1998
[Boltanski, Christian], *After Auschwitz: Responses to the Holocaust in Contemporary Art* (ed. Monica Bohm-Duchen), Lund Humphries, 1995
Bonnefoy, Yves, *L'Arrière-Pays*, Skira, Geneva 1972 and 1992
  [Stephen Romer's fine translation (*The Hinterland*) is to be published later by Chicago University Press]
— *La Vérité de parole*, Mercure de France, Paris 1988
  [in particular the essays on Nerval and Borges]
Borges, Jorge Luis, *Dreamtigers*, E. P. Dutton, New York 1970
— *Labyrinths*, Penguin, 1969
Brainard, Joe, *I Remember*, Full Court Press, New York 1975
  [The identical Penguin New York edition (1995) contains a helpful afterword by Ron Padgett]
Broner, Esther, *Mornings and Mourning: A Kaddish Journal*, HarperCollins, San Francisco 1994

Brooke-Rose, Christine, *Remake*, Carcanet, Manchester 1996

Brown, Norman O., *Apocalypse and/or Metamorphosis*, University of California Press, 1991

Butler, Samuel, *The Way of All Flesh*, Penguin, 1986

Canary, R. H. and Kozicki, H. (eds), *The Writing of History: Literary Form and Historical Understanding*, University of Wisconsin Press, 1978

Canetti, Elias, *The Secret Heart of the Clock*, André Deutsch, 1991

Cooper, William, *From Early Life*, Macmillan, 1990

Daiches, David, *Two Worlds: An Edinburgh Jewish Childhood*, Canongate Classics, Edinburgh 1997 (reprint)

— *A Third World*, Sussex University Press, 1971

[The first of these two Daiches autobiographies is a moving, subtle, intelligent and well-written evocation of the author's early life, culminating in his student years. The sequel is its opposite in all respects. Why? Perhaps because the child and adolescent is a character in someone else's script and, thus, to write about that character need not involve strategies of self-protection. On the other hand, telling the life of the adult who was once that character risks the dangers of vanity and self-importance, defensiveness and triviality. In volume one you are, as it were, a character in search of an author. In volume two the roles are reversed. In volume one you take the book seriously but not yourself. In volume two, where you cannot disavow personal responsibility for the implication of your lived life, you take yourself seriously but not the book.]

Davis, Philip, *Memory and Writing*, Liverpool University Press, 1983

— *The Experience of Reading*, Routledge Kegan Paul, 1992

de la Mare, Walter, *Complete Poems*, Faber and Faber, 1969

Derrida, Jacques, *L'Ecriture et la différence*, Le Seuil, Paris 1967

Deutsch, Gitta, *The Red Thread*, Ariadne Press, California 1996

Diderot, Denis, *Le Supplément au voyage de Bougainville*, 1769

Duras, Marguerite, *La Mer écrite*, Marval, Paris 1996

Edwards, Ken, *3,600 Weekends*, Oasis Books, 1993

Eliot, T. S., *Collected Poems*, Faber and Faber, 1974

Esterson, Aaron, *The Leaves of Spring: Schizophrenia, Family and Sacrifice*, Penguin, 1972

FitzGerald, Edward, 'The Rubaiyat of Omar Khayyam', in *An Anthology of World Poetry* (ed. M. Van Doren), Cassell, 1929
[Complete in Van Doren. An extract from FitzGerald's great poem can be found in the successor volume to Van Doren: K. Washburn's and J. S. Major's *World Poetry*, Norton 1998. W. G. Sebald's *The Rings of Saturn* (see below) contains a superb meditation on FitzGerald]
Fitzgerald, F. Scott, *The Great Gatsby*, Grey Walls Press, 1948
Fortune, R. F., *Sorcerers of Dobu: The Social Anthropology of the Dobu Islanders of the Western Pacific*, Dutton, New York 1963

Gosse, Edmund, *Father and Son*, Penguin, 1986
Gunn, Thom, *My Sad Captains*, Faber and Faber, 1961

Harwood, Lee and Bailey, Peter, *The Empty Hill*, Skylark Press, Hove 1992
Hazlitt, William, *Selected Essays of William Hazlitt*, Nonesuch Press, 1946
[The reviews of Tom Paulin's new book on Hazlitt had me reaching for the Nonesuch *Hazlitt* I nicked a few years ago from my mother's house when she wasn't looking. Given the context of *The Arithmetic of Memory*, I re-read two of his classic essays: 'Why Distant Objects Please' and 'On the Feeling of Immortality in Youth'. The last three pages of the latter essay are among the most heartfelt and unsparing words he ever wrote. I'm glad I did not have them in mind before I started writing this book . . . Hazlitt would surely have agreed with the young Rilke: 'To be awake and to be alive are deeds not states']
Heaney, Seamus, *Field Work*, Faber and Faber, 1979
Helman, Cecil, 'Medicine in the Cultural Context' in *The Therapist*, 5/3, Summer 1998
Hemingway, Ernest, *A Moveable Feast*, Bantam Books, New York 1965
Heschel, Abraham Joshua, *The Earth is the Lord's: The Inner World of the Jew in Eastern Europe*, Farrer, Straus and Giroux, New York 1949
Heller, Michael, *Living Root*, unpublished memoir
Hiller, Susan, *After the Freud Museum*, Book Works, 1995
Hirsch, Robin, *Last Dance at the Hotel Kempinski*, University of New England Press, 1995
Hoffman, Eva, *Lost in Translation*, Heinemann, 1989
Hopkins, Gerard Manley, *Poems*, Oxford University Press, 1952

Howell, Anthony, *In the Company of Others*, Marion Boyars, 1986

Hyde, Lewis, *The Gift: Imagination and the Erotic Life of Property*, Vintage, New York 1983

Jacobson, Dan, *Heschel's Kingdom*, Hamish Hamilton, 1998

Jimenez, Juan Ramon, *Time and Space: A Poetic Autobiography*, Paragon House, New York 1988

Jones, David, *In Parenthesis*, Faber and Faber, 1969

— *The Tribune's Visitation*, Fulcrum Press, 1969

— *The Anathemata*, Faber and Faber, 1972

Josipovici, Gabriel, *The Inventory*, Gollancz, 1968

Joubert, Joseph, *Selected Thoughts*, Duckworth, 1898
   [This edition, translated by Katharine Lyttelton, has a preface by Mrs Humphrey Ward, and also contains a few translations by Matthew Arnold taken from his essay on the aphorist]

— *The Notebooks* (ed./tr. Paul Auster), North Point Press, San Francisco 1983
   [Contains an afterword by Maurice Blanchot]

Joyce, James, *A Portrait of the Artist as a Young Man*, Penguin, 1990

Kochan, Lionel, *Beyond the Graven Image: A Jewish View*, Macmillan, 1997

Kravtsov, Sergei, 'Defining Jewish Architecture' (int'v. AR), *Jewish Quarterly* 159, 1995

Laing R. D. and Cooper, D. G., *Reason and Violence*, Tavistock, 1971

Langley, Lee, *Change of Address*, Mandarin, 1995

Lanzmann, Claude, *Shoah*, Fayard, Paris 1985

Levi, Primo, *The Periodic Table*, Michael Joseph, 1985

— *If Not Now, When?*, Summit Books, New York 1985

Lévi-Strauss, Claude, *La Pensée sauvage*, Plon, Paris 1962

— *Totemism* (intro. R. Poole), Penguin, 1969

[Lévi-Strauss, Claude], *The Structural Study of Myth and Totemism* (ed. Edmund Leach), Tavistock, London 1967
   [contains an excellent essay by Michael Mendelsohn. I use one of his quotes from the old hot gospeller as the third epigraph to my Themes/ Motifs chapter. There is a fascinating diagram on page 137. One day I shall try to convert some of my theoretical fancies into a diagram]

[Lévi-Strauss, Claude], see Octavio Paz book below

Lowell, Robert, *Life Studies*, Vintage Books, New York 1959
— *For the Union Dead*, Faber and Faber, 1965

Mandelstam, Osip (tr. Clarence Brown), *Prose*, Princeton University Press, 1967
[My para 5.C.i.5: translation slightly amended after discussion with Richard McKane]
Matthews, Harry, *20 Lines a Day*, Dalkey Archive Press, Illinois 1989
Miller, Alice, *The Drama of Being a Child*, Virago, 1987
— *The Untouched Key*, Virago, 1990
— *Pictures of a Childhood*, Virago, 1995
Moore, Marianne, *Collected Poems*, Faber and Faber, 1951
Morrison, Blake, *And when did you last see your Father?*, Granta/Penguin, 1994

Nora, Pierre, *Les Lieux de mémoire 1*, Gallimard, Paris 1984

Pasternak, Boris, *An Essay in Autobiography*, Collins Harvill, 1959
Paz, Octavio, *Claude Lévi-Strauss*, Cape Editions, 1971
[My para 4.A.3: translation of sentence amended after discussion with Jason Wilson]
Péguy, Charles, *Clio*, Gallimard, Paris 1932
Perec, Georges, *Je me souviens*, Hachette, Paris 1993
— *Species of Space and Other Pieces*, Penguin, 1997
[Perec, Georges], *Je me souviens de Je me souviens* (by Roland Brasseur), Le Castor Astral, Paris 1998
Picon, Gaëtan, *Admirable tremblement du temps*, Skira, Geneva 1970
Pinsky, Robert, *Poetry and the World*, The Ecco Press, New York 1988
[contains essays on his childhood]
Ponge, Francis, *Le Parti pris des choses*, Gallimard, Paris 1967
Popa, Vasco, *Collected Poems*, Anvil Press, 1997

Raine, Craig, *Rich*, Faber and Faber, 1984
Rego, Paula, *Nursery Rhymes*, The Folio Society, 1994
Reznikoff, Charles, *Selected Letters* (ed. Milton Hindus), Black Sparrow Press, California 1997
[Afterword reference (para. 20) is to the letter to Albert Lewin dated March 1932]

Ricks, Christopher, *Keats and Embarrassment*, Oxford University Press, 1976

Riding, Laura, *Collected Poems*, Cassell, 1938

Rilke, Rainer Maria, *Diaries of a Young Poet*, Norton, 1997

— *The Notebooks of Malte Laurids Brigge*, Norton, 1964

Robbe-Grillet, Alain, *Le Miroir qui revient*, Les Editions de Minuit, Paris 1984

Roden, Claudia, *The Book of Jewish Food*, Knopf, New York 1998

Rose, Evelyn, *The Complete International Jewish Cookbook*, Pan Books, 1978

Roth, Cecil, *Short History of the Jewish People*, East and West Library, 1953

Roth, Henry, *Call it Sleep*, Avon Books, New York 1965

Roth, Joseph, *Flight without End*, J. M. Dent, 1984

Roth, Philip, *The Facts: A Novelist's Autobiography*, Penguin, 1988

Roubaud, Jacques, *La Boucle*, Le Seuil, Paris 1993

Rudolf, Anthony, *The Same River Twice*, Carcanet, Manchester 1976

— *After the Dream*, Cauldron Press, St Louis 1979

— *Broccoli* (etching by Paul Coldwell), Culford Press, 1989

— *Everything is Prepared for the Feast: On the Triple Threshold of Religion, Politics and Literature* (unpublished), 1998

Salomon, Charlotte, *Life or Theatre? (An Autobiographical Play)*, (intro. by Judith Herzberg), The Viking Press, New York 1981

[Salomon, Charlotte], *To Paint her Life: Charlotte Salomon in the Nazi Era* (by Mary Lowenthal Felstiner), HarperPerennial, New York 1995

Sarraute, Nathalie, *L'Ere du soupçon*, Idées (NRF), Paris 1964

— *Tropismes*, 10|18, Paris 1971

— *L'Enfance*, Gallimard, Paris 1983

— *Ici*, Gallimard, 1995

Schatzman, Morton, *Soul Murder: Persecution in the Family*, Penguin, 1976

Scholem, Gershom, *The Messianic Idea in Judaism*, Schocken, New York 1971

Schulz, Bruno, *Sanatorium under the Sign of the Hour*, Picador, 1979

— *The Street of Crocodiles*, Picador, 1980

Sebald, W. G., *The Emigrants*, New Directions, New York 1996

— *The Rings of Saturn*, Harvil Press, 1998

Shakespeare, William, *Collected Plays* (3 volumes), Oxford University Press, 1948

— *The Complete Works* (eds Stanley Wells and Gary Taylor), Clarendon Press, Oxford 1986

   [NB The prose passage containing the sentence which gave me my title (see epigraph) is often omitted from modern editions. It is from the Second Quarto. The 1986 Oxford Shakespeare has additional passages at the end of plays]

Silkin, Jon, *The First Twenty-Four years*, Contemporary Authors Autobiography Series, No 5, 1987
[This is a wonderful, bizarre, characteristically personal and very important essay by one of the best poets of our time]

Sillitoe, Alan, *Life without Armour*, Flamingo, 1996

Spark, Muriel, *Curriculum Vitae*, Penguin, 1993

Spiegelman, Art, *Maus*, vols 1 & 2, Penguin, 1987/92

Stavans, Ilan, *On Borrowed Words: A Memoir of Language*, Viking, 2000

Steiner, George, *Errata: An Examined Life*, Weidenfeld and Nicolson, 1997

Stevens, Wallace, *Collected Poems*, Faber and Faber, 1984

Sylvester, David, *Conversations with Bacon* (3rd edition), Thames and Hudson, 1993

Taggart, John, *Remaining in Light: Ant Meditations on a Painting by Edward Hopper*, State University of New York Press, New York 1993

[Travers Herford, R. (ed. and trs.)], *The Sayings of the Fathers*, Schocken Books, New York 1962

Turnbull, Gael, *A Year and a Day*, Mariscat Press, Glasgow 1985

Vigée, Claude, *Un Panier de houblon*, vols 1 and 2, J. C. Lattès, Paris 1994 and 1995

Wall, Alan, *Bless the Thief*, Secker and Warburg, 1997

Warren, Robert Penn, *Portrait of a Father*, University Press of Kentucky, 1988

Williams, W. C., *Collected Earlier Poems*, Magibbon and Kee, 1965

— *Collected Later Poems*, Magibbon and Kee, 1967

Wittgenstein, L., *Tractatus Logico-Philosophicus*, Routledge Kegan Paul, 1969

Wordsworth William, *The Prelude* (ed. E. de Selincourt/S. Gill), Oxford University Press, 1970

Young, Augustus, *The Credit*, books 1, 2 & 3, The Menard Press, 1980/1986

[in the *Tanakh* volume], *The Torah* (Masoretic text), Jewish Publication Society of America, Philadelphia 1985

Discography

The Beatles, *Sgt Pepper's Lonely Hearts Club Band*, EMI (LP), PCF 7027, 1967
Half Man Half Biscuit, *Back in the DHSS*, Probe Plus (LP), Probe 4, 199?
Lipatti, Dinu, *The Art of Dinu Lipatti*, EMI/HMV (4 LPs), 1980
— *Chopin Waltzes* [number ?], LP, 1958?
Pires, Maria Joao, *Chopin: The Nocturnes*, Deutsche Grammophon 447 096-2
    (2 CDs), 1996
— *Le Voyage Magnifique: Schubert's Impromptus*, Deutsche Grammophon,
    457 550-2 (2 CDs), 1997
Schiff, Andras, *Schubert's Piano Sonatas* (7 CDs), Decca 1992–5
Waits, Tom, *Frank's Wild Years*, Polygram ICM2024, 1993
    [Tracks include two versions of 'Innocent While You Dream']

Index of Names and Places

Names and places found in the *specialised* sections, such as Reading (1.E) or Sport (1.J) or The Arts in Paris (4.D.ii) or Politics (5.E), are not listed in this index. The references below to Denis Compton, for example (who else?), relate not to sport but to his appearance in advertisements and in a book.

NAMES

Edwin Abbott Abbott 4.C.ii.I.6

Chimen Abramsky 5.C.ii.4

H. C. Andersen 5.B.6

Kingsley Amis 4.C.ii.I.6

John Arlott 1.G.18

Matthew Arnold 4.C.iv.I.3, 5.A.i.19, 5.B.7

Michael Apted 4.C.ii.II.9

Margaret Atwood 5.A.i.15

Paul Auster 1.D.1, 1.F.ii.7, 5.A.i.19

A. J. Ayer 3.E.ii.4, 4.C.ii.II.5

Isaac Babel 1.A.7

Gaston Bachelard 5.A.v.7

Balzac 3.C.6, 4.D.i.5, 5.A.vi.7

Hastings Banda 5.A.vi.7

Roland Barthes 4.D.ii.9

The Beatles 1.D.5

Samuel Beckett 4.D.ii.3

Menachem Begin 5.C.i.2

Ben-Bag Bag Afterword 6

W. Benjamin 1.D.5, 3.B.5, 4.D.ii.11, 5.A.iv.5, Afterword *passim*

Shmuel H. Bergmann 5.A.ii.16

Beverley Sisters 5.D.ii.1

Tony Blair 1.B.2

Issie Bonn 1.E.22

Maurice Blanchot 4.C.iv.II.7

Rabbi L.Blue 3.A.4, 5.B.7

Yves Bonnefoy 5.A.ii.4

Jorge Luis Borges 2.A.12, 2.A.23, 4.B.ii.1, Afterword 10

Keith Bosley 2.A.15

Joe Brainard 1.A.5, Afterword 1

Georges Brassens 1.F.ii.15, 4.C.iii.3, 4.D.ii.8

Mike Brearley 4.C.i.16, 4.C.ii.II.2, 4.C.iv.I.8

D. G. Bridson 1.G.16

Christine Brooke-Rose 4.C.i.7

Norman O. Brown Afterword 17

Bum-Bum Lady 2.B.7

Samuel Butler 5.A.i.19

Albert Camus 4.C.i.7, 5.E.4

Elias Canetti Afterword 19

PLACES OUTSIDE THE SUBURB

1. IN LONDON

2. OUTSIDE LONDON

Marvellous tremor of time

CHATEAUBRIAND